Modern Midges

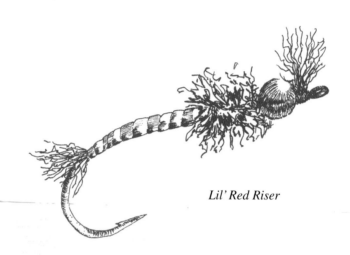

Lil' Red Riser

Modern Midges

TYING AND FISHING
THE WORLD'S MOST EFFECTIVE
PATTERNS

Rick Takahashi and Jerry Hubka
Photos by Brian Yamauchi and Mark Tracy

HEADWATER
BOOKS

STACKPOLE
BOOKS

To my wife, Susan Lynn Sandell-Takahashi—without your support,
I could not have written this book. To my children, Haley Maria Tokiko Takahashi and
Joshua Randall Chikara Takahashi, who are my inspiration.
To my parents, Henry and Clara Takahashi, and my stepmother, Jessie Takahashi.
And to three of my biggest fans, my sisters Dee Dee Lee, Becky Larsen, and Caprice Benz.
RT

To my wife, Joyce, whose love and support has allowed me to pursue my art
and my hobbies and who is always there when my line gets tangled.
JH

Copyright © 2009 by Headwater Books

Published by
HEADWATER BOOKS
531 Harding Street
New Cumberland, PA 17070
www.headwaterbooks.com

STACKPOLE BOOKS
5067 Ritter Road
Mechanicsburg, PA 17055
www.stackpolebooks.com

All illustrations by the authors

Printed in China

First edition

10 9 8 7 6 5 4 3 2

ISBN: 978-1-934753-00-2

Library of Congress Control Number: 2009923108

CONTENTS

ACKNOWLEDGMENTS

I COULD NOT have written this book without the support of my family. Being a Takahashi has provided me with the genes of creativity. My entire clan is made up of creative and artistic people; I hope I bring them honor. This book is for my family.

When I was eight years old, my uncle Ted Takahashi bought me my first fly-tying kit—the catalyst for a lifetime pursuit for knowledge and understanding of this thing called tying flies. My uncle Paul first showed me how to draw and gave me the gift of art, which has served me well as an art educator.

I'll always be indebted to Dr. Donn Johnson for instructing me in the finer aspects of fly fishing, and for instilling in me an appreciation for the aesthetics of the well-tied fly and the joy of angling art and literature. My gratitude goes to one of the most gifted fly tiers I know, Tim England, for helping me develop a sense of craftsmanship and the notion of always trying to make the next tie better than the last. My thanks to Ross Purnell for giving me the opportunity to write and illustrate for *Fly Fisherman*. To Steve Solano of the Rocky Mountain Fly Shop and Gordon Waldmier of Angler's Roost who allowed me to work and teach fly tying at their shops. A special thanks to Bruce Olson for the honor and opportunity to design flies for Umpqua Feather Merchants. Also, I could not have undertaken this project with out the help of my closest friend, my fishing partner and co-author Jerry Hubka. —RT

***

My personal fly-fishing history began on the Frying Pan River, in my late teens, and faded away until 20 years ago, when Rick Takahashi reintroduced me to this lost passion. We've spent many days catching trout on the rivers and lakes in the Rocky Mountain region. Though I thought we were just having fun, little did I know that this was also research for his creative and productive fly patterns and, eventually, the substance for this book. Rick is one of the best people I know, and his humor, friendship, generosity, and gentle way with people has taught me much more than simply how and where to catch trout.

To my fishing friends Scott Kemp, Ron Yoshimura, Sandy and Dave Beegle, and all those others who allowed me to join them on the water and experience the joy of catching trout. To my friend and teaching colleague, T. S. Berger, who said to me one day, thirty-four years ago, that he appreciated people who actually do what they say they are going to do, instead of just talking about it; thanks for the lifelong "push" and for the thirty years of teaching art and making pottery together. And finally to my mother, Helen Hubka, for teaching me kindness, responsibility, independence, and that, despite perceptions to the contrary, "only children" are not always spoiled. And, in memory of Ralph Coffman, who took the time to start a young man off on a lifetime of fly-fishing adventures. —JH

***

Both of us would like to thank Brian Yamauchi, for his beautiful photography and his creative midge patterns, and Mark Tracy for his product photography. Thanks also to Brian Chan for the excellent photographs and information provided regarding midge entomology. We would like to thank those companies that contributed flies and other items for this book, including Umpqua Feather Merchants, Regal Vise, Solitude Fly Company, Renzetti, Pacific Fly Group, Spirit River, Rainy's, Montana Fly Company, Tiemco, Daiichi, Gamakatsu, Hedron, Danville, and Targus Fly and Feather. And we would like to thank Joann Vota, who fed and housed all those fly fishing boys.

Writing this book has been a dream of ours for over twenty years. We have spent countless hours writing, drawing, and, of course, fishing—to bring this book to the angling community. To all the talented tiers who contributed flies and fishing advice to this book, we offer our sincere thanks. Last but not least, this book is for you—our fellow fly fishers. Our goal was to share what we have learned, and also to share with you our enjoyment of fly fishing.

Our special thanks go to Jay Nichols at Headwater Books for launching us on this creative journey. His enormous knowledge of the publishing and fly fishing worlds allowed us to realize our dream. Jay's wealth of knowledge and professionalism made this journey a true pleasure. Let's go fishing.

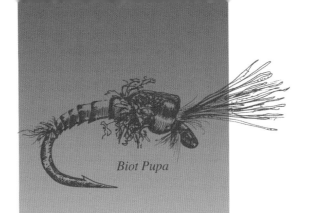

Biot Pupa

Discovering the Midge

FORTUNE DEALT ME a kind hand when I met my wife, Susan, whose mother lived in the southwestern town of Durango, Colorado. Durango is a short distance from the San Juan River, which is just across the border in northern New Mexico, and in short order I found it easy to convince Susan that we should visit her mother. Perhaps, if she didn't mind, I could fish for a few days on the Juan?

I had read countless articles and heard a number of friends discussing how fantastic fishing was on the fabled waters of the San Juan River. This scenic river, nestled in the semi-desert of a southwest landscape that includes piñon pines, sagebrush, rolling hills, and sandstone, is home to some of the best midge fishing in the United States.

Before I ever fished this river, I considered midges just small versions of dry-fly patterns, like diminutive Adamses or Black Gnats. Whenever I encountered trout feeding on midges I avoided matching the hatch, instead flogging away with the larger patterns that were easier for me to see. I often left the river without a single hookup. But through the kindness of strangers, and with some help from Scott Donovan (a former

Guide Monroe Coleman helps net a fish that guide Gary Okazaki caught on the lower section of the South Platte River.

1

Brian Yamauchi's midge pupa is a near perfect imitation of a natural chironomid pupa. It is important to sample the naturals in the stream for precise imitations.

student), I started to understand that I needed to master the minutiae to be successful.

I spent hours watching trout behavior in shallow water. It was clear that the primary food for the trout—at least in the upper reaches below Navajo Dam—was midges. They thrived in the river's constant cold temperatures and silty bottom, and the trout absolutely gorged on them. I sampled the water, pumped the throats of the fish I caught, and most of what I saw was midges. Though I found larvae, pupae, and adults, most of what I sampled were pupae.

To be more successful, I learned as much as I could about midges, their life cycles and habitats, how to fish them, and how to imitate them. I read books and magazines, watched the action onstream, talked with friends, and visited local fly shops. This quest has led me and Jerry on a journey that has occupied a great deal of our fishing and fly-tying time together, and we have studied these fascinating creatures for the better part of two decades.

—RT

I LEARNED TO fly fish on Colorado's Frying Pan River in 1966, two years before Ruedi Reservoir dammed the river. My girlfriend (and future wife) Joyce lived with her grandparents in Basalt during the summers while she worked in Aspen. I would take a week off work and spend it in Basalt with Joyce and her family. Ralph Coffman, a family friend, owned a "house and lot" (really more of a cabin) on the Frying Pan, and volunteered to teach me how to fly fish. Ralph was also the inventor of the famous House and Lot fly that President Eisenhower loved to fish with during his visits to Colorado.

Twenty-six years passed before I began tying my own flies, right after I first started fly fishing with Rick Takahashi, in 1992, on the South Platte River. At some point during that initial fishing trip with Rick I realized that my one-and-only fly box—full of large mayfly nymphs and three dry flies—was not going to help me keep up with his experience and expert-

Co-authors Jerry Hubka and Rick Takahashi hold a pair of rainbow trout caught on Bow Tie Buzzers in Wyoming.

ise on the river. I needed more fly boxes, and a lot more flies to fill them.

The next weekend, I attended a Saturday morning fly-tying demonstration at our local fly shop, where Rick worked and conducted fly-tying classes. When I left the shop, three hours later, Rick had loaded me up with over a hundred dollars worth of tying materials and hooks—in a very small bag. For the next two weeks, I tied some ridiculously small patterns on #18-22 hooks in preparation for my first trip to the Green River. With two boxes full of small flies, Joyce and I headed off to Vernal, Utah.

When driving through Vernal, we stopped at a fly shop and purchased several patterns that were recommended for the Green. I remember that one of the patterns I had purchased was called a WD-40 midge, size 20. We arrived at Little Hole on the Green in the afternoon, and I hurriedly tied on the WD-40 and headed for the water. To my great surprise, I caught and released six nice fish that day with it. For the next two days I experimented with many of the small patterns I had tied, and found that they really did catch fish. However, I did not understand much about what midges actually were; just that they were small flies that could catch big trout.

After Rick began fishing the San Juan in northern New Mexico, I started making a trip or two each year with him to learn more about the river. My knowledge—of midge fishing, midge patterns, and how to fish them—has increased over the last two decades, thanks to Rick and the many fishing friends we have met, and fished with, on the rivers in the Rocky Mountain region. Just how important do I think midges are to the trout's diet? I currently have twenty-three boxes of flies that I have tied over the last sixteen years, and ten of those boxes are filled exclusively with midge patterns.

—JH

Why Midges?

MIDGE IS A COMMON term used by anglers to describe small fly patterns, though technically (and in the context of this book) the term applies to insects of the order Diptera ("two wings"), some of which are not so small. Midges live in both streams and stillwaters and come in a variety of sizes, shapes, and colors. The immense variety of insects in the Dipteran order, family Chironomidae, is estimated to be well over 20,000, with more being identified every year. Midges are distributed throughout the world, and most species live in water, making them a valuable food source for fish. These aquatic insects are tolerant of a wide range of environmental conditions. Chironomids are found in swift-moving streams; deep, slow-moving rivers; stagnant ditches; and in lakes and ponds that are rich in decomposing organic matter.

Trout eat midges—lots and lots of midges. Unlike some of the more seasonal hatches of mayflies or caddis, trout consistently eat midges all year long, so depending on the fish's habitat, this minute insect can make up a large part of their

Clear weather brings out a large contingency of fly fishermen who try and take advantage of trout putting on weight during a chironomid hatch on a plains lake in Colorado.

3

Midges are simple to tie and work almost anywhere. A beautiful brown, caught on a midge, goes back to the water.

diet. Because trout have to balance the amount of energy they expend with the energy they take in, they must consume a huge number of midges to stay alive. Fortunately, nature has supplied them with abundance. The sheer number of midges available to trout combined with the relative safety of the depth of the water where these organisms live provide for prime feeding conditions that encourage healthy growth rates on many rivers. All the trout have to do is hold in the current and allow the smorgasbord to come to them. In a lake or reservoir, trout can feed in relative safety as they intercept the midge in deeper water, safe from predators above.

Because trout feed on every stage of the midge's life cycle, whether in moving or still waters, fishing imitations of them is an effective method for consistently fooling fish year-round. Midges are so diverse in their distribution that patterns imitating them can take trout when no other patterns seem to work. Midges are covered extensively in the entomological and scientific world, but information on midge patterns and fishing techniques is scarce. However, in recent decades, more and more information about midges and midge fishing has become available, and there have been extremely creative endeavors from fly tiers all around the world to imitate the various life cycles of the midge.

Throughout the course of our research, we have marveled at the number of individuals from all over the world who have also been afflicted with "midge madness." We are delighted to have received over 1,000 patterns for this book and feel that we've really only begun to scratch the surface of what is available out there from the midge fanatics who work away at their craft.

Midges are, for the most part, simple to tie. In this book, we demonstrate basic tying techniques of the larva, pupa, and adult life-cycle stages as well as the transitional emerger stage. We also include three cluster patterns. The following tying instructions are meant to give the novice midge fly tier a basic idea of the construction of the various stages. As with all endeavors, practice makes perfect, and taking time to learn the techniques demonstrated here will have you becoming proficient in a short period of time.

If you want to learn more about tying accurate midge patterns, invest some time collecting samples of each of the life stages of the midge from as many locations as possible. We carry a portable entomology kit that includes a carrying container, a small white tray to examine what we've collected, tweezers, collection bottles with preserving fluid, labels, a fine-tipped permanent pen, a small clipboard, and a collecting net. You can purchase a preserving fluid from a biological supply dealer, or in a pinch, you can use a mixture of 50 percent water and 50 percent Vodka.

When collecting samples, it is nice to have one person to hold the net while you walk upstream and kick the bottom to release any of the immature insects into the current, and into your net. We place what we collect in the small tray with a little water so that we can examine our findings and collect any immature insects for later study. This is a good method to ease you into learning about the entomology of the streams you are fishing. You will gain insight into what the fish eat, and the size, shape, and color of the insects that you should be imitating at the vise.

Midge Life Cycle Overview

Chironomid larvae are segmented and wormlike in shape. Most larvae live in simple tubecases or shelters in the bottom of the lake or river. Under ideal conditions, there can be as many as 600 or more larvae living in a 6-inch cube of bottom substrate. Larvae feed on organic matter that collects in these benthic, or bottom, areas. In lakes, chironomid larvae can be found living at the bottom in several feet to well beyond 70 feet in depth. Many species have adapted to living in almost anoxic conditions by storing hemoglobin in their primitive respiratory system. This allows them to survive in the deepest parts of the water, where oxygen is almost nonexistent. These larvae, often referred to as bloodworms, are blood-red in color.

The most common larvae colors are red or maroon, and various shades of green. Larvae pupate within the larval tube or cocoon while at the stream or lake bottom. The fully developed pupae break out of the old larval tubes and ascend to the surface. This pupal ascent is aided by gases trapped under the pupal shuck, which also creates a silvery appearance in the majority of the pupae as they near the surface. Once at the surface, the adult emerges from the old pupal shuck, dries its wings, and flies off to mate, beginning the cycle again.

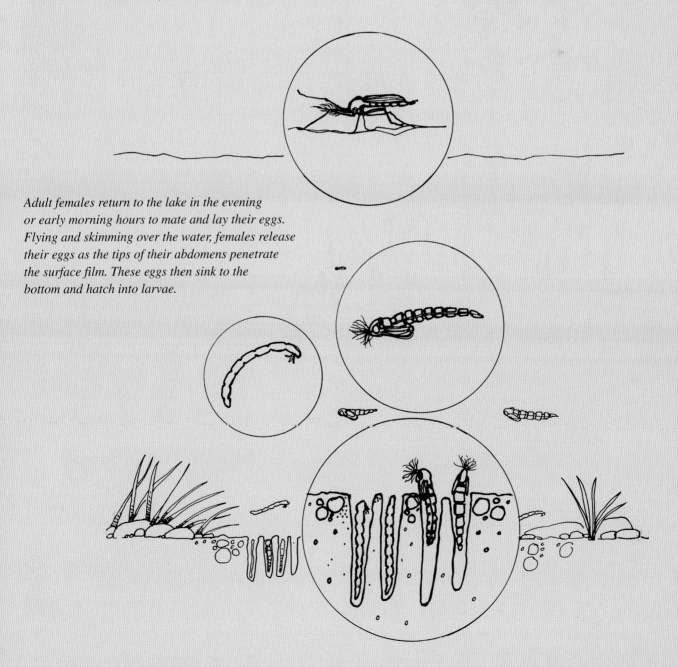

Adult females return to the lake in the evening or early morning hours to mate and lay their eggs. Flying and skimming over the water, females release their eggs as the tips of their abdomens penetrate the surface film. These eggs then sink to the bottom and hatch into larvae.

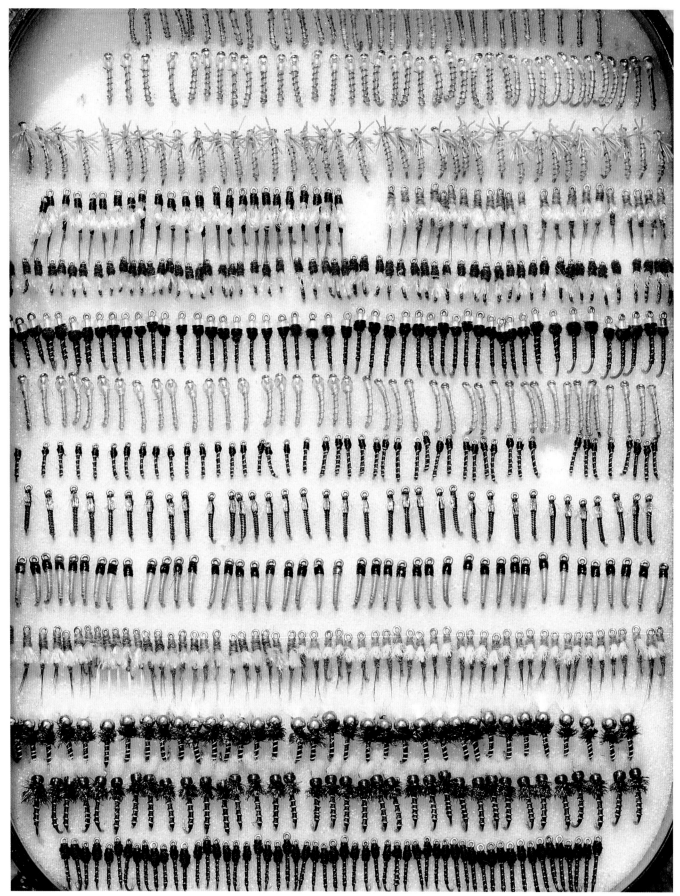

A close up look at one of Pat Dorsey's midge boxes—a great example of a well stocked fly box with a variety of sizes and colors to match the naturals.

Tying Midges

Tak's Mini Bow Tie Buzzer

Tying the Larva

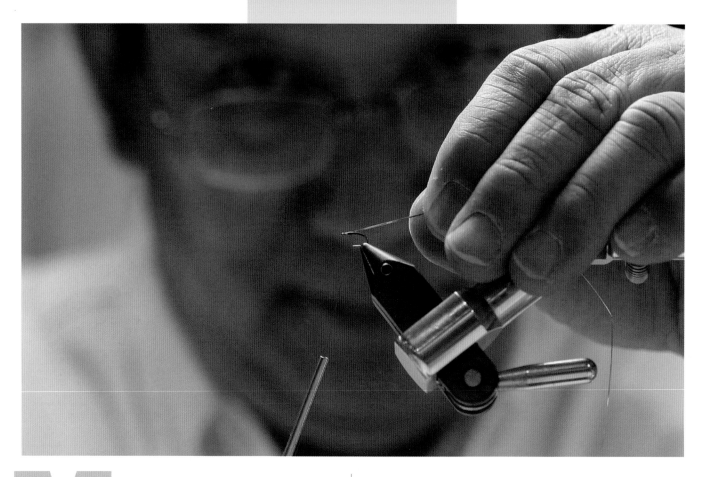

MIDGE LARVAE ARE wormlike in shape and are generally found on or near the bottom of their watery habitat. They prefer to stay out of the drift and like to remain secure, but they are often washed into the stream flow, becoming available food for trout. Larvae often prefer the low-oxygen environments found on the bottom of lakes and streams. Some larvae store oxygen, in the form of hemoglobin, thus giving them a reddish appearance. Larvae come in a variety of shades and colors, including cream, tan, olive, and brown, but red is one

of the most common. This reddish appearance also gives rise to the term bloodworm. Due to physical similarities, some fly fishers mistakenly refer to the midge larvae as an annelid (aquatic worm), but on closer examination, you will see the absence of the clitellum, a swelling found on earthworms, and the presence of prolegs, which are small appendages.

We demonstrate three types of larvae: the first has a simple thread body and rib; the second has a plastic tubing material wrapped over a thread base for segmentation; and the third

Midge larvae patterns can be constructed with nothing more than thread and floss, yet they are deadly. Author Rick Takahashi starts to tie one of several midges for a trip to the Cache La Poudre River near his hometown of Fort Collins, Colorado.

Choosing the Right Thread

HOOK SIZE	RECOMMENDED THREAD
#8-12	Uni 3/0, 6/0; Danville Flymaster 6/0 and Plus, Ultra Thread (UTC) 140- and 210-denier, Lagartun X-Strong 95- and 150-denier
#12-16	Uni 8/0; UTC 70-denier, Danville Flymaster 6/0, Lagartun X-Strong 74- and 95-denier, Orvis 6/0, Giorgio Benecchi 10/0, 12/0
#18-24	Uni 8/0, 17/0, Caenis (20-denier); UTC GSP 50-denier, Gordon Griffiths 14/0, Danville Spiderweb 18/0
#26 and smaller	Uni 17/0, Danville Spiderweb 18/0

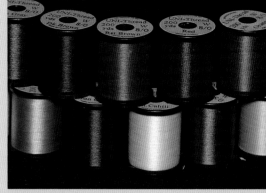
Uni-Thread

The threads in the chart are just guidelines. When tying midges, it is better to go with a smaller thread than one that is too heavy, as you will learn to apply a good deal of pressure with even the lightest threads. The key is learning to apply maximum pressure without breaking the thread. When we want to tie a pattern that is tiny or needs to have a slim profile, we use the 17/0 thread regardless of hook size, though using it takes some practice. The 17/0 comes in white only, and is 40 denier (a unit of measurement of linear density of textile fiber mass). This thread lays flat, does not create bulk, and takes colored markers. Coat the thread with a thinned-out head cement to protect the color and the thread from the fish's sharp teeth. Because of the fine diameter of the thread, we like to use a whip-finisher to tie off the heads rather than doing it by hand. A half-hitch tool is useful for putting a single knot in the thread to keep various materials you tie on from unraveling.

Danville

When using thread to form bodies and ribs, the size of the fly is an important consideration. For larger flies where you need to form bulk, such as Buzzers, choose a floss or larger thread such as Uni 3/0 or 6/0; Danville 3/0; or Ultra Thread (UTC) 140- or 210-denier. All these threads come in a wide range of colors.

Uni-Thread is available in 3/0 (266-denier), 6/0 (135-denier), 8/0 (72-denier), 17/0 (40-denier) in white only, and Caenis (20-denier) in black and white. You can color white threads with permanent markers.

Danville is available in 3/0, Flymaster 6/0 (70-denier), Flymaster Plus (140- and 210-denier), and Spiderweb (30-denier) in white only. Danville 3/0 is useful for tying some of the larger chironomid patterns, such as Bow Tie Buzzers.

Ultra Thread's shiny finish makes it look almost like floss, and we recommend it when you need to wrap the thread flat on the hook. You can also twist it into a tight rope, by spinning the bobbin clockwise, creating a riblike appearance. The 70-denier is ideal for midge patterns down to size 32.

Ultra Thread

Heavier threads such as **Coats & Clarks** (sewing thread) or **Gudebrod** rod-winding threads are also useful for creating abdomens on midge larvae and pupae. A large Griffin bobbin is great for holding these thread spools. Merco Product's Rite Bobbin is a useful tool for thicker types of thread, such as Danville's 2/0 and Ultra Thread's 140- and 210-denier.

Coats & Clarks and Gudebrod

Larvae come in a variety of shades and colors, including cream, tan, olive, and brown, but red is one of the most common. This reddish appearance also gives rise to the term bloodworm.

uses latex. Each pattern will be tied on a #18 Tiemco 200R, but you could substitute a Dai-Riki 270, which has a similar design. The longer shank length and the slight curve of these hooks closely resembles the curved shape of the larvae. We often coat these patterns with head cement to help protect the materials, to protect the color if using a water-based marker, or to lend transparency to the body.

Thread Body Larva

This simple pattern is constructed entirely with tying thread, except for the coating of thinned head cement. The ribbing is created by spinning the bobbin to twist the thread, which creates segmentation when it is wrapped around the body. Most of the midge larvae we tie are red; however, olive, cream, tan, white, and yellowish tan are also good patterns to carry. With some markers, and a little creativity, you can achieve natural, contrasting effects with one color of thread, or combine two colors. For instance, you can build an abdomen with one color, then color the thread with a darker permanent marker for the next section, then spin the thread clockwise to create a rope, and rib the fly with the darker thread.

Materials

Hook:	#18 Tiemco 200R
Thread:	Red 8/0 Uni or 70-denier UTC
Body:	Tying thread
Rib:	Tying thread, twisted
Head:	Tying thread coated with Griff's Thin Head Cement

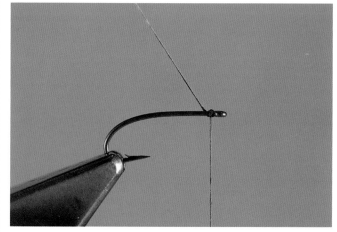

1. Attach the thread just behind the hook eye, and take six to eight wraps back over the thread to secure it.

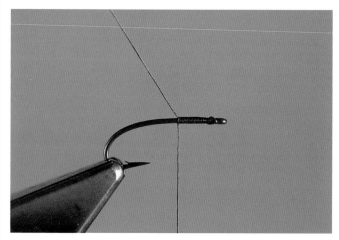

2. Wrap the tying thread in touching wraps back toward the hook bend. Holding the tag end of the tying thread at a 45-degree angle will help to make tighter touching wraps by sliding the thread next to the previous wrap.

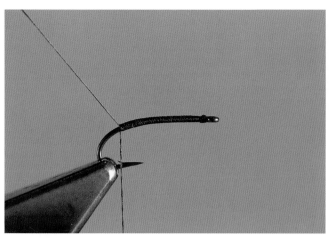

3. Continue to wrap the thread back to a point on the shank just above the barb.

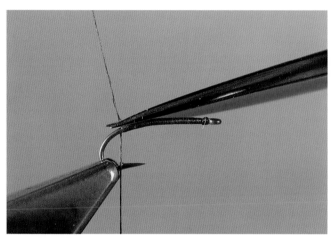

4. Grasp the tag end of the tying thread and trim it as close to the hook as possible.

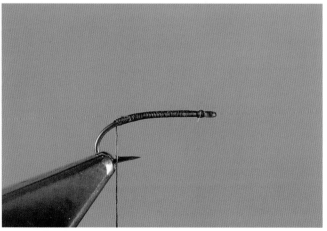

5. Spin the bobbin clockwise to twist the thread. The twisted thread will create a pronounced rib when wrapped over the thread body.

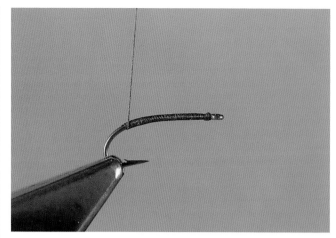

6. Begin wrapping the thread forward with evenly spaced wraps.

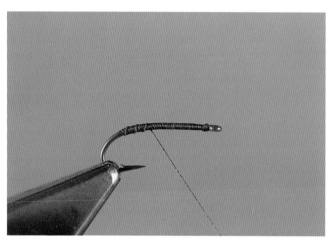

7. Wrap the tying thread forward in evenly spaced wraps.

8. Continue to wrap the thread to the hook eye.

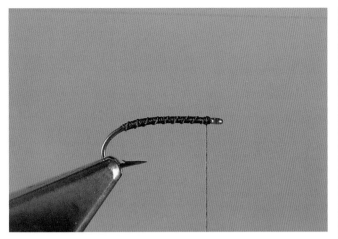

9. Stop when you reach one hook eye width behind the eye.

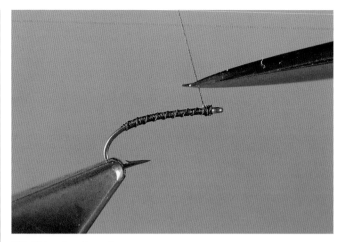

12. Trim the thread.

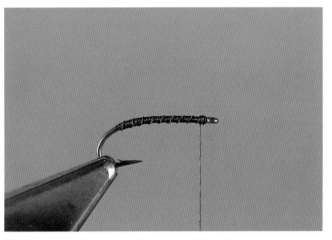

10. Take several wraps to form a small head.

13. If desired, leave a small tag. This can be used to simulate the prolegs of the natural.

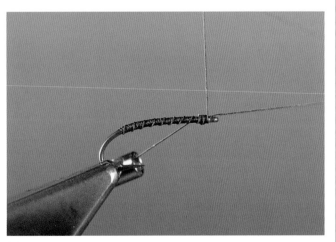

11. Whip-finish the head of the fly.

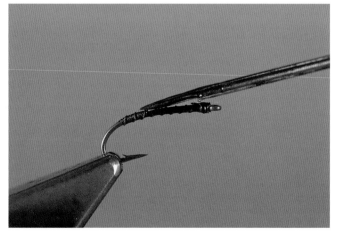

14. Coat the entire length of the body with Griff's Thin Head Cement.

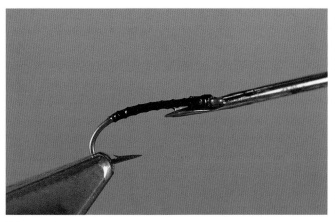

15. Apply a second coat of Griff's Thin Head Cement. Coat the underside of the body.

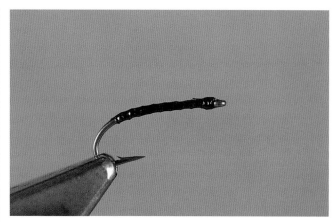

16. The 200R hook provides a long hook shank to imitate the wormlike appearance of the natural. The thin coat of head cement makes the fly look transparent, imitating the translucency of the natural. Do not apply a thick coat of cement or the fly will crack when you grip it with hemostats to remove it from a fish's mouth.

D Rib Larva

Plastic tubing creates a colorful, yet translucent, segmented body. One of our favorite materials, D Rib, comes in a wide variety of colors and sizes. D Rib has a semicircular cross-section, and when wrapped with the flat side down, the rounded side creates a nice segmented effect. Once you learn how to work with it, you can adapt the techniques to working with other types of plastic tubing.

The many varieties of plastic tubing on the market provide ample opportunities to create realistic bodies on midges. Each material has its advantages. Some tubing stretches a lot, such as the aptly named Stretch Magic, which is a common ingredient in many of the patterns included in this book. Some tubing such as Tier's Lace or Larva Lace is hollow. You can also use Micro Tubing (Hareline), which is a small-diameter tubing that will collapse when wrapped around the hook shank. It is transparent and hollow, which enables you to insert flash into the tube, or it can be filled with liquid to achieve different effects.

Materials
Hook:	#18 Tiemco 200R
Thread:	Red 70-denier UTC
Body:	UTC Vinyl D Rib
Cement:	Griff's Thin Head Cement

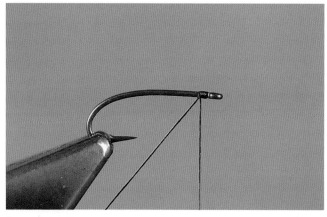

1. Attach the thread to the hook eye, taking six to eight wraps back over the thread to secure it.

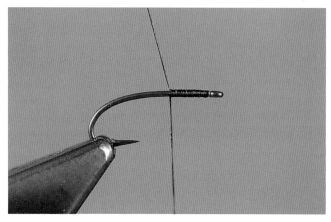

2. Wrap the tying thread in touching wraps back toward the hook bend. Holding the tag end of the tying thread at a 45-degree angle will help to make tighter touching wraps by sliding the thread up next to the previous wrap.

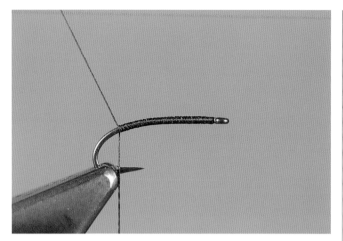

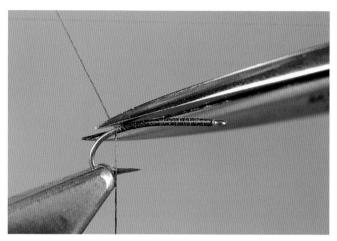

3. Continue to wrap the thread back to the hook bend opposite the barb.

4. Grasp the tag end of the tying thread, and trim it as close to the hook as possible.

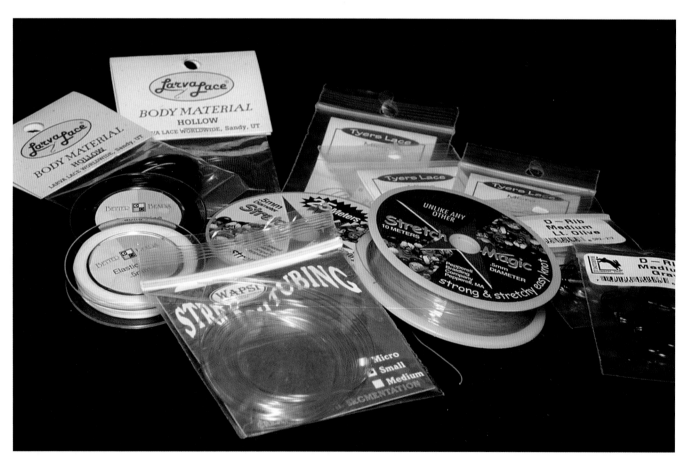

Tubing is available in round, half round, solid, and hollow. With translucent tubing materials, the color of your underbody shows through. Using thread, Flashabou, or Krystal Flash as a base can create interesting effects on your flies. You can also try weaving smaller diameter tubing.

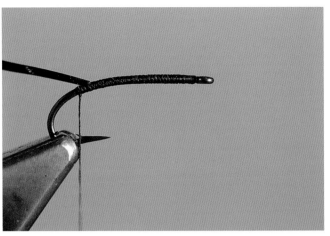

5. Cut the end of the D Rib to a point and tie the tapered end in, which helps create a smoother tie-in area.

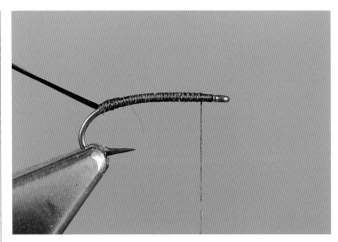

8. Wrap the thread to within one eye width back from the hook eye.

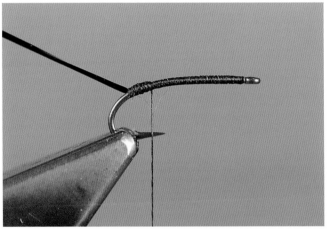

6. Continue to take several tight wraps of thread in touching wraps, moving forward toward the hook eye.

9. Grasp the D Rib and pull it tight to stretch it out while you make the first three wraps. This will help form a tapered body.

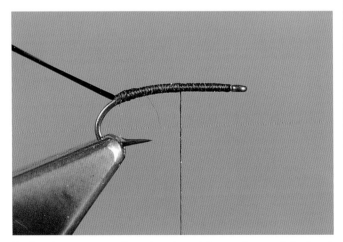

7. Continue to wrap the tying thread forward toward the hook eye.

10. Continue to wrap the D Rib forward in touching wraps.

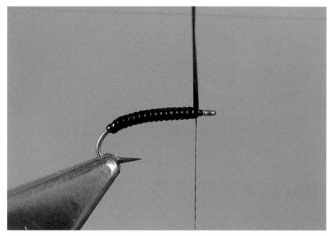

11. Wrap the D Rib forward to within one eye width behind the hook eye.

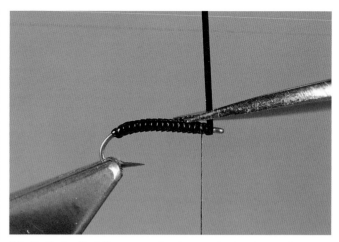

14. Pull the D Rib perpendicular to the hook shank, away from the tying thread, and trim excess material.

12. Position the tying thread over the D Rib, and prepare to secure it.

15. Take several wraps of thread over the exposed end of the D Rib that has been trimmed.

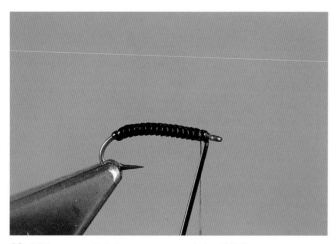

13. Make several tight wraps around the D Rib.

16. Wrap a small tapered head.

17. Whip-finish the head.

18. The head should be about this big after whip-finishing.

19. Trim the tying thread flush to the hook.

20. When you trim the thread, you can leave a small tag to imitate the natural's prolegs, but this is optional.

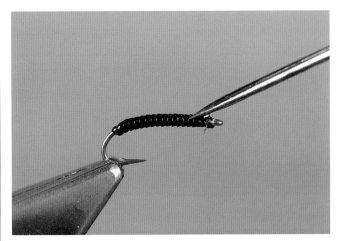

21. The trimmed thread with a small tag to imitate the prolegs.

22. Apply a small amount of head cement to the thread head.

Latex Larva

Latex is a versatile material that allows you to quickly make midge larvae and pupae patterns. It comes in many colors, takes markers well, and you can trim it to any size. Latex (Scud Back and similar products will also work) comes in strips, in sheets, or you can cut your own from high quality medical gloves. In addition to using it for midges, it also makes good scud imitations, which are also popular trout foods in many places that midges are found.

Brian Yamauchi, one of the best fly tiers we know, has developed a series of midge patterns using latex, which are featured in the fly pattern section. Brian's patterns closely mimic the naturals—from their abdomens to eyes. Latex is a major component in all of Brian's fly patterns to date. He wants to create the translucence of the naturals and finds that latex covered with UV Knot Sense, epoxy, or fingernail polish meets those requirements. Brian pays close attention to detail, creating mottled effects in his patterns to simulate internal organs and external colors of the naturals, as well as adds details such as eyes. Some may think that the patterns he creates are too realistic or that they don't fish very well, but we can attest to the fact that his patterns catch lots of fish.

Materials

Hook:	#18 Tiemco 200R
Thread:	Red 8/0 or white 17/0 Uni
Body:	Thin latex strip, coated with Griff's Thin Head Cement

You can cut your own latex from high-quality medical gloves (over-the-counter latex gloves tend to be too thin). A rotary cutter or razor make cutting latex a snap. Use a straightedge when cutting narrow strips.

Latex is available in various thicknesses from several suppliers. Hareline offers ⅛-inch-wide strips of natural latex that is our favorite material for creating the abdomens of midge pupae. Scud Back, which comes in ¼- or ⅛-inch-wide strips, is highly elastic, easily colored, and you can use it in the same way as latex.

1. Attach the thread to the hook eye, taking six to eight wraps back over the thread to secure it.

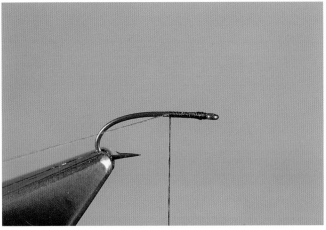

2. Wrap the tying thread in touching wraps back toward the hook bend. Hold the tag end at an angle as with the previous patterns.

3. Continue to wrap the thread back to the hook bend opposite the barb.

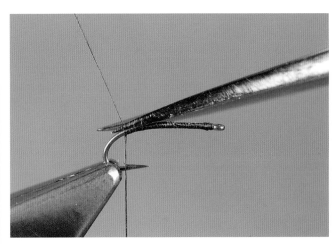

4. Grasp the tag end of the tying thread, and trim as close to the hook as possible.

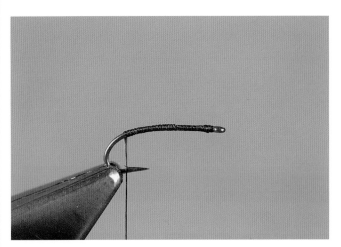

5. This is how the thread base should look.

6. Advance the tying thread forward toward the hook eye two-thirds of the distance along the hook shank.

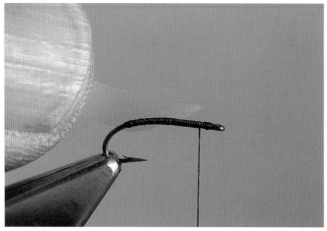

7. Cut a point in the end of the latex strip, and position it about one-third of the way back on the hook shank.

8. Tie in the latex strip by the point, taking several wraps to ensure that the latex is secure.

9. Pull the latex taut, and wrap over the latex strip in touching turns.

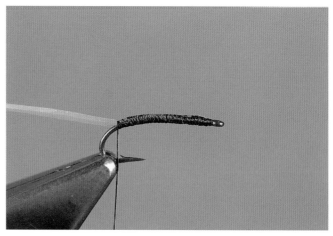

10. Continue to wrap the tying thread over the latex back to the hook bend opposite the barb.

11. Pull the latex back over the hook bend, and take three wraps forward with tying thread.

12. Grasp the latex strip and fold forward over the top half of the hook shank. Take two to three wraps of thread to form a rib.

13. Fold the latex strip back out of the way and make three more wraps of tying thread in front of it.

14. Fold the latex strip forward over the top half of the hook shank. Take two to three wraps of thread to form the second rib.

15. Fold the latex strip back out of the way and take three more wraps of tying thread in front of it.

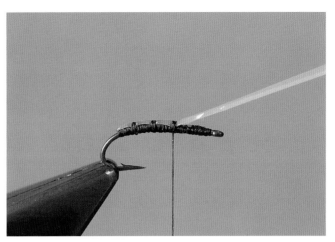

16. Fold the latex strip forward over the top half of the hook shank. Take two to three wraps of thread to form the third rib.

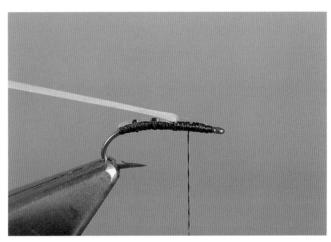

17. Fold the latex strip back out of the way, and make three more wraps of tying thread in front of it.

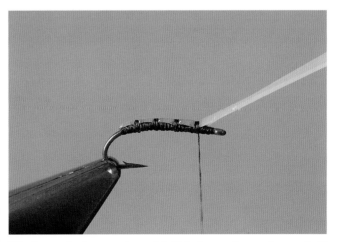

18. Grasp the latex strip and fold it forward over the top half of the hook shank. Take two to three wraps of thread to form the fourth rib.

19. Fold the latex strip back out of the way and wrap the tying thread in front of it to a point just behind the hook eye.

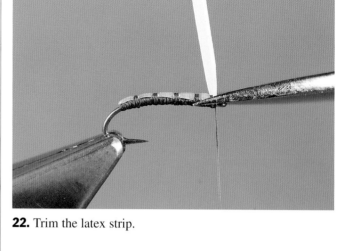

22. Trim the latex strip.

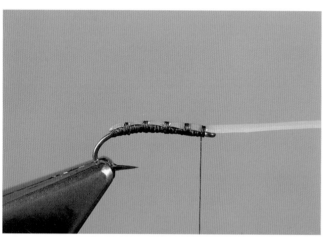

20. Take three more wraps of tying thread over the latex strip behind the hook eye.

23. Wrap a neat tapered head.

21. Fold the latex strip back, and take several wraps of thread behind the hook eye to secure it.

24. Whip-finish and trim the thread flush with hook. Sometimes your thread will fray during the whip-finish. You can either cut them away or roll with it and use the stray fibers to imitate the prolegs.

25. Color the latex with permanent marker.

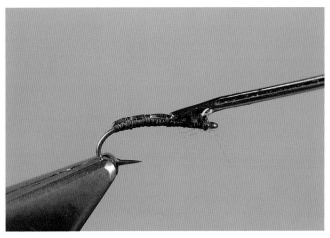

27. Coat the entire body with Sally Hansen Hard As Nails, Loon UV Knot Sense, or Griff's Thick Head Cement.

26. The colored body.

28. Finished Latex Larva

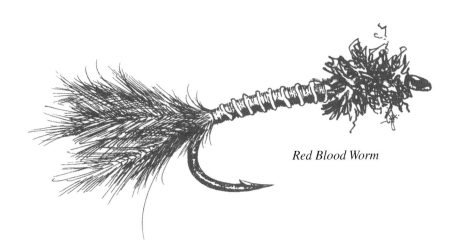

Red Blood Worm

Larva Patterns

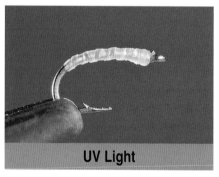

UV Light

Originator: Chris Karl
Tier: Rick Takahashi

Hook: #18-26 Tiemco 2488
Thread: White 17/0 Uni
Body: Tying thread
Rib: Pearl UV Krystal Flash
Head: Tying thread
Note: Coat entire fly with Griff's Thin Head Cement or Loon UV Knot Sense. Other hook(s): Tiemco 2487, 2475, or Dai-Riki 125.

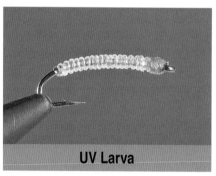

UV Larva

Originator: Chris Karl
Tier: Rick Takahashi

Hook: #18-26 Tiemco 200R
Thread: White 8/0 Uni
Body: Pearl UV Krystal Flash
Rib: Clear .5mm Stretch Magic
Head: Tying thread colored with tan Pantone marker
Note: Coat head with Griff's Thin Head Cement. Other hook(s): Dai-Riki 270.

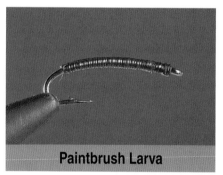

Paintbrush Larva

Originator: Unknown
Tier: Rick Takahashi

Hook: #18-26 Tiemco 200R
Thread: Olive dun 8/0 Uni
Body: Tying thread
Rib: Olive polyester paintbrush fiber
Note: Other hook(s): Dai-Riki 270.

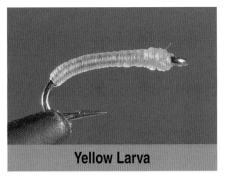

Yellow Larva

Originator: Paul Freeman
Tier: Paul Freeman

Hook: #20-22 Tiemco 200R
Thread: Yellow 8/0 Uni
Body: Yellow Micro Tubing
Head: Tying thread
Note: Other hook(s): Tiemco 2487 or Dai-Riki 125.

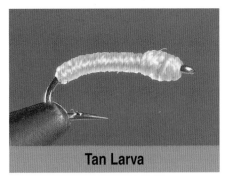

Tan Larva

Originator: Paul Freeman
Tier: Paul Freeman

Hook: #20-22 Tiemco 200R
Thread: Tan 8/0 Uni
Body: Tying thread
Head: Tying thread
Note: Other hook(s): Tiemco 2487 or Dai-Riki 125.

Chocolate Larva

Originator: Paul Freeman
Tier: Paul Freeman

Hook: #20-24 Tiemco 2487
Thread: Black 8/0 Uni
Body: Summer brown (54A) Coats & Clark
Head: Tying thread
Note: Other hook(s): Tiemco 2487 or Dai-Riki 125.

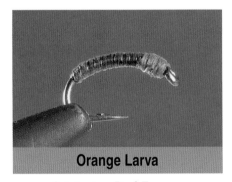

Orange Larva

Originator: Paul Freeman
Tier: Paul Freeman

Hook: #18-24 Tiemco 2487
Thread: Hot orange 8/0 Uni
Underbody: Orange Krystal Flash
Body: Orange Micro Tubing
Head: Tying thread
Note: Other hook(s): Tiemco 2457 or Dai-Riki 135.

Red Larva

Originator: Paul Freeman
Tier: Paul Freeman

Hook: #16-24 Tiemco 2487
Bead: Red glass
Thread: Red 8/0 Uni
Body: Red Micro Tubing
Note: Other hook(s): Tiemco 2457 or Dai-Riki 135.

Chocolate Larva

Originator: Paul Freeman
Tier: Paul Freeman

Hook: #20-24 Tiemco 2487
Thread: Black 8/0 Uni
Body: Tan 10/0 Gudebrod
Rib: Clear Micro Tubing
Head: Black 8/0 Uni
Note: Other hook(s): Tiemco 2457 or Dai-Riki 135.

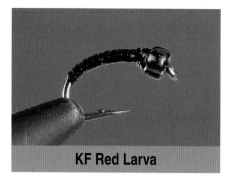

KF Red Larva

Originator: Paul Freeman
Tier: Paul Freeman

Hook: #16-24 Tiemco 2487
Bead: Red glass
Thread: Red 8/0 Uni
Underbody: Red Krystal Flash
Body: Red Micro Tubing
Note: Other hook(s): Tiemco 2457 or Dai-Riki 135.

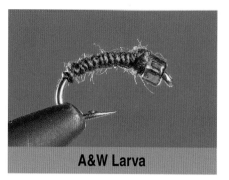

A&W Larva

Originator: Paul Freeman
Tier: Paul Freeman

Hook: #18-24 Tiemco 2487
Bead: Root beer glass
Thread: Tan 8/0 Uni
Body: Summer brown (54A) Coats & Clark
Note: Other hook(s): Tiemco 2487 or Dai-Riki 135.

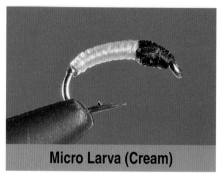

Micro Larva (Cream)

Originator: Paul Freeman
Tier: Paul Freeman

Hook: #20-26 Tiemco 2487
Thread: White 8/0 Uni
Body: Clear Micro Tubing over white thread
Head: Black 8/0 Uni
Note: Other hook(s): Tiemco 2457 or Dai-Riki 135.

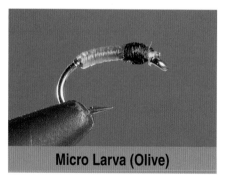

Micro Larva (Olive)

Originator: Paul Freeman
Tier: Paul Freeman

Hook: #20-24 Tiemco 2487
Thread: Olive 70-denier UTC
Body: Olive Micro Tubing
Head: Black 8/0 Uni
Note: Other hook(s): Tiemco 2457 or Dai-Riki 135.

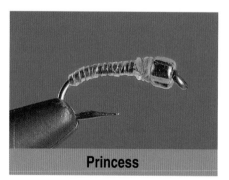

Princess

Originator: Johnny Gomez
Tier: Paul Freeman

Hook: #18-24 Tiemco 100
Bead: Orange glass
Thread: Fire orange 8/0 Uni
Body: Orange Krystal Flash
Note: Other hook(s): Dai-Riki 125.

Flashback Larva

Originator: Rick Takahashi
Tier: Rick Takahashi

Hook: #20-24 Tiemco 200R
Thread: Light cahill 6/0 Uni
Body: Tying thread
Back: Root beer Krystal Flash
Rib: Clear .5mm Stretch Magic
Head: Tying thread
Note: Color the tying thread with sand Chartpak marker for the head and coat with Griff's Thick Head Cement. Other hook(s): Dai-Riki 270.

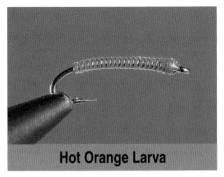

Hot Orange Larva

Originator: Rick Takahashi
Tier: Rick Takahashi

Hook: #18-22 Tiemco 200R
Thread: Hot orange 70-denier UTC
Body: Tying thread
Rib: Clear .5mm Stretch Magic
Head: Tying thread
Note: Coat head with Griff's Thick Head Cement. Other hook(s): Dai-Riki 270.

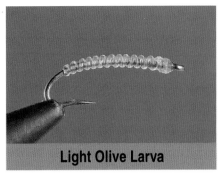

Light Olive Larva

Originator: Rick Takahashi
Tier: Rick Takahashi

Hook: #18-22 Tiemco 200R
Thread: Light olive 6/0 Uni
Body: Tying thread
Rib: Clear .5mm Stretch Magic
Note: Coat head with Griff's Thick Head Cement. Other hook(s): Dai-Riki 270.

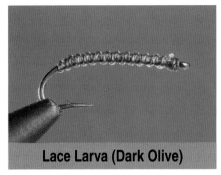

Lace Larva (Dark Olive)

Originator: Rick Takahashi
Tier: Rick Takahashi

Hook: #18-22 Tiemco 200R
Thread: Dark olive 6/0 Uni
Body: Tying thread
Rib: Clear .5mm Stretch Magic
Head: Tying thread
Note: Coat head with Griff's Thick Head Cement. Other hook(s): Dai-Riki 270.

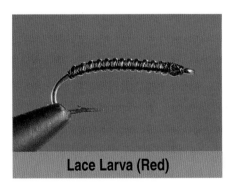

Lace Larva (Red)

Originator: Rick Takahashi
Tier: Rick Takahashi

Hook: #18-22 Tiemco 200R
Thread: Red 70-denier UTC
Body: Tying thread
Rib: Clear .5mm Stretch Magic
Head: Tying thread
Note: Coat head with Griff's Thick Head Cement. Other hook(s): Dai-Riki 270.

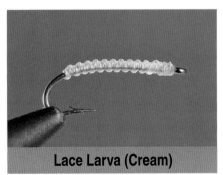

Lace Larva (Cream)

Originator: Rick Takahashi
Tier: Rick Takahashi

Hook: #18-20 Tiemco 200R
Thread: Light cahill 8/0 Uni
Body: Tying thread
Rib: Clear .5mm Stretch Magic
Note: Coat head with Griff's Thick Head Cement. Other hook(s): Dai-Riki 270.

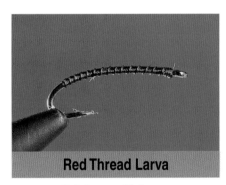

Red Thread Larva

Originator: Unknown
Tier: Rick Takahashi

Hook: #18-22 Tiemco 200R
Thread: Red 70-denier UTC
Body: Tying thread
Rib: Tying thread, twisted
Note: Coat head with Griff's Thin Head Cement. Other hook(s): Dai-Riki 270.

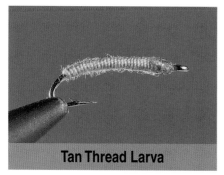

Tan Thread Larva

Originator: Rick Takahashi
Tier: Rick Takahashi

Hook: #18-22 Tiemco 200R
Thread: Light cahill 8/0 Uni
Body: Tying thread, twisted
Head: Tying thread
Note: Color tying thread with tan
Chartpak marker for the body. Coat
head with Griff's Thick Head Cement.
Other hook(s): Dai-Riki 270.

Flashabou Midge Larva (Pearl)

Originator: Unknown
Tier: Solitude Fly Company

Hook: #18-22 Daiichi 1270
Thread: White 8/0 Uni
Body: Pearl Flashabou
Thorax: Peacock herl

Flashabou Midge Larva (Olive)

Originator: Unknown
Tier: Solitude Fly Company

Hook: #18-22 Daiichi 1270
Thread: Olive 8/0 Uni
Body: Olive Flashabou
Thorax: Peacock herl

Flashabou Midge Larva (Red)

Originator: Unknown
Tier: Solitude Fly Company

Hook: #18-22 Daiichi 1270
Thread: Red 8/0 Uni
Body: Red Flashabou
Thorax: Peacock herl

Marabou Larva (Red)

Originator: Unknown
Tier: Solitude Fly Company

Hook: #18-20 Daiichi 1270
Thread: Red 6/0 Danville
Body: Red marabou
Rib: Red Flashabou

Marabou Larva (Olive)

Originator: Unknown
Tier: Solitude Fly Company

Hook: #18-20 Daiichi 1270
Thread: Olive 6/0 Danville
Body: Olive marabou
Rib: Olive Flashabou

Midge Larva (Black)

Originator: Shane Stalcup
Tier: Solitude Fly Company

Hook: #18-22 Daiichi 1120
Thread: Black 6/0 Danville
Body: Black Midge Tubing
Head: Tying thread coated with epoxy

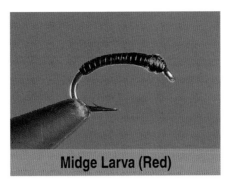

Midge Larva (Red)

Originator: Shane Stalcup
Tier: Solitude Fly Company

Hook: #18-22 Daiichi 1120
Thread: Red 6/0 Danville
Body: Red Midge Tubing
Head: Tying thread

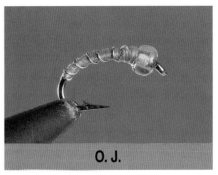

O. J.

Originator: Unknown
Tier: Float n Fish Fly Shop

Hook: #14-16 Tiemco 2487
Bead: Orange glass
Thread: Orange 8/0 Uni
Body: Tying thread
Rib: Copper Ultra Wire (extra small)

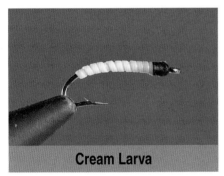

Cream Larva

Originator: Unknown
Tier: Float n Fish Fly Shop

Hook: #18-22 Tiemco 200R
Thread: Black 8/0 Uni
Body: White Micro Tubing
Head: Black 8/0 Uni

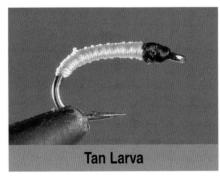

Tan Larva

Originator: Unknown
Tier: Float n Fish Fly Shop

Hook: #18-22 Tiemco 2488
Body: Tan 70-denier UTC
Head: Black 8/0 Uni

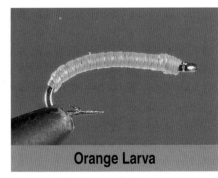

Orange Larva

Originator: Unknown
Tier: Float n Fish Fly Shop

Hook: #18-22 Tiemco 200R
Thread: Orange 8/0 Uni
Body: Orange Micro Tubing
Head: Orange 8/0 Uni

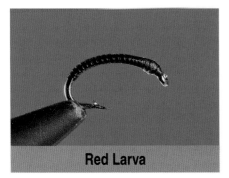

Red Larva

Originator: Unknown
Tier: Float n Fish Fly Shop

Hook:	#18-22 Tiemco 2457
Thread:	Red 8/0 Uni
Body:	Red Micro Tubing
Head:	Red 8/0 Uni

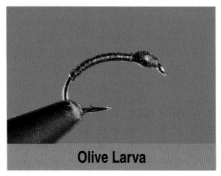

Olive Larva

Originator: Unknown
Tier: Float n Fish Fly Shop

Hook:	#18-22 Tiemco 2457
Thread:	Olive 8/0 Uni
Body:	Olive Micro Tubing
Head:	Olive 8/0 Uni

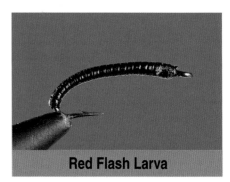

Red Flash Larva

Originator: Unknown
Tier: Float n Fish Fly Shop

Hook:	#18-22 Tiemco 200R
Thread:	Red 8/0 Uni
Body:	Red Micro Tubing
Head:	Red 8/0 Uni

Big Mac (Gray)

Originator: John Tavenner
Tier: Pacific Fly Group

Hook:	#18-22 Tiemco 200R
Thread:	Iron gray 8/0 Uni
Body:	Tying thread
Rib:	Clear Micro Tubing
Thorax:	Black Super Fine

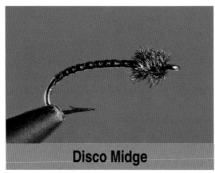

Disco Midge

Originator: Unknown
Tier: Umpqua Feather Merchants

Hook:	#20-24 Tiemco 200R
Thread:	Red 8/0 Uni
Body:	Red Krystal Flash
Thorax:	Peacock herl

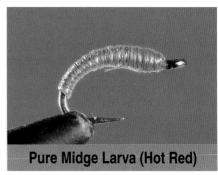

Pure Midge Larva (Hot Red)

Originator: John Barr
Tier: Umpqua Feather Merchants

Hook:	#20-22 Daiichi 1273
Thread:	Fl. red 70-denier UTC
Underbody:	Tying thread
Body:	Red Micro Tubing
Head:	Thread covered with Sally Hansen Hard As Nails

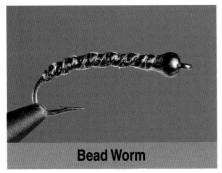

Bead Worm

Originator: Bruce Smith
Tier: Bruce Smith

Hook: #14 Tiemco 200R
Bead: Black nickel metal
Thread: Orange 8/0 Uni
Body: Red Holographic
Flashabou
Rib 1: Clear V Rib (medium)
Rib 2: Copper Ultra Wire (small)
Note: Other hook(s): Dai-Riki 270.

Red Midge

Originator: Ron Yoshimura
Tier: Ron Yoshimura

Hook: #16-22 Tiemco 2487
Bead: Red glass
Thread: Red 8/0 Uni
Body: Red ostrich herl
Rib: Gold Lagartun wire (fine)

Midge Larva

Originator: Brian Yamauchi
Tier: Brian Yamauchi

Hook: #18-22 Tiemco 2487
Thread: White 17/0 Uni
Body: Red UTC Vinyl D Rib
Note: Crimp the Vinyl D Rib with
serrated forceps; cover the body and
thorax with Loon UV Knot Sense.

Black Fly Larva

Originator: Brian Yamauchi
Tier: Brian Yamauchi

Hook: #18 Gamakatsu C15
Thread: White 17/0 Uni
Body: Latex colored with tan
Chartpak marker
Note: Color the end of the body dark
brown to represent head. Build up the
eye of the hook with Loon UV Knot
Sense. Other hook(s): Tiemco 206BL
(#20).

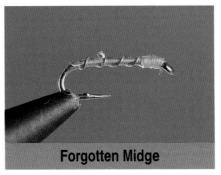

Forgotten Midge

Originator: Austin Haacke
Tier: Austin Haacke

Hook: #18-24 Tiemco 3761
Thread: Light olive 6/0 Uni
Body: Tying thread
Rib: Gold Lagartun wire
(extra fine)
Head: Tying thread

High Water Larva (Red)

Originator: Jerry Saiz
Tier: Jerry Saiz

Hook: #18-22 Daiichi 1273
Bead: Red glass
Thread: Red 14/0 Gordon Griffiths
Abdomen: Red Midge Tubing
Thorax: Red Super Fine

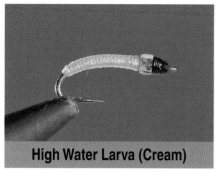

High Water Larva (Cream)

Originator: Jerry Saiz
Tier: Jerry Saiz

Hook: #18-22 Tiemco 200R
Bead: Gold glass
Thread: Black 8/0 Uni
Body: Cream Gudebrod rod
             wrapping thread
Head: Tying thread

High Water Larva (Yellow)

Originator: Jerry Saiz
Tier: Jerry Saiz

Hook: #18-22 Daiichi 1273
Thread: Red 8/0 Uni
Bead: Red glass
Abdomen: Light Goldenstone Midge
              Tubing
Thorax: Red Super Fine

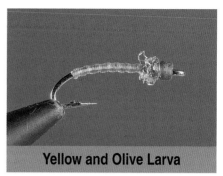

Yellow and Olive Larva

Originator: Rick Takahashi
Tier: Rick Takahashi

Hook: #18-22 Tiemco 200R
Bead: Gunmetal brown glass
Thread: White 17/0 Uni
Body: Tying thread
Rib: Olive Micro Tubing
Collar: Rusty brown Ice Dub
Note: Color thread with yellow Chartpak
marker.

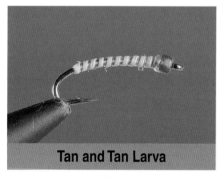

Tan and Tan Larva

Originator: Rick Takahashi
Tier: Rick Takahashi

Hook: #18-22 Tiemco 200R
Bead: Gunmetal brown glass
Thread: White 17/0 Uni
Body: Tying thread
Rib: Buckskin Micro Tubing
Note: Color thread with sand Chartpak
marker.

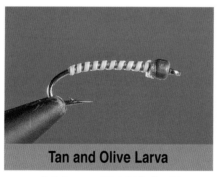

Tan and Olive Larva

Originator: Rick Takahashi
Tier: Rick Takahashi

Hook: #18-22 Tiemco 200R
Bead: Gunmetal olive glass
Thread: White 17/0 Uni
Body: Tying thread
Rib: Buckskin Micro Tubing
Note: Color thread with olive Chartpak
marker.

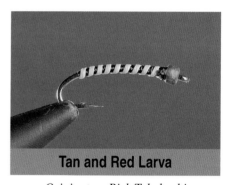

Tan and Red Larva

Originator: Rick Takahashi
Tier: Rick Takahashi

Hook: #18-22 Tiemco 200R
Bead: Gunmetal brown glass
Thread: White 17/0 Uni
Body: Tying thread
Rib: Buckskin Micro Tubing
Note: Color thread with red Sharpie
marker.

Candy Cane Larva

Originator: Unknown
Tier: Rick Takahashi

Hook: #18-22 Tiemco 200R
Bead: Flat white glass
Thread: White 17/0 Uni
Body: Tying thread
Rib: Red Krystal Flash
Collar: Rust Ice Dub
Note: Color thread with light tan
Chartpak marker.

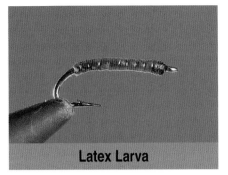

Latex Larva

Originator: Rick Takahashi
Tier: Rick Takahashi

Hook: #14-18 Tiemco 200R
Thread: White 8/0 Uni
Body: Latex colored with red
Sharpie

Chironomid Larva (Bloodworm)

Originator: John Shewey
Tier: Rainy's Fly Company

Hook: #12-16 Tiemco 200R
Thread: Black 8/0 Uni
Body: Red Danville floss
Rib: Gold Ultra Wire (small)
Thorax: Peacock herl

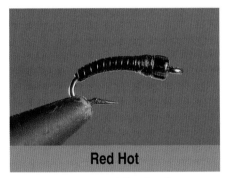

Red Hot

Originator: John Gordon
Tier: John Gordon

Hook: #22 Tiemco 200R
Bead: Red glass
Thread: Red 8/0 Uni
Underbody: Tying thread
Body: Blood red D Rib
Head: Tying thread
Note: Other hook(s): Daiichi 1270.

Black Fly Larva

Originator: John Gordon
Tier: John Gordon

Hook: #22 Tiemco 200R
Thread: Black 8/0 Uni
Body: DMC embroidery threads
#732 olive and #762 light
gray

Shelmore Buzzer

Originator: Dennis Shaw
Tier: Dennis Shaw

Hook: #16-20 Kamasan B420
Thread: Olive 6/0 Uni
Body: Bottle green Lagartun wire
(fine)
Thorax: Thread
Note: Cover the entire fly with varnish
or epoxy.

Crystal Method

Originator: Chad Gauerke
Tier: Chad Gauerke

Hook: #18 Dai-Riki 270
Bead: Silver Czech
Thread: White 10/0 Gudebrod
Body: Clear .5mm Stretch Magic
Thorax: Rainbow Sow Scud
Dubbing

Plum's Crystal Method

Originator: Chad Gauerke
Tier: Chad Gauerke

Hook: #20 Dai-Riki 270
Thread: Wine 8/0 Uni
Bead: Red glass
Body: Red .5mm Stretch Magic
Thorax: Claret Ice Dub

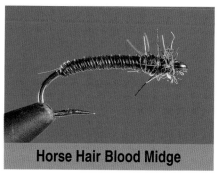

Horse Hair Blood Midge

Originator: Chad Gauerke
Tier: Chad Gauerke

Hook: #20 Dai-Riki 270
Thread: White 10/0 Uni
Body: Red dyed horse hair
Thorax: Scarlet red Spectrablend
dubbing

Rainbow Warrior

Originator: Chad Gauerke
Tier: Chad Gauerke

Hook: #20 Dai-Riki 125
Thread: White 10/0 Uni
Body: Olive Come's Alive Fish
Scale
Thorax: Rainbow Wapsi Sow Scud
Dubbing

Trout Crack

Originator: John Wilson
Tier: Russell Stanton

Hook: #20 Tiemco 100
Thread: 7X tippet
Body: Tan Antron
Rib: 7X tippet
Back: Brown UTC Vinyl D Rib

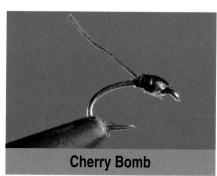

Cherry Bomb

Originator: Chris (Swizz) Evenstad
Tier: Chris (Swizz) Evenstad

Hook: #20-22 Tiemco 2487
Thread: Red 8/0 Uni
Body: Red Super Floss, split
Thorax: Red Krystal Flash coated
with epoxy

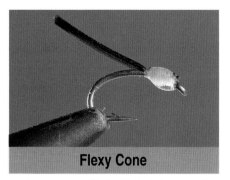

Flexy Cone

Originator: Chris (Swizz) Evenstad
Tier: Chris (Swizz) Evenstad

Hook:	#20-22 Tiemco 2487
Thread:	White 8/0 Uni
Body:	Bark brown Super Floss, split
Thorax:	White 10/0 coated with epoxy

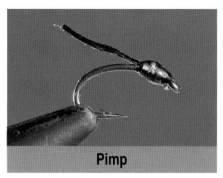

Pimp

Originator: Chris (Swizz) Evenstad
Tier: Chris (Swizz) Evenstad

Hook:	#20-22 Tiemco 2487
Thread:	Purple 8/0 Uni
Body:	Purple Super Floss, split
Thorax:	Black Holographic Tinsel coated with epoxy

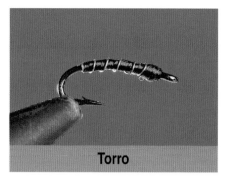

Torro

Originator: Kelli Sandoval
Tier: Kelli Sandoval

Hook:	#18-22 Daiichi 1273
Thread:	Red 70-denier UTC
Body:	Tying thread
Rib:	Copper Ultra Wire (extra small)
Head:	Tying thread

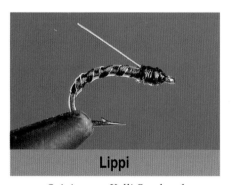

Lippi

Originator: Kelli Sandoval
Tier: Kelli Sandoval

Hook:	#22-26 Tiemco 2488
Thread:	Red 70-denier UTC
Body:	Tying thread
Rib:	Pearl Krystal Flash
Wing:	Pearl Krystal Flash
Head:	Tying thread

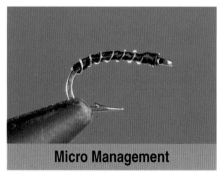

Micro Management

Originator: Kelli Sandoval
Tier: Kelli Sandoval

Hook:	#22-26 Tiemco 2488
Thread:	Black 70-denier UTC
Body:	Tying thread
Rib:	Copper Lagartun wire (extra fine)
Head:	Tying thread

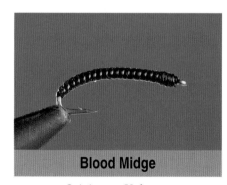

Blood Midge

Originator: Unknown
Tier: Spirit River

Hook:	#18-22 Spear It CS200
Thread:	Black 8/0 Uni
Body:	Red V Rib (extra small)
Head:	Tying thread
Note:	Other hook(s): Daiichi 1270.

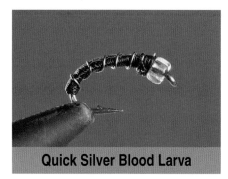

Quick Silver Blood Larva

Originator: Unknown
Tier: Spirit River

Hook: #12-18 Spear-It CS048
Bead: Clear glass
Thread: Black 8/0 Uni
Back: Pearl Crystal Splash
Body: Tying thread
Rib: Copper Lagartun wire (fine)
Note: Other hook(s): Daiichi 2230.

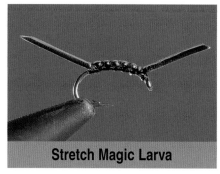

Stretch Magic Larva

Originator: Rick Takahashi
Tier: Rick Takahashi

Hook: #18-20 Tiemco 2457
Thread: Red 70-denier UTC
Rib: Tying thread
Body: Red .5mm Stretch Magic

Alien Larva

Originator: Unknown
Tier: Chad Gauerke

Hook: #20 Dai-Riki 270
Thread: Olive 8/0 Uni
Backing: Light olive Magic Shrimp Foil
Rib: Clear Stretch Rib (small)
Head: Thread colored with black marker
Body: Callibaetis Buggy Nymph Dubbing

Rainbow Pearlescent

Originator: Chad Gauerke
Tier: Chad Gauerke

Hook: #18 Skalka P Midge
Thread: Wine 8/0 Uni
Body: Rainbow Pearlescent Fly Flash
Head: Black 8/0 Uni
Note: Cover body with Sally Hansen Hard As Nails.

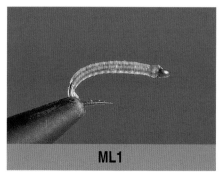

ML1

Originator: Deward Yocum
Tier: Deward Yocum

Hook: #18-22 Tiemco 200R
Thread: Light cahill 8/0 Uni
Body: Cream latex
Note: Color latex with light tan marker. Seal body with Hard Headed by Angling Evolutions.

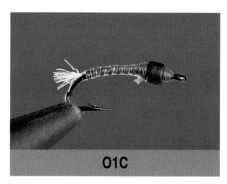

O1C

Originator: Deward Yocum
Tier: Deward Yocum

Hook: #18-22 Daiichi 1273
Thorax: Black glass bead
Thread: Fire orange 70-denier UTC
Tail: White Antron
Body: Tying thread
Rib: Pearl Flashabou

Red Zen

Originator: Deward Yocum
Tier: Deward Yocum

Hook: #18-22 Tiemco 200R
Bead: Red glass
Thread: Red 8/0 Uni
Body: Tying thread
Rib: Silver Lagartun wire (fine)
Thorax: Purple and red Super Fine, mixed

Blondie

Originator: Deward Yocum
Tier: Deward Yocum

Hook: #18-22 Tiemco 200R
Body: Cream (116) Coats & Clark
Rib: Pearl Flashabou
Head: Gray brown 70-denier UTC

San Juan Flasher

Originator: Deward Yocum
Tier: Deward Yocum

Hook: #18-22 Tiemco 200R
Body: Summer brown (54A) Coats & Clark
Rib: Pearl Flashabou
Head: Black 8/0 Uni

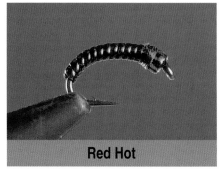

Red Hot

Originator: Unknown
Tier: Pacific Fly Group

Hook: #16-22 Daiich 1130
Bead: Red glass
Thread: Red 8/0 Uni
Abdomen: Red Micro Tubing

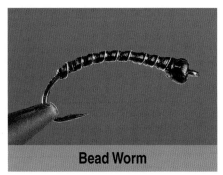

Bead Worm

Originator: Phil Rowley
Tier: Phil Rowley

Hook: #14-16 Partridge PX15BN
Bead: Red glass
Thread: Red 8/0 Uni
Body: Red Holographic Mylar
Rib 1: Red Stillwater Solutions Midge Stretch Floss
Rib 2: Silver Lagartun wire (fine)

Green and Red Midge Larva

Originator: Brian Chan
Tier: Brian Chan

Hook: #10-14 Mustad C53S
Bead: Red glass
Thread: Red 8/0 Uni
Underbody: Bright green Flashabou
Body: Red Stretch Floss
Rib: Silver Ultra Wire (small)
Note: Other hook(s): Tiemco 2302.

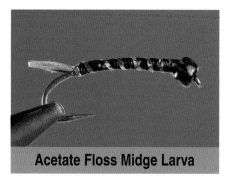

Acetate Floss Midge Larva

Originator: Brian Chan
Tier: Brian Chan

Hook: #10-14 Mustad C53S
Bead: Maroon silver-lined glass
Thread: Red 8/0 Uni
Tail: Red Stretch Floss
Body: Red Stretch Floss
Rib: Small gold Holographic Tinsel
Overbody: Red Stretch Floss
Note: Dip completed fly in acetone to melt and fuse the acetate floss. Other hook(s): Tiemco 2302.

Red Larva

Originator: ATF Fly Shop
Tier: Tim Mack

Hook: #18-22 Daiichi 1260
Thread: Red 70-denier UTC
Body: Red Flex-Floss

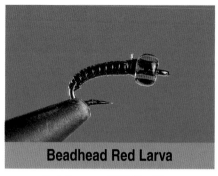

Beadhead Red Larva

Originator: ATF Fly Shop
Tier: Tim Mack

Hook: #18-22 Daiichi 1273
Bead: Red glass
Thread: Red 70-denier UTC
Body: Red Micro Tubing

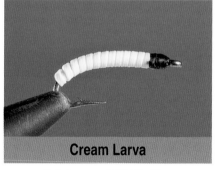

Cream Larva

Originator: ATF Fly Shop
Tier: Tim Mack

Hook: #20-24 Tiemco 200R
Thread: Black 10/0 Bennechi
Body: Cream Micro Tubing
Head: Thread

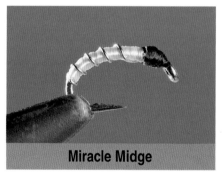

Miracle Midge

Originator: Unknown
Tier: Duranglers Fly Shop

Hook: #18-24 Tiemco 2487
Thread: Black 8/0 Uni
Body: Cream 70-denier UTC
Rib: Copper Lagartun wire (fine)
Head: Tying thread

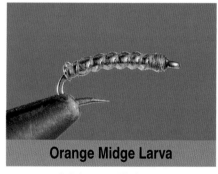

Orange Midge Larva

Originator: Unknown
Tier: Duranglers Fly Shop

Hook: #18-22 Tiemco 200R
Thread: Hot orange 8/0 Uni
Underbody: Tying thread
Body: Orange Micro Tubing
Rib: Tying thread
Head: Tying thread

Otter's Chironomid Larva (Olive)

Originator: Walt Mueller
Tier: Montana Fly Company

Hook:	#10-14 MFC 7002
Thread:	Light olive 6/0 Uni
Tail:	White Gator Hair
Underbody:	Tying thread
Body:	Clear Larva Lace
Thorax:	March Brown Frog's Hair

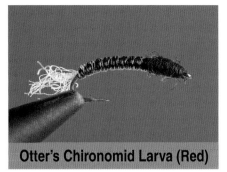

Otter's Chironomid Larva (Red)

Originator: Walt Mueller
Tier: Montana Fly Company

Hook:	#10-14 MFC 7002
Thread:	Red 8/0 Uni
Tail:	White Gator Hair
Underbody:	Tying thread
Body:	Clear Larva Lace
Thorax:	Black Frog's Hair

Otter's Blackfly Larva (Gray)

Originator: Walt Mueller
Tier: Montana Fly Company

Hook:	#20-22 MFC 7002
Thread:	Rust brown 8/0 Uni
Underbody:	Dun Antron Body Wool
Body:	Clear UTC Vinyl D Rib
Head:	Rust Frog's Hair

Otter's Micro Midge Larva (Gray)

Originator: Walt Mueller
Tier: Montana Fly Company

Hook:	#20-22 MFC 7000
Thread:	Gray 8/0 Uni
Body:	Clear Larva Lace
Head:	Adams gray Frog's Hair
Tail:	White Antron

Martin's Midge Larva (Pearl)

Originator: Jason Goodale
Tier: Jason Goodale

Hook:	#16-24 Tiemco 200R
Thread:	White 10/0 Bennechi
Underbody:	Pearl Krystal Flash
Body:	Clear Micro Tubing
Head:	Black 10/0

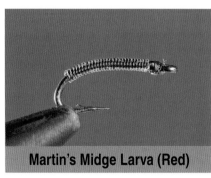

Martin's Midge Larva (Red)

Originator: Jason Goodale
Tier: Jason Goodale

Hook:	#16-24 Tiemco 200R
Thread:	Red 10/0 Bennechi
Underbody:	Tying thread
Body:	.005 clear mono
Head:	Tying thread

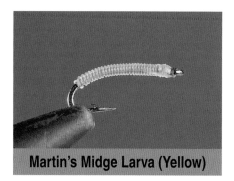

Martin's Midge Larva (Yellow)

Originator: Jason Goodale
Tier: Jason Goodale

Hook: #16-24 Tiemco 200R
Thread: Yellow 10/0 Bennechi
Underbody: Tying thread
Body: .005 clear mono
Head: Tying thread

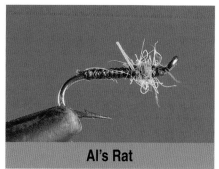

Al's Rat

Originator: Allen Miller
Tier: Bob Magill

Hook: #20-24 Daiichi 1330
Thread: Brown Danville Monocord
Thorax: Dark muskrat fur

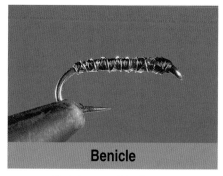

Benicle

Originator: Jim Auman
Tier: Jim Auman

Hook: #18-24 Tiemco 100
Thread: Black 10/0
Body: Red 10/0 Gudebrod
Rib 1: Copper Lagartun wire (extra fine)
Rib 2: Pearl Krystal Flash

Cream Midge Larva

Originator: Rob Jiron
Tier: Rob Jiron

Hook: #18-22 Tiemco 200R
Body: Cream Coats and Clark sewing thread
Head: Light cahill 8/0 Uni

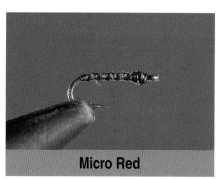

Micro Red

Originator: Ron Donahue
Tier: Ron Donahue

Hook: #26 Tiemco 101
Thread: Red 14/0 Gordon Griffiths
Body: Orange red 8/0 Uni
Rib: Red 14/0 Gordon Griffiths, twisted
Head: Tying thread

Mercury Sparkle Root Beer

Originator: Ron Donahue
Tier: Ron Donahue

Hook: #22-24 Tiemco 200R
Bead: Mercury glass
Thread: Yellow 14/0 Gordon Griffiths
Body: Root beer Ice Dub Braid
Thorax: Tying thread

Sally's Secret

Originator: Sally Sheets
Tier: Sally Sheets

Hook: #18-22 Daiichi 1273
Thread: Red 8/0 Uni
Body: Red Vernille
Rib: Silver Lagartun wire (fine)
Note: Burn the Vernille on both ends.

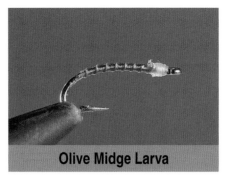

Olive Midge Larva

Originator: Rob Jiron
Tier: Rob Jiron

Hook: #18-22 Tiemco 200R
Body: Olive 8/0 Uni
Rib: Tying thread, twisted
Head: Light cahill 8/0 Uni

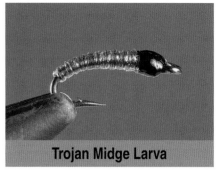

Trojan Midge Larva

Originator: Jude Duran
Tier: Jude Duran

Hook: #18-22 Tiemco 200R
Thread: Olive brown 70-denier
               UTC
Body: Clear Scud Back
Head: Black 12/0 Bennechi
               coated with Sally Hansen
               Hard As Nails.

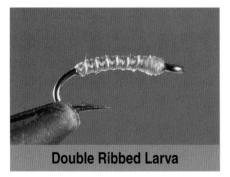

Double Ribbed Larva

Originator: Jude Duran
Tier: Jude Duran

Hook: #18-22 Tiemco 200R
Thread: Cream 8/0 Uni
Rib 1:   Clear Micro Tubing
Rib 2:   Light olive size A Belding
               Corticelli silk
Head: Tying thread

Black Fly Larva

Originator: Brian Yamauchi
Tier: Brian Yamauchi

Hook: #18-24 Tiemco 2487
Thread: White 17/0 Uni
Body: UTC Vinyl D Rib
Note: Color the teeth of the forceps with
dark brown marker before crimping the
D Rib. Coat the body with Loon UV
Knot Sense.

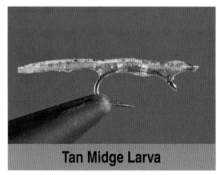

Tan Midge Larva

Originator: Brian Yamauchi
Tier: Brian Yamauchi

Hook: #18-24 Tiemco 2487
Thread: White 17/0 Uni
Body: Clear UTC Vinyl D Rib
Note: Crimp the D Rib with hemostats
colored with tan Chartpak marker. Coat
entire body with Loon UV Knot Sense.

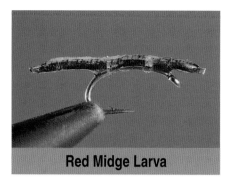

Red Midge Larva

Originator: Brian Yamauchi
Tier: Brian Yamauchi

Hook: #18-24 Tiemco 2487
Thread: White 17/0 Uni
Body: Red UTC Vinyl D Rib
Note: Crimp the D Rib with hemostats. Coat entire body with Loon UV Knot Sense.

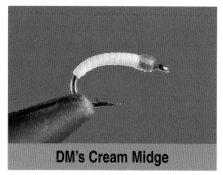

DM's Cream Midge

Originator: Dennis Martin
Tier: Dennis Martin

Hook: #18-24 Tiemco 2488
Thread: Ginger 14/0 Gordon Griffiths
Body: White Midge Tubing
Head: Tying thread

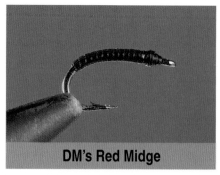

DM's Red Midge

Originator: Dennis Martin
Tier: Dennis Martin

Hook: #18-24 Tiemco 2488
Thread: Black 14/0 Gordon Griffiths
Body: Red Midge Tubing
Head: Tying thread

Weikert Run Midge Larva

Originator: Don Holbrook
Tier: Kevin Compton

Hook: #20 Grip 11911BL
Thread: Rusty brown 10/0 Gudebrod
Body: DMC Floss #3013 Light Khaki
Rib: DMC Floss #712 Cream
Head: Tying thread

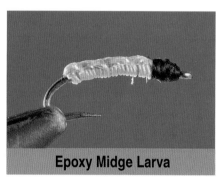

Epoxy Midge Larva

Originator: Bubba Smith
Tier: Bubba Smith

Hook: #18-22 Tiemco 200R
Body: Size "A" tan Gudebrod thread
Back: Pearl Midge Braid covered with epoxy
Rib: Tan 12/0 Bennechi
Head: Black 12/0 Bennechi

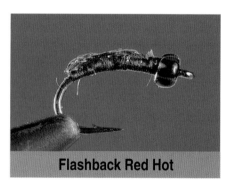

Flashback Red Hot

Originator: Unknown
Tier: Bubba Smith

Hook: #18-24 Tiemco 2488
Bead: Red glass
Thread: Red 8/0 Uni
Back: Red Midge Braid
Body: Tying thread

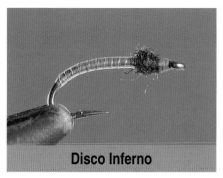

Disco Inferno

Originator: Unknown
Tier: Bruce Hopper

Hook: #18-24 Tiemco 200R
Thread: Flame-orange 70-denier UTC
Body: Tying thread
Rib: Pearl Krystal Flash
Thorax: Black Super Fine

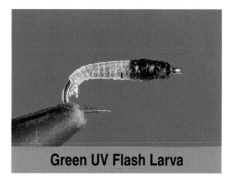

Green UV Flash Larva

Originator: John Larson
Tier: John Larson

Hook: #22-24 Tiemco 101
Thread: Black 14/0 Gordon Griffiths
Body: Chartreuse Danville Glo Flash
Head: Black UV Krystal Flash
Note: Coat body with Wet and Wild Rock Solid Nail Polish.

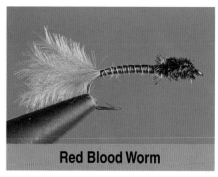

Red Blood Worm

Originator: Unknown
Tier: John Nichols

Hook: #14-18 Daiichi 1720
Thread: Red 8/0 Uni
Tail: Red marabou
Rib: Gold Ultra Wire (extra small)
Body: Red floss
Thorax: Peacock herl

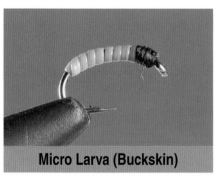

Micro Larva (Buckskin)

Originator: Paul Freeman
Tier: Paul Freeman

Hook: #18-24 Tiemco 2487
Thread: Black 8/0 Uni
Body: Buckskin Micro Tubing
Head: Black 8/0 Uni
Note: Other hook(s): Tiemco 2457 or Dai-Riki 135.

4

Tying the Pupa

TROUT FEED ON pupae as they emerge from their larval cases, from the bottom to the surface, where they transform into adults. It is generally thought that pupae are poor swimmers and just drift along in the water, ascending slowly and giving trout ample opportunities to capture them. However, Ralph and Lisa Cutter's DVD, *Bugs of the Underworld,* shows footage of a midge pupa ascending to the surface very quickly. Because the factors that influence the various speeds of this pupal journey are relatively unknown, it makes sense for

anglers to experiment with retrieves until they find what works. After countless hours spent watching fish feed and noticing that we catch most of our fish on pupa patterns, we believe that trout feed more on midge pupae than any other stage.

We love tying flies for this stage of the midge life cycle, and with new materials becoming available each year, we've spent hours at the vise coming up with variations of and experimenting with new midge pupa patterns. One important aspect of the midge pupa to consider when tying imitations is the size

Brian Yamauchi's Latex Pupa does its job again. The pupal stage is the most important stage of a midge's life for fly fishers to imitate.

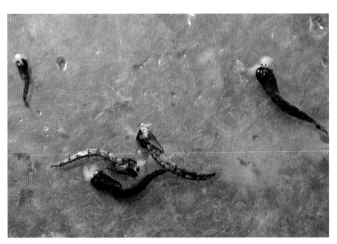

Midge pupae are short and stubby and have well-segmented abdomens and a larger thorax that encases the developing wings and legs. They have feathery gills and wing pads tucked close to their thoraxes.

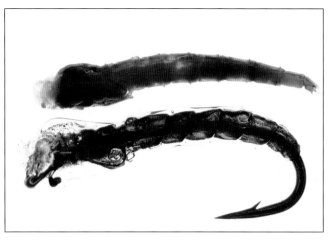

The hundreds and hundreds of available pupa patterns cover a broad spectrum of colors and range from simple to elaborate creations. We've found the most effective colors to be earth tones in shades of brown, tan, olive, gray, cream, and black.

differences between samples—especially between those collected in rivers and those collected in lakes and reservoirs. In general, stream midges appear to be smaller—approximately equivalent to size 18 to 28 hooks. Stillwater anglers should have midges as large as size 8.

On tailwaters such as the San Juan, the average size of the midge pupae falls in the range of size 20 to 26 hooks. That doesn't mean that you can't catch fish using larger imitations,

but smaller sizes usually work best. Of course, presentation is a key factor in whether or not the fish will elect to eat the pattern you are drifting toward them.

In the following steps we show three out of an untold number of techniques used to imitate the midge pupa. Generally, most pupa patterns tend to be more impressionistic in their design, though one of the techniques we demonstrate results in a realistic pattern.

Thread Body Pupa

The Thread Body Pupa uses sewing thread to form the body, but you can substitute a variety of other thread types to meet your tying needs. You can tie fairly small flies using sewing thread, or you may use a larger-diameter tying thread. The main reason for using sewing thread is to create segmentation by twisting the thread into a tight cord and wrapping it on the shank. We try to incorporate this segmentation into most of the pupa patterns we tie because it seems to work well. Even though these patterns are small, don't underestimate the effectiveness of paying attention to such details as segmentation, a larger thorax, and the head.

Materials

Hook:	#18-26 Tiemco 2487, 2488, 100, or Dai-Riki 060
Thread:	Black 8/0 Uni or 70-denier UTC
Abdomen:	Coats & Clark sewing thread
Thorax/head:	Tying thread

1. Attach the sewing thread at the midpoint of the hook, and wrap forward toward the eye. Wrap to within one eye width back from the eye.

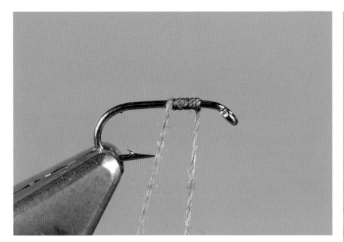

2. Begin wrapping the sewing thread back toward the hook bend, over the previous wraps.

3. Wrap the sewing thread back to the midpoint of the hook.

4. Trim the sewing thread.

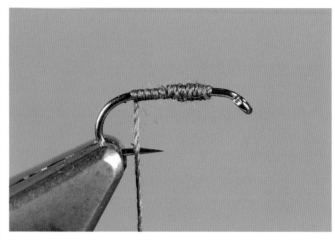

5. Wrap the sewing thread back toward the hook bend, stopping between the barb and the hook point.

6. Spin the bobbin clockwise to twist the thread. This helps create a segmented abdomen.

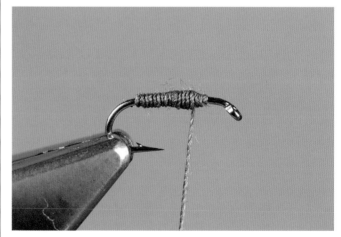

7. Wrap the sewing thread forward in touching wraps to within two wraps of the front end of the previous wraps.

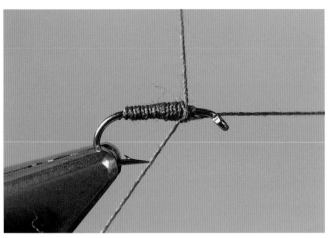

8. Whip-finish the sewing thread with two wraps.

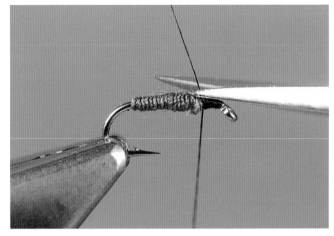

11. Trim the tag end of the tying thread.

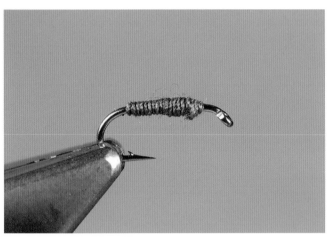

9. Trim the sewing thread flush with the body.

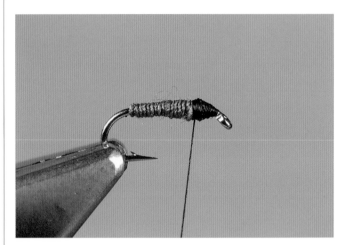

12. Create a tapered head, with the rear portion slightly larger than the body.

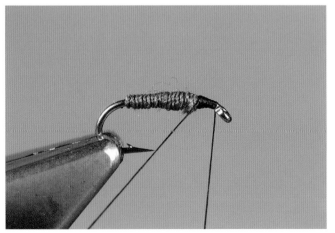

10. Attach tying thread at the hook eye, and wrap back toward the body.

13. Whip-finish at the rear of the head.

14. Trim the tying thread flush to the hook.

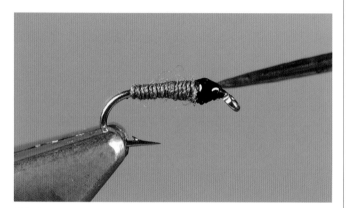

15. Apply Griff's Thick Head Cement to create a shiny head.

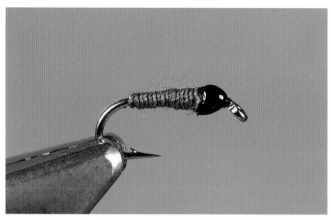

16. Finished Thread Body Pupa. This impressionistic version of the midge pupa mimics the size, shape, and color of the natural. The segmented effect of the thread and the shiny head are important components of this pattern. Change the thread color to match naturals in the waters you are fishing.

Mercury Black Beauty

Pat Dorsey's Black Beauty is a simple but deadly pattern. You can select any color bead and thread to represent the midge pupae where you're fishing. The reason you see so many patterns with beads is because they are so effective. Beads may represent the natural's thorax, the chironomid's silvery appearance right before emergence, or just add a little extra sparkle that catches the fish's attention.

Beads come in a host of colors and sizes. Spirit River markets Hi-Lite Glass Beads in silver-lined, metallic, or transparent finishes. The most useful sizes for midges (#16-22) are extra small (15/0). Wapsi markets glass beads under the name Killer Caddis that are available in a similar midge size. Spirit River's Hump-Bak glass beads have an offset hole, which allows the hook to sit on top of the hook shank. You can also purchase beads from craft stores, but we have found the most useful beads for fly tying at bead specialty shops that carry beads down to size 18/0. These specialty beads come in a huge selection of colors.

Hook Size to Bead Size

HOOK SIZE	BEAD SIZE
#22-26	$\frac{1}{16}$ inch (1.5 mm)
#18-22	$\frac{5}{64}$ inch (2.0 mm)
#16-18	$\frac{3}{32}$ inch (2.5 mm)
#14-16	$\frac{7}{64}$ inch (3.0 mm)
#12-14	$\frac{1}{8}$ inch (3.5 mm)
# 8-10	$\frac{5}{32}$ inch (4.0 mm)

Note: This is a universal measurement chart, but some beads may not fit on the hook size listed because of variations in hook models.

Materials

Hook:	#18-24 Tiemco 2457 or 2488; Dai-Riki 135 or 125
Bead:	Spirit River Mercury clear glass
Thread:	Black 8/0 Uni or 70-denier UTC
Abdomen:	Tying thread
Rib:	Silver Lagartun wire (fine)
Thorax/head:	Black Super Fine

Glass beads come in a variety of colors and sizes—clear or colored with metallic or colored centers. The variety is endless.

Wire can be used to add weight to the fly, provide flash, and also provide contrast to the underbody colors. Lagartun and Ultra Wire both have nontarnishing copper finishes in a variety of colors and sizes.

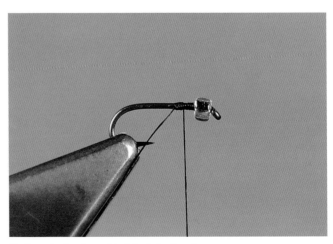

Metal beads are available in copper, silver, gold, and black colors and in brass or tungsten. Tungsten is heavier than brass and more expensive. They range in size from the smallest 1.5mm ($^1/_{16}$) to the largest 5.5mm ($^7/_{32}$). See bead chart for suggested sizing.

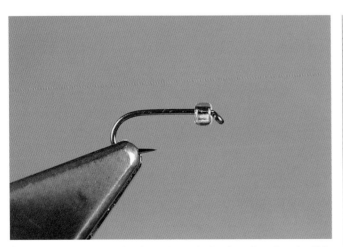

1. Insert the hook point into the hole in the glass bead, slide the bead to the hook eye, and place the hook in the vise.

2. Attach the thread behind the bead.

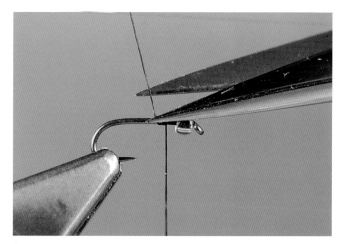

3. Trim the tag end of the tying thread.

4. Tie in the wire, leaving the tag end of the wire exposed.

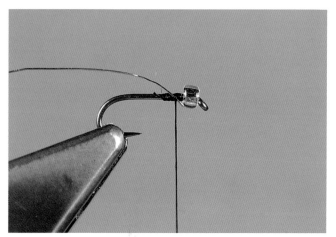

5. Pull the wire until the tag end slides underneath the tying thread.

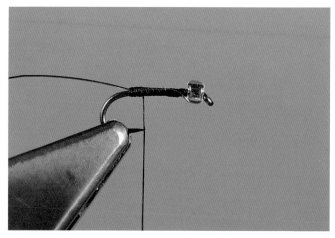

6. Continue to wrap the tying thread over the wire to the hook bend opposite the barb. Start wrapping the thread forward toward the bead.

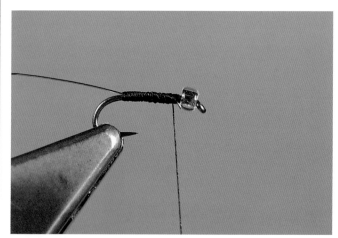

7. Continue wrapping the thread to the bead.

8. Wrap the thread back and forth to build up the thorax.

9. Wrap the thread to the bead.

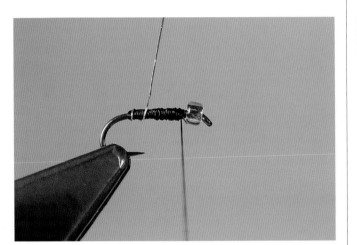

10. Begin wrapping the wire forward toward the bead.

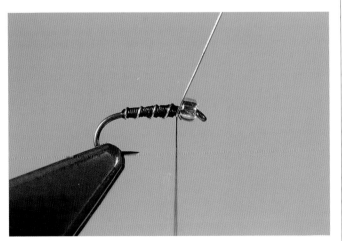

11. Continue wrapping the wire forward in evenly spaced wraps to the bead.

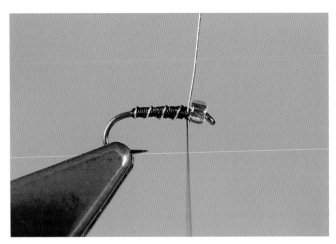

12. Wrap tying thread around the wire to secure it.

13. Trim the excess wire.

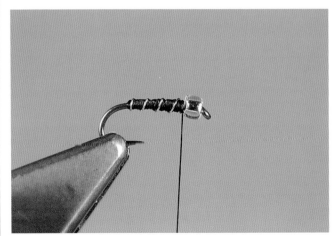

14. When the wire is trimmed, the fly should look like this.

15. Apply a small amount of dubbing to the thread.

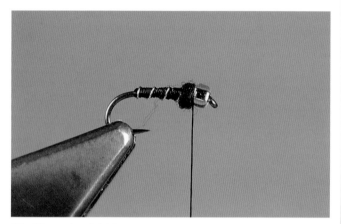

16. Wrap the dubbing to create a small oval-shaped ball for the thorax.

17. Whip-finish behind the bead.

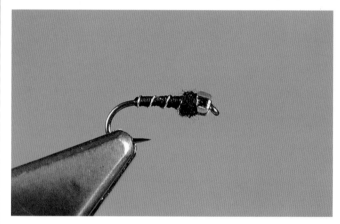

18. Trim the tying thread flush to the hook, and the Mercury Black Beauty is finished.

Mini Bow Tie Buzzer

We first started tying Bow Tie Buzzers after reading about them in Gary Borger's *Designing Trout Flies*. We've used several different materials to represent the wing buds of the pupa, but favor biots for their ease of use. Mylar also seemed a logical choice after collecting pupae that exhibited a shiny appearance when emerging. Greg Garcia, the creator of the Rojo Midge, showed us how to use Oral-B Ultra Floss for the gills. The long, fine, yarnlike strands of the dental floss flare out when cut short and tied in, giving a fuzzy appearance that looks like breathing gills.

To finish these flies, coat them with Loon Outdoors UV Knot Sense or Sally Hansen Hard As Nails. The UV Knot Sense cures when it is exposed to the sun's UV rays, and was originally used for strengthening and protecting knots. However, many fly tiers now use it as an alternative to epoxy, which requires the time-consuming steps of mixing a catalyst into a resin in order for the epoxy to harden. A UV light is good for setting up the UV Knot Sense but further curing in sunlight is recommended.

Materials

Hook:	#18-26 Tiemco 3761 or 2488; Dai-Riki 125 or 070
Thread:	Black 70- or 140-denier UTC
Abdomen:	Tying thread
Rib:	Silver Flashabou Holographic Tinsel
Wing buds:	Brown biot
Wing case:	Mirage Tinsel
Gills:	Oral-B Ultra Floss

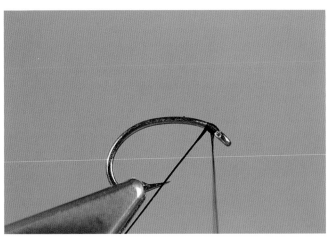

1. Attach the thread behind the hook eye.

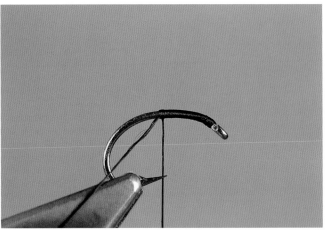

2. Wrap the thread back to the midpoint of the hook shank. This will start the build-up of thread for the thorax.

3. Wrap the tying thread forward to the hook eye and trim the tag end.

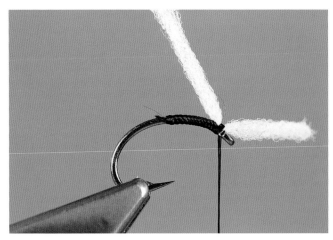

4. Attach the dental floss with two wraps of tying thread.

5. Twist the dental floss so that it is perpendicular to the hook shank.

6. Wrap the thread in a crisscross pattern over the top of the dental floss, then under the floss, and back over the top. Repeat.

7. Trim each end of the dental floss short.

8. Wrap the tying thread toward the hook bend and stop at the midpoint of the hook shank.

9. Tie in the Holographic Tinsel.

10. Wrap the tying thread over the Holographic Tinsel in touching wraps, wrapping back to the hook bend opposite the barb.

11. Take two more wraps back down the hook bend.

12. Begin wrapping the tying thread forward in touching wraps.

13. Continue wrapping the tying thread forward toward the hook eye.

14. Wrap the thread back toward the hook bend and stop at the midpoint on the hook shank.

15. Begin wrapping the Holographic Tinsel forward toward the midpoint of the hook shank.

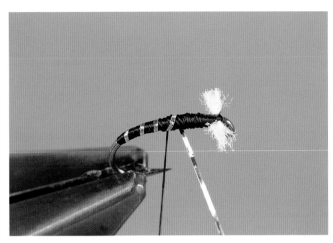

16. Continue to wrap the Holographic Tinsel forward to the midpoint of the body.

17. Tie off the tinsel with several wraps.

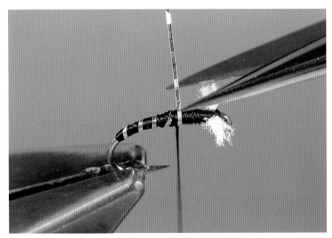

18. Trim the excess tinsel.

19. Tie in a piece of Mylar tinsel on top of the hook at the midpoint of the body.

22. Wrap the tying thread to a point behind the gills. Fold the near-side biot toward the gills, and tie it off with two wraps of tying thread.

20. Tie in the goose biot by its tip with the fiber curving away from the body on the near side of the hook.

23. Fold the far-side biot toward the gills, and tie it off with two wraps of thread.

21. Tie in a biot on the far side of the hook shank at the midpoint of the hook.

24. Top view.

25. Trim the ends of the biots flush to the thorax.

28. Trim the excess Mylar tinsel close to the thorax.

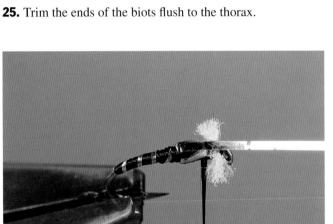

26. Fold the Mylar tinsel over the top of the thorax.

29. Whip-finish the thread behind the gills.

27. Tie off the Mylar tinsel with two wraps of thread.

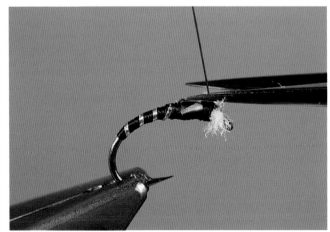

30. Trim the tying thread flush to the hook.

31. Completed Mini Bow Tie Buzzer, before adding clear coats to the body.

34. Turn the fly over in vise, and apply the same coating on the underside.

32. Apply a finish coat of Sally Hansen Hard As Nails or UV Knot Sense over the top half of the thorax.

35. Finished Mini Bow Tie Buzzer. Apply one or two additional layers of coating, as needed.

33. Apply coating over the abdomen.

36. Top view of the Mini Bow Tie Buzzer.

Pupa Patterns

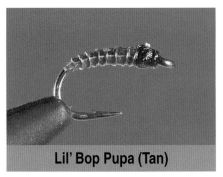

Lil' Bop Pupa (Tan)

Originator: Rick Takahashi
Tier: Rick Takahashi

Hook:	#18-26 Tiemco 2488
Thread:	White 17/0 Uni
Body:	Tying thread
Rib:	Gold Lagartun wire (extra fine)
Flash:	Pearl Krystal Flash
Thorax:	Tying thread

Note: Color the tying thread with sand Chartpak marker for the body and dark brown Pantone for the thorax. Coat entire fly with Griff's Thin Head Cement. Other hook(s): Tiemco 2487 or 2457, or Dai-Riki 125 or 060.

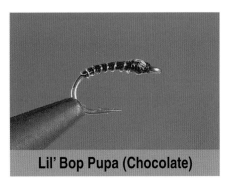

Lil' Bop Pupa (Chocolate)

Originator: Rick Takahashi
Tier: Rick Takahashi

Hook:	#18-26 Tiemco 2488
Thread:	White 17/0 Uni
Body:	Tying thread
Rib:	Gold Lagartun wire (extra fine)
Flash:	Pearl Krystal Flash
Thorax:	Tying thread

Note: Color the tying thread with dark brown Chartpak marker for the body and dark brown Pantone for the thorax. Coat entire fly with Griff's Thin Head Cement. Other hook(s): Tiemco 2487 or 2457, or Dai-Riki 125 or 060.

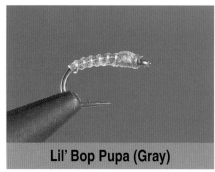

Lil' Bop Pupa (Gray)

Originator: Rick Takahashi
Tier: Rick Takahashi

Hook:	#18-26 Tiemco 2488
Thread:	White 17/0 Uni
Body:	Tying thread
Rib:	Silver Lagartun wire (extra fine)
Flash:	Pearl Krystal Flash
Thorax:	Tying thread

Note: Color the tying thread with gray Chartpak marker for the body and gray Pantone for the thorax. Coat entire fly with Griff's Thin Head Cement. Other hook(s): Tiemco 2487 or 2457, or Dai-Riki 125 or 060.

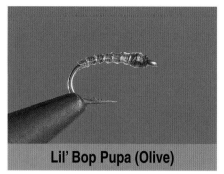

Lil' Bop Pupa (Olive)

Originator: Rick Takahashi
Tier: Rick Takahashi

Hook: #18-26 Tiemco 2488
Thread: White 17/0 Uni
Body: Tying thread
Rib: Gold Lagartun wire (extra fine)
Flash: Pearl Krystal Flash
Thorax: Tying thread
Note: Color the tying thread with olive Chartpak marker for the body and olive Pantone for the thorax. Coat entire fly with Griff's Thin Head Cement. Other hook(s): Tiemco 2487 or 2457, or Dai-Riki 125 or 060.

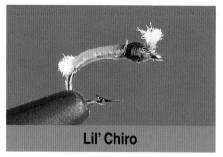

Lil' Chiro

Originator: Rick Takahashi
Tier: Rick Takahashi

Hook: #18-26 Tiemco 2488
Thread: White 17/0 Uni
Tail/Gills: Oral-B Ultra Floss
Body: Cream latex strip
Thorax: Tying thread
Head: Tying thread
Note: Color the cream latex with tan Pantone marker, the tying thread with dark brown Pantone marker for the thorax, and the tying thread with tan Pantone marker for the head. Coat entire fly with Griff's Thin Head Cement or Loon UV Knot Sense. Other hook(s): Tiemco 2487 or 2457, or Dai-Riki 125 or 060.

Latex Pupa (Cream)

Originator: Rick Takahashi
Tier: Rick Takahashi

Hook: #18-26 Tiemco 2488
Thread: White 17/0 Uni
Body: Cream latex strip
Head: Tying thread
Tail/Gills: Oral-B Ultra Floss
Note: Color the latex strip and the tying thread used for the head with tan Pantone marker. Coat entire fly with Griff's Thin Head Cement or Loon UV Knot Sense. Other hook(s): Tiemco 2487 or 2457, or Dai-Riki 125 or 060.

Latex Pupa (Tan/Cream)

Originator: Rick Takahashi
Tier: Rick Takahashi

Hook: #18-26 Tiemco 2488
Thread: White 17/0 Uni
Body: Cream latex strip
Head: Tying thread
Note: Color the latex strip with tan Pantone marker and the tying thread used for the head with brown Pantone marker. Coat entire fly with Griff's Thin Head Cement or Loon UV Knot Sense. Other hook(s): Tiemco 2487 or 2457, or Dai-Riki 125 or 060.

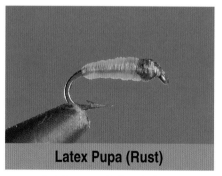

Latex Pupa (Rust)

Originator: Rick Takahashi
Tier: Rick Takahashi

Hook: #18-22 Dai-Riki 060
Thread: White17/0 Uni
Body: Latex
Head: Tying thread
Note: Color the latex with sand Chartpak marker and color the tying thread with black Sharpie to form the head.

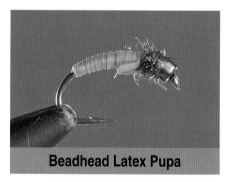

Beadhead Latex Pupa

Originator: Rick Takahashi
Tier: Rick Takahashi

Hook: #18-24 Tiemco 2457
Bead: Root beer glass
Thread: White 8/0 Uni
Body: Latex
Wing buds: Rust goose biot
Collar: Peacock Ice Dub
Note: Color the latex with olive Chartpak marker.

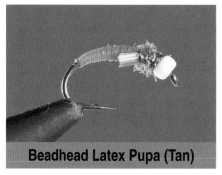

Beadhead Latex Pupa (Tan)

Originator: Rick Takahashi
Tier: Rick Takahashi

Hook: #18-24 Tiemco 2457
Bead: White glass
Thread: White 8/0 Uni
Body: Latex
Wing buds: Rust goose biot
Collar: Rust Ice Dub
Note: Color the latex with olive
Chartpak marker.

Pure Latex Pupa

Originator: Rick Takahashi
Tier: Rick Takahashi

Hook: #18-24 Tiemco 2457
Bead: Root beer glass
Thread: White 8/0 Uni
Body: Latex
Wing buds: Rust goose biot
Collar: Rust Ice Dub

Olive Flashback

Originator: Rick Takahashi
Tier: Rick Takahashi

Hook: #18-26 Tiemco 2488
Thread: White 17/0 Uni
Body: Tying thread
Rib: Tying thread
Flash: Pearl Midge Flash
Head: Tying thread
Note: For the body color the tying
thread with olive Chartpak marker.
Color the thread for the rib and the head
with a black Sharpie marker. Coat head
with Griff's Thin Head Cement. Other
hook(s): Dai-Riki 125.

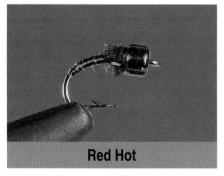

Red Hot

Originator: Unknown
Tier: Rick Takahashi

Hook: #18-26 Tiemco 2488
Thread: White 17/0 Uni
Bead: Red glass
Body: Tying thread
Thorax: Black Super Fine
Note: For the body, color the tying
thread with a red Sharpie marker. Other
hook(s): Dai-Riki 125.

Brown Thread Flash Pupa

Originator: Unknown
Tier: Rick Takahashi

Hook: #18-22 Dai-Riki 060
Body: Summer brown (54A)
                Coats & Clark
Flash: Pearl Krystal Flash, pearl
                Flashabou, pearl Mirage
                Tinsel
Head: Black 8/0 Uni
Note: Coat head with Griff's Thin
Cement.

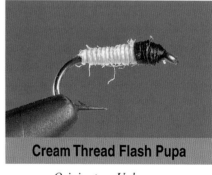

Cream Thread Flash Pupa

Originator: Unknown
Tier: Rick Takahashi

Hook: #18-22 Dai-Riki 060
Body: Cream Coats & Clark
Flash: Pearl Krystal Flash, pearl
                Flashabou, pearl Mirage
                Tinsel
Head: Black 8/0 Uni
Note: Coat head with Griff's Thin Head
Cement.

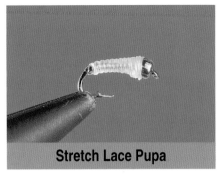

Stretch Lace Pupa

Originator: Rick Takahashi
Tier: Rick Takahashi

Hook: #18-22 Dai-Riki 060
Bead: Root beer glass
Thread: Light cahill 8/0 Uni
Underbody: Tying thread
Body: Clear .5mm Stretch Magic

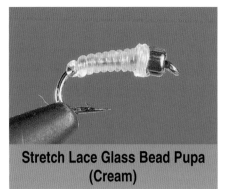

Stretch Lace Glass Bead Pupa (Cream)

Originator: Rick Takahashi
Tier: Rick Takahashi

Hook: #18-22 Dai-Riki 060
Bead: Root beer glass
Thread: Cream 70-denier UTC
Body: Tying thread
Rib: Clear .5 mm Stretch Magic
Thorax: Tying thread

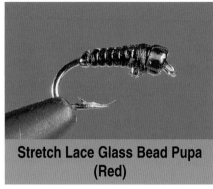

Stretch Lace Glass Bead Pupa (Red)

Originator: Rick Takahashi
Tier: Rick Takahashi

Hook: #18-22 Dai-Riki 060
Bead: Red glass
Thread: Red 70-denier UTC
Body: Tying thread
Rib: Clear .5 mm Stretch Magic
Thorax: Tying thread

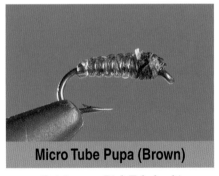

Micro Tube Pupa (Brown)

Originator: Rick Takahashi
Tier: Rick Takahashi

Hook: #18-22 Dai-Riki 060
Thread: White 17/0 Uni
Body: Pheasant tail Micro Tubing
Thorax: Tying thread
Note: For the thorax, color the tying thread with black Sharpie. Coat head with Griff's Thin Head Cement.

Stretch Lace Pupa (Brown)

Originator: Rick Takahashi
Tier: Rick Takahashi

Hook: #18-22 Dai-Riki 060
Thread: White 17/0 Uni
Underbody: Tying thread
Body: Clear .5mm Stretch Magic
Thorax: Tying thread
Note: For the underbody, color the tying thread with brown Chartpak marker and color the tying thread with black Sharpie for the thorax.

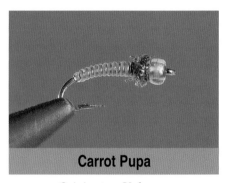

Carrot Pupa

Originator: Unknown
Tier: Rick Takahashi

Hook: #18-26 Tiemco 200R
Bead: Green glass
Thread: Hot orange 70-denier UTC
Body: Tying thread
Rib: Clear .5mm Stretch Magic
Thorax: Peacock Ice Dub
Note: Other hook(s): Dai-Riki 270.

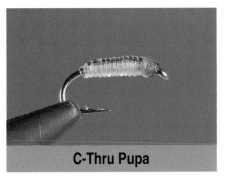

C-Thru Pupa

Originator: Rick Takahashi
Tier: Rick Takahashi

Hook: #18-22 Dai-Riki 060
Thread: Light cahill 8/0 Uni
Body: Tying thread
Dorsal line: Root beer Krystal Flash
Rib: Clear .5mm Stretch Magic
Head: Tying thread
Note: Color the tying thread with sand Chartpak marker for the head.

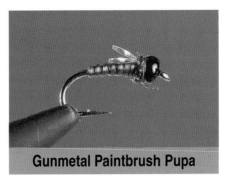

Gunmetal Paintbrush Pupa

Originator: Rick Takahashi
Tier: Rick Takahashi

Hook: #18-22 Dai-Riki 060
Bead: Gunmetal glass
Thread: Olive dun 8/0 Uni
Body: Olive polyester paintbrush fiber
Thorax: Peacock Ice Dub
Wing: Pearl Krystal Flash

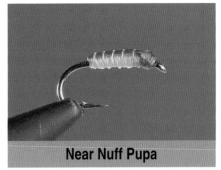

Near Nuff Pupa

Originator: Rick Takahashi
Tier: Rick Takahashi

Hook: #18-22 Dai-Riki 060
Thread: Light cahill 8/0 Uni
Body: Tying thread
Dorsal line: Two olive polyester paintbrush fibers
Rib: Tying thread
Head: Tying thread
Note: For the head, color the thread with tan Chartpak marker.

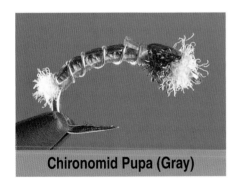

Chironomid Pupa (Gray)

Originator: Rick Takahashi
Tier: Rick Takahashi

Hook: #18-26 Tiemco 2487
Thread: Gray 8/0 Uni
Body: Tying thread
Dorsal line: Gray Swiss Straw
Tail/Gills: Oral-B Ultra Floss
Wing case: Gray Swiss Straw
Thorax: Peacock herl
Note: Other hook(s): Dai-Riki 125.

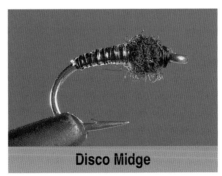

Disco Midge

Originator: Unknown
Tier: Rick Takahashi

Hook: #18-26 Tiemco 2488
Thread: Black 8/0 Uni
Body: Pearl Krystal Flash
Thorax: Black Super Fine.
Note: Other hook(s): Tiemco 2457 or Dai-Riki 125.

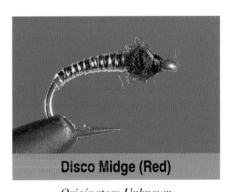

Disco Midge (Red)

Originator: Unknown
Tier: Rick Takahashi

Hook: #18-26 Tiemco 2488
Thread: Red 8/0 Uni
Body: Pearl Krystal Flash
Thorax: Black Super Fine
Note: Other hook(s): Tiemco 2487 or Dai-Riki 125.

Green Hornet

Originator: Paul Freeman
Tier: Paul Freeman

Hook: #20-22 Tiemco 2487
Bead: Green glass
Thread: Olive 70-denier UTC
Body: Tying thread
Rib: Black Super Hair
Note: Other hook(s): Tiemco 2457 or Dai-Riki 135.

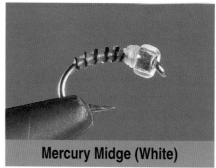

Mercury Midge (White)

Originator: Paul Freeman
Tier: Paul Freeman

Hook: #20-24 Tiemco 2487
Bead: Mercury glass
Thread: White 8/0 Uni
Body: Tying thread
Rib: Black Super Hair
Note: Other hook(s): Tiemco 2457 or Dai-Riki 135.

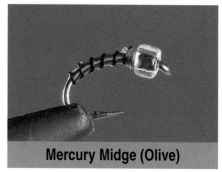

Mercury Midge (Olive)

Originator: Paul Freeman
Tier: Paul Freeman

Hook: #20-24 Tiemco 2487
Thread: Olive 70-denier UTC
Bead: Mercury glass
Body: Tying thread
Rib: Black Super Hair
Note: Other hook(s): Tiemco 2457 or Dai-Riki 135.

Bumble Bee

Originator: Paul Freeman
Tier: Paul Freeman

Hook: #20-26 Tiemco 2487
Thread: Yellow 8/0 Uni
Body: Tying thread
Rib: Black Super Hair
Head: Black 8/0 Uni
Note: Other hook(s): Tiemco 2457 or Dai-Riki 135.

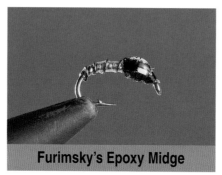

Furimsky's Epoxy Midge

Originator: Ben Furimsky
Tier: Montana Fly Company

Hook: #10-12 MFC 7048
Thread: Black 8/0 Uni
Body: Tying thread
Rib: Copper Ultra Wire
Head: Pearl High Voltage
Note: Cover the head with epoxy

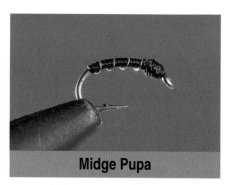

Midge Pupa

Originator: Paul Freeman
Tier: Paul Freeman

Hook: #20-24 Tiemco 2487
Thread: Black 8/0 Uni
Body: Tying thread
Rib: Copper Lagartun wire (extra fine)
Head: Black 8/0 Uni
Note: Other hook(s): Tiemco 2457 or Dai-Riki 135.

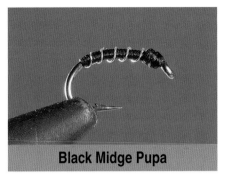

Black Midge Pupa

Originator: Paul Freeman
Tier: Paul Freeman

Hook: #20-24 Tiemco 2487
Thread: Black 8/0 Uni
Body: Tying thread
Rib: Silver Lagartun wire (extra fine)
Head: Black 8/0 Uni
Note: Other hook(s): Tiemco 2457 or Dai-Riki 135.

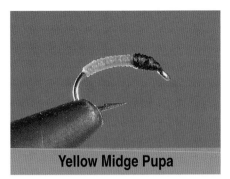

Yellow Midge Pupa

Originator: Paul Freeman
Tier: Paul Freeman

Hook: #20-24 Tiemco 2487
Thread: Yellow 8/0 Uni
Body: Tying thread
Head: Black 8/0 Uni
Note: Other hook(s): Tiemco 2457 or Dai-Riki 135.

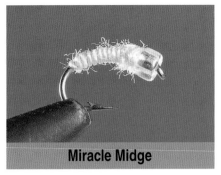

Miracle Midge

Originator: Unknown
Tier: Paul Freeman

Hook: #20-24 Tiemco 2487
Bead: Clear or mercury glass
Thread: White Coats & Clarks
Body: Tying thread
Thorax: White Super Fine
Note: Other hook(s): Tiemco 2457 or Dai-Riki 135.

Ultra Pupa (Olive)

Originator: Rick Takahashi
Tier: Rick Takahashi

Hook: #20-24 Tiemco 2487
Thread: White 17/0 Uni
Underbody: Tying thread
Body: Clear .5mm Stretch Magic
Wing buds: Tan biots
Gills: Oral-B Ultra Floss
Note: For the underbody, color the tying thread with light olive Chartpak marker. Other hook(s): Dai-Riki 125.

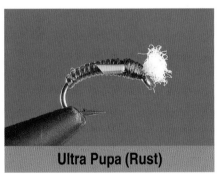

Ultra Pupa (Rust)

Originator: Rick Takahashi
Tier: Rick Takahashi

Hook: #20-24 Tiemco 2487
Thread: White 17/0 Uni
Underbody: Tying thread
Body: Clear .5mm Stretch Magic
Wing buds: Tan biots
Gills: Oral-B Ultra Floss
Note: For the underbody, color the tying thread with rust Chartpak marker. Other hook(s): Dai-Riki 125.

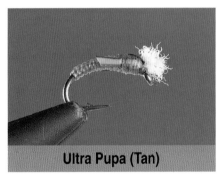

Ultra Pupa (Tan)

Originator: Rick Takahashi
Tier: Rick Takahashi

Hook: #20-24 Tiemco 2487
Thread: White 17/0 Uni
Underbody: Tying thread
Body: Clear .5mm Stretch Magic
Wing buds: Tan biots
Gills: Oral-B Ultra Floss
Note: For the underbody, color the tying thread with tan Chartpak marker. Other hook(s): Dai-Riki 125.

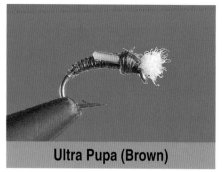

Ultra Pupa (Brown)

Originator: Rick Takahashi
Tier: Rick Takahashi

Hook: #20-24 Tiemco 2487
Thread: White 17/0 Uni
Underbody: Tying thread
Body: Clear .5mm Stretch Magic
Wing buds: Tan biots
Gills: Oral-B Ultra Floss
Note: For the underbody, color the tying thread with brown Chartpak marker. Other hook(s): Dai-Riki 125.

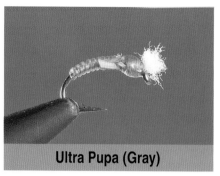

Ultra Pupa (Gray)

Originator: Rick Takahashi
Tier: Rick Takahashi

Hook: #20-24 Tiemco 2487
Thread: White 17/0 Uni
Underbody: Tying thread
Body: Clear .5mm Stretch Magic
Wing buds: Tan biots
Gills: Oral-B Ultra Floss
Note: For the underbody, color the tying thread with gray Chartpak marker. Other hook(s): Dai-Riki 125.

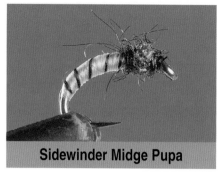

Sidewinder Midge Pupa

Originator: Bear Goode
Tier: Solitude Fly Company

Hook: #20-26 Daiichi 1130
Thread: Yellow 6/0 Uni
Body: Yellow 6/0 Uni
Rib: Black 6/0 Uni
Head: Black rabbit dubbing

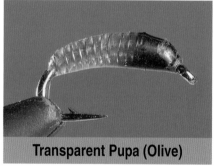

Transparent Pupa (Olive)

Originator: Rick Takahashi
Tier: Rick Takahashi

Hook: #20-24 Tiemco 2487
Thread: White 17/0 Uni
Underbody: Tying thread
Body: Clear .5mm Stretch Magic
Rib: Silver Lagartun wire (extra fine)
Head: Tying thread
Note: For the underbody color the tying thread with light olive Chartpak marker and color the tying thread with dark brown Pantone marker for the head. Cover head with Loon UV Knot Sense, Sally Hansen Hard As Nails, or Griff's Thick Head Cement. Other hook(s): Dai-Riki 125.

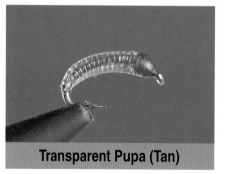

Transparent Pupa (Tan)

Originator: Rick Takahashi
Tier: Rick Takahashi

Hook: #20-24 Tiemco 2487
Thread: White 17/0 Uni
Underbody: Tying thread colored
Body: Clear .5mm Stretch Magic
Rib: Gold Lagartun wire (extra fine)
Head: Tying thread
Note: For the underbody color the tying thread with tan Chartpak marker and color the tying thread with tan Pantone marker for the head. Cover head with Loon UV Knot Sense, Sally Hansen Hard As Nails, or Griff's Thick Head Cement. Other hook(s): Dai-Riki 125.

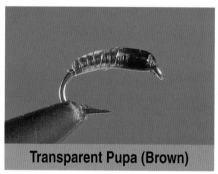

Transparent Pupa (Brown)

Originator: Rick Takahashi
Tier: Rick Takahashi

Hook: #20-24 Tiemco 2487
Thread: White 17/0 Uni
Underbody: Tying thread
Body: Clear .5mm Stretch Magic
Rib: Copper Lagartun wire (extra fine)
Head: Tying thread
Note: For the underbody color the tying thread with rust Chartpak marker and color the tying thread with dark brown Pantone marker for the head. Cover head with Loon UV Knot Sense, Sally Hansen Hard As Nails, or Griff's Thick Head Cement. Other hook(s): Dai-Riki 125.

GB Biot Pupa (Olive)

Originator: Rick Takahashi
Tier: Rick Takahashi

Hook: #20-24 Tiemco 2487
Bead: Gunmetal glass
Thread: White 17/0 Uni
Body: Olive goose biot
Thorax: Rust Ice Dub
Wing case/Gills: White organza
Note: Other hook(s): Tiemco 2457 or Dai-Riki 125.

GB Biot Pupa (Brown)

Originator: Rick Takahashi
Tier: Rick Takahashi

Hook: #20-24 Tiemco 2487
Bead: Root beer glass
Thread: White 17/0 Uni
Body: Brown goose biot
Thorax: Rust Ice Dub
Wing case/Gills: White organza
Note: Other hook(s): Tiemco 2457 or Dai-Riki 125.

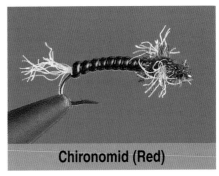

Chironomid (Red)

Originator: Unknown
Tier: Solitude Fly Company

Hook: #12-18 Daiichi 1270
Thread: Black 6/0 Uni
Tail: White Hi-Vis
Body: Red UTC Vinyl D Rib over red Flashabou
Thorax: Peacock herl
Wing case/Gills: White Hi-Vis

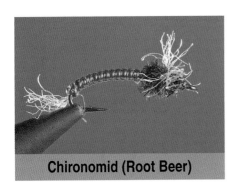

Chironomid (Root Beer)

Originator: Unknown
Tier: Solitude Fly Company

Hook: #12-18 Daiichi 1270
Thread: Black 6/0 Uni
Tail: White Hi-Vis
Body: Amber UTC Vinyl D Rib over pearl Flashabou
Thorax: Peacock herl
Wing case/Gills: White Hi-Vis

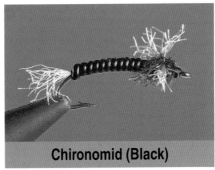

Chironomid (Black)

Originator: Unknown
Tier: Solitude Fly Company

Hook: #12-18 Daiichi 1270
Thread: Black 6/0 Uni
Tail: White Hi-Vis
Body: Black UTC Vinyl D Rib over black Flashabou
Thorax: Peacock herl
Wing case/Gills: White Hi-Vis

Glass Bead Midge (Olive)

Originator: Unknown
Tier: Solitude Fly Company

Hook: #18-22 Daiichi 1270
Bead: Green glass
Thread: Olive 8/0 Uni
Body: Olive Danville floss
Rib: Pheasant tail
Thorax: Peacock herl

Glass Bead Midge (Gray)

Originator: Unknown
Tier: Solitude Fly Company

Hook:	#18-22 Daiichi 1270
Bead:	Clear glass
Thread:	Gray 8/0 Uni
Body:	Gray Danville floss
Rib:	Pheasant tail
Thorax:	Peacock herl

Glass Bead Midge (Black)

Originator: Unknown
Tier: Solitude Fly Company

Hook:	#18-22 Daiichi 1270
Bead:	Black glass
Thread:	Black 8/0 Uni
Body:	Black Danville floss
Rib:	Pheasant tail
Thorax:	Peacock herl

Tungsten Midge (Olive)

Originator: Unknown
Tier: Solitude Fly Company

Hook:	#16-22 Daiichi 1120
Bead:	Gold tungsten
Thread:	Black 6/0 Danville
Body:	Olive goose biot
Wing case:	Pearl Flashabou
Thorax:	Peacock herl

Tungsten Midge (Red)

Originator: Unknown
Tier: Solitude Fly Company

Hook:	#16-22 Daiichi 1120
Bead:	Gold tungsten
Thread:	Black 6/0 Danville
Body:	Red goose biot
Wing case:	Pearl Flashabou
Thorax:	Peacock herl

Tungsten Midge (White)

Originator: Unknown
Tier: Solitude Fly Company

Hook:	#16-22 Daiichi 1120
Bead:	Gold tungsten
Thread:	Black 6/0 Danville
Body:	White goose biot
Wing case:	Pearl Flashabou
Thorax:	Peacock herl

BH SLF Midge (Red)

Originator: John Harrington
Tier: Solitude Fly Company

Hook:	#18-22 Daiichi 1120
Bead:	Red glass
Thread:	Red 6/0 Danville
Body:	Crimson SLF dubbing
Rib:	Copper Ultra Wire (extra small)

BH SLF Midge (Brown)

Originator: John Harrington
Tier: Solitude Fly Company

Hook: #18-22 Daiichi 1120
Bead: Root beer glass
Thread: Tan 6/0 Danville
Body: Fiery brown SLF dubbing
Rib: Copper Ultra Wire
(extra small)

BH SLF Midge (Black)

Originator: John Harrington
Tier: Solitude Fly Company

Hook: #18-22 Daiichi 1120
Bead: Black glass
Thread: Black 6/0 Danville
Body: Fiery black SLF dubbing
Rib: Black Ultra Wire
(extra small)

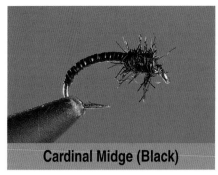

Cardinal Midge (Black)

Originator: John Harrington
Tier: Solitude Fly Company

Hook: #18-24 Daiichi 1120
Thread: Black 6/0 Danville
Body: Black Flashabou
Thorax: Fiery black SLF dubbing

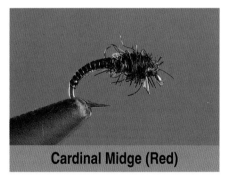

Cardinal Midge (Red)

Originator: John Harrington
Tier: Solitude Fly Company

Hook: #18-24 Daiichi 1120
Thread: Red 6/0 Danville
Body: Red Flashabou
Thorax: Fiery black SLF dubbing

VC Midge (Purple)

Originator: Brian Schmidt
Tier: Solitude Fly Company

Hook: #16-26 Daiichi 1130
Thread: Purple 8/0 Uni
Body: Tying thread
Wing case/Gills: White CDC
Thorax: Gray Super Fine
Rib: Silver Lagartun wire (fine)

VC Midge (Black)

Originator: Brian Schmidt
Tier: Solitude Fly Company

Hook: #16-26 Daiichi 1130
Thread: Black 8/0 Uni
Body: tying thread
Wing case/Gills: White CDC
Thorax: UV black Ice Dub
Rib: Gold Lagartun wire (fine)

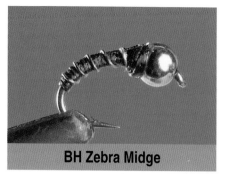

BH Zebra Midge

Originator: Unknown
Tier: Solitude Fly Company

Hook: #16-20 Daiichi 1120
Bead: Silver Cyclops
Thread: Black 8/0 Uni
Body: Tying thread
Rib: Silver Ultra Wire
             (extra small)
Thorax: Tying thread

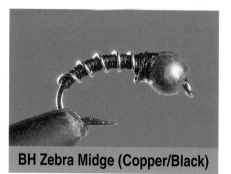

BH Zebra Midge (Copper/Black)

Originator: Unknown
Tier: Solitude Fly Company

Hook: #16-20 Daiichi 1120
Bead: Copper Cyclops
Thread: Black 8/0 Uni
Body: Tying thread
Rib: Copper Ultra Wire
             (extra small)
Thorax: Tying thread

BH Zebra Midge (Copper/Rust)

Originator: Unknown
Tier: Solitude Fly Company

Hook: #16-20 Daiichi 1120
Bead: Copper Cyclops
Thread: Red 8/0 Uni
Body: Tying thread
Rib: Copper Ultra Wire (extra
             small)
Thorax: Tying thread

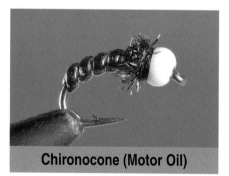

Chironocone (Motor Oil)

Originator: Unknown
Tier: Solitude Fly Company

Hook: #10-20 Daiichi 1120
Bead: White metal
Thread: Black 6/0 Danville
Body: Brown UTC Vinyl D Rib
             over brown Flashabou
Thorax: Peacock herl

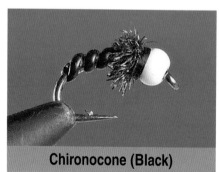

Chironocone (Black)

Originator: Unknown
Tier: Solitude Fly Company

Hook: #10-20 Daiichi 1120
Bead: White metal
Thread: Black 6/0 Danville
Body: Black UTC Vinyl D Rib
             over black Flashabou
Thorax: Peacock herl

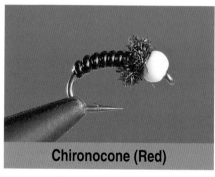

Chironocone (Red)

Originator: Unknown
Tier: Solitude Fly Company

Hook: #10-20 Daiichi 1120
Bead: White metal
Thread: Black 6/0 Danville
Body: Red UTC Vinyl D Rib over
             red Flashabou
Thorax: Peacock herl

Chironocone (Olive)

Originator: Unknown
Tier: Solitude Fly Company

Hook:	#10-20 Daiichi 1120
Bead:	White metal
Thread:	Olive 6/0 Danville
Body:	Olive UTC Vinyl D Rib over olive Flashabou
Thorax:	Peacock herl

BH Cimarron Special (Red)

Originator: Greg Faught
Tier: Solitude Fly Company

Hook:	#14-20 Daiichi 1120
Bead:	Gold Cyclops
Thread:	Tan 6/0 Danville
Body:	Red Ultra Wire (extra small)
Thorax:	Natural hare's ear dubbing and pearl Ice Dub

BH Cimarron Special (Wine)

Originator: Greg Faught
Tier: Solitude Fly Company

Hook:	#14-20 Daiichi 1120
Bead:	Black Cyclops
Thread:	Black 6/0 Danville
Body:	Wine Ultra Wire (extra small)
Thorax:	Natural hare's ear dubbing and pearl Ice Dub

Chironomid (Black)

Originator: Shane Stalcup
Tier: Solitude Fly Company

Hook:	#14-16 Daiichi 1260
Thread:	Black 6/0 Danville
Tail:	White ostrich herl
Body:	Black UTC Vinyl D Rib
Wing:	Z-Wing
Thorax:	Brown and black Super Fine, mixed
Wing case:	Medium gray Medallion Sheeting
Gills:	White ostrich herl

Chironomid (Olive)

Originator: Shane Stalcup
Tier: Solitude Fly Company

Hook:	#14-16 Daiichi 1260
Thread:	Black 6/0 Danville
Tail:	White ostrich herl
Body:	Olive UTC Vinyl D Rib
Wing:	Z-Wing
Thorax:	Brown and black Super Fine, mixed
Wing case:	Medium gray Medallion Sheeting
Gills:	White ostrich herl

Maggot Midge

Originator: Shane Stalcup
Tier: Solitude Fly Company

Hook:	#18-22 Daiichi 1120
Thread:	Black 6/0 Danville
Body:	White Micro Tubing
Thorax:	Black rabbit dubbing

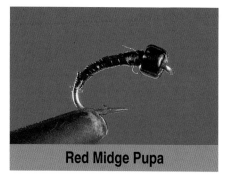

Red Midge Pupa

Originator: Unknown
Tier: Float n Fish Fly Shop

Hook:	#18-24 Tiemco 2457
Bead:	Red glass
Thread:	Red 8/0 Uni
Body:	Red Flashabou

Orange Midge Pupa

Originator: Unknown
Tier: Float n Fish Fly Shop

Hook:	#18-22 Tiemco 2457
Thread:	Orange 8/0 Uni
Body:	Orange V Rib
Thorax:	Fl. orange dubbing
Head:	Orange 8/0 Uni

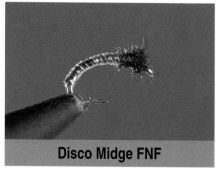

Disco Midge FNF

Originator: Unknown
Tier: Float n Fish Fly Shop

Hook:	#18-24 Tiemco 2457
Thread:	Black 8/0 Uni
Body:	Pearl Flashabou
Thorax:	Black rabbit dubbing

Desert Storm

Originator: Unknown
Tier: Float n Fish Fly Shop

Hook:	#18-22 Tiemco 2457
Thread:	Pink 8/0 Uni
Body:	Tying thread
Rib:	Pearl Flashabou
Thorax:	Black dubbing
Head:	Pink 8/0 Uni

PT Pupa

Originator: Bear Goode
Tier: Bear Goode

Hook:	#18-22 Tiemco 200R
Thread:	Black 8/0 Uni
Tail:	Pheasant tail
Body:	Pheasant tail
Rib:	Copper Ultra Wire (extra small)
Thorax:	Cream rabbit dubbing

Zebra (Black and Silver)

Originator: Unknown
Tier: Float n Fish Fly Shop

Hook:	#18-22 Tiemco 2488
Thread:	Black 8/0 Uni
Body:	Tying thread
Rib:	Silver Ultra Wire (extra small)
Thorax:	Black Super Fine

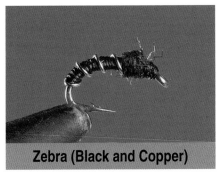

Zebra (Black and Copper)

Originator: Unknown
Tier: Float n Fish Fly Shop

Hook: #18-22 Tiemco 2457
Thread: Black 8/0 Uni
Body: Tying thread
Rib: Copper Ultra Wire
          (extra small)
Thorax: Black Super Fine

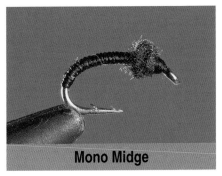

Mono Midge

Originator: Unknown
Tier: Ray Johnston

Hook: #18-26 Tiemco 2457
Thread: Black 70-denier UTC
Body: Tying thread
Thorax: Black Super Fine

Chocolate Midge Pupa

Originator: Unknown
Tier: Ray Johnston

Hook: #18-26 Tiemco 2488
Thread: Light brown 70-denier
          UTC
Body: Tying thread
Rib: Copper Ultra Wire
          (extra small)
Thorax: Tan Super Fine

Gray Midge Pupa

Originator: Unknown
Tier: Ray Johnston

Hook: #18-26 Tiemco 2488
Thread: Gray 70-denier UTC
Body: Tying thread
Rib: Silver Ultra Wire
          (extra small)
Thorax: Light gray Super Fine

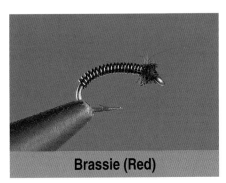

Brassie (Red)

Originator: Unknown
Tier: Solitude Fly Company

Hook: #14-20 Daiichi 1130
Thread: Black 6/0 Danville
Body: Red Ultra Wire
          (extra small)
Thorax: Black rabbit dubbing

Brassie (Copper)

Originator: Unknown
Tier: Solitude Fly Company

Hook: #14-20 Daiichi 1130
Thread: Black 6/0
Body: Copper Ultra Wire
          (extra small)
Thorax: Black rabbit dubbing

Olive Chironomid

Originator: Unknown
Tier: Umpqua Feather Merchants

Hook:	#12-14 Tiemco 2302
Thread:	Light olive 6/0 Uni
Body:	Tying thread
Rib:	Silver Lagartun wire (fine)
Thorax:	Peacock herl
Back:	Cock pheasant tail
Gills:	White Antron

Pheasant Tail Chironomid

Originator: Unknown
Tier: Umpqua Feather Merchants

Hook:	#12-14 Tiemco 5230
Thread:	Dark brown 6/0 Uni
Tail:	White Antron
Body:	Natural pheasant tail
Rib:	Copper Ultra Wire (extra small)
Thorax:	Peacock herl
Back:	Cock pheasant tail
Gills:	White Antron

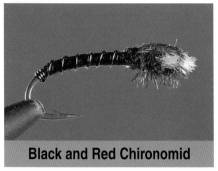

Black and Red Chironomid

Originator: Unknown
Tier: Umpqua Feather Merchants

Hook:	#12-14 Tiemco 2302
Thread:	Black 6/0 Uni
Tag:	Red Ultra Wire (extra small)
Body:	Black Frostbite Mylar
Rib:	Red Ultra Wire (extra small)
Thorax:	Peacock herl
Back:	Cock pheasant tail
Gills:	White Antron

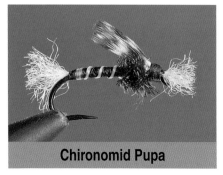

Chironomid Pupa

Originator: Randall Kaufmann
Tier: Umpqua Feather Merchants

Hook:	#16-20 Tiemco 900BL
Thread:	Black 6/0 Uni
Tail:	Clear Antron
Gills:	Clear Antron
Body:	Tying thread
Rib:	White silk thread
Wing:	Grizzly hen hackle tips
Thorax:	Peacock herl

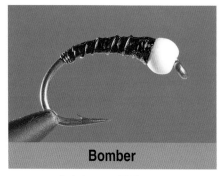

Bomber

Originator: Unknown
Tier: Umpqua Feather Merchants

Hook:	#10-12 Tiemco 2457
Bead:	White metal
Thread:	Red 6/0 Uni
Body:	Black Frostbite Mylar
Rib:	Red Ultra Wire (extra small)

Desert Storm

Originator: Unknown
Tier: Umpqua Feather Merchants

Hook:	#20-24 Tiemco 2457
Bead:	Black glass
Thread:	Fl. orange 8/0 Uni
Body:	Tying thread
Rib:	Pearl Flashabou

Frostbite Chironomid Pupa

Originator: Unknown
Tier: Umpqua Feather Merchants

Hook:	#12-18 Tiemco 2457
Bead:	Copper metal
Thread:	Black 6/0 Uni
Body:	Red Frostbite Mylar
Rib:	Silver Lagartun wire (small)
Gills:	White poly yarn
Thorax:	Peacock herl

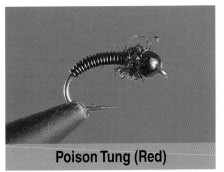

Poison Tung (Red)

Originator: Charlie Craven
Tier: Umpqua Feather Merchants

Hook:	#16-22 Tiemco 2487
Bead:	Black tungsten
Thread:	Black 70-denier UTC
Body:	Red Ultra Wire (small)
Thorax:	Black peacock Ice Dub

Poison Tung (Black)

Originator: Charlie Craven
Tier: Charlie Craven

Hook:	#16-22 Tiemco 2487
Bead:	Black tungsten
Thread:	Black 70-denier UTC
Body:	Black Ultra Wire (small)
Thorax:	Black peacock Ice Dub

Poison Tung (Olive and Black)

Originator: Charlie Craven
Tier: Charlie Craven

Hook:	#16-22 Tiemco 2487
Bead:	Black tungsten
Thread:	Black 70-denier UTC
Body:	Olive Ultra Wire (Brassie) and black Ultra Wire (small)
Thorax:	Black peacock Ice Dub

Poison Tung (Deep Blue)

Originator: Charlie Craven
Tier: Charlie Craven

Hook:	#16-22 Tiemco 2487
Bead:	Silver tungsten
Thread:	Gray 8/0 Uni
Body:	Tying thread
Rib:	Peacock blue Lagartun wire (fire)
Thorax:	UV gray Ice Dub

Shuckin Midge (Claret)

Originator: Stan Benton
Tier: Umpqua Feather Merchants

Hook:	#20-22 Tiemco 2487
Bead:	Black metal
Thread:	Claret 8/0 Uni
Tail:	Claret Krystal Flash and red Antron
Body:	Tying thread
Collar:	Claret beaver dubbing

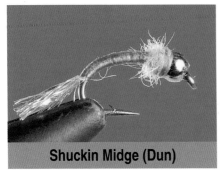

Shuckin Midge (Dun)

Originator: Stan Benton
Tier: Umpqua Feather Merchants

Hook:	#20-22 Tiemco 2487
Bead:	Silver metal
Thread:	Gray 8/0 Uni
Tail:	Blue dun Krystal Flash and gray Antron
Body:	Tying thread
Collar:	Dun beaver dubbing

Shuckin Midge (Olive)

Originator: Stan Benton
Tier: Umpqua Feather Merchants

Hook:	#20-22 Tiemco 2487
Bead:	Copper metal
Thread:	Olive 8/0 Uni
Tail:	Olive Krystal Flash and olive Antron
Body:	Tying thread
Collar:	Olive beaver dubbing

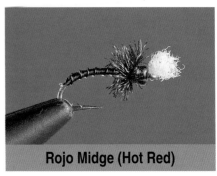

Rojo Midge (Hot Red)

Originator: Greg Garcia
Tier: Umpqua Feather Merchants

Hook:	#18-22 Tiemco 200R
Bead:	Red glass
Thread:	Red 8/0 Uni
Body:	Tying thread
Rib:	Red Lagartun wire (fine)
Thorax:	Peacock herl
Gills:	Oral-B Ultra Floss

Rojo Midge (Tan)

Originator: Greg Garcia
Tier: Umpqua Feather Merchants

Hook:	#18-22 Tiemco 200R
Bead:	Red glass
Thread:	Tan 8/0 Uni
Body:	Tying thread
Rib:	Copper Lagartun wire (fine)
Thorax:	Peacock herl
Gills:	Oral-B Ultra Floss

Rojo Midge (Black)

Originator: Greg Garcia
Tier: Umpqua Feather Merchants

Hook:	#18-22 Tiemco 200R
Bead:	Red glass
Thread:	Black 8/0 Uni
Body:	Tying thread
Rib:	Copper Lagartun wire (fine)
Thorax:	Peacock herl
Gills:	Oral-B Ultra Floss

Rojo Midge (Olive)

Originator: Greg Garcia
Tier: Umpqua Feather Merchants

Hook:	#18-22 Tiemco 200R
Bead:	Red glass
Thread:	Olive 8/0 Uni
Body:	Tying thread
Rib:	Olive Lagartun wire (fine)
Thorax:	Peacock herl
Gills:	Oral-B Ultra Floss

Tungsten Zebra Midge (Black/Copper)

Originator: Greg Garcia
Tier: Umpqua Feather Merchants

Hook: #16-20 Tiemco 2487
Bead: Copper tungsten
Thread: Black 3/0 Danville
Body: Tying thread
Rib: Copper Lagartun wire (fine)

Tungsten Zebra Midge (Black/Silver)

Originator: Greg Garcia
Tier: Umpqua Feather Merchants

Hook: #16-20 Tiemco 2488H
Bead: Silver tungsten
Thread: Black 3/0 Danville
Body: Tying thread
Rib: Silver Lagartun wire (fine)

Tungsten Zebra Midge (Red)

Originator: Greg Garcia
Tier: Umpqua Feather Merchants

Hook: #16-20 Tiemco 2488H
Bead: Gold tungsten
Thread: Red 3/0 Danville
Body: Tying thread
Rib: Silver Lagartun wire (fine)

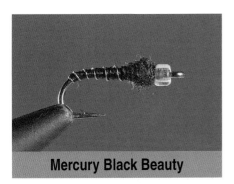

Mercury Black Beauty

Originator: Pat Dorsey
Tier: Umpqua Feather Merchants

Hook: #18-24 Dai-Riki 310
Bead: Mercury glass
Thread: Black 8/0 Uni
Body: Tying thread
Rib: Copper Lagartun wire (fine)
Thorax: Black Fine and Dry
Note: Other hook(s): Tiemco 501.

Halo Midge

Originator: Mark Boname
Tier: Stone Creek

Hook: #16-20 Tiemco 3761
Thread: Black 70-denier UTC
Rib: Silver Holographic Tinsel
Body: Tying thread
Wing case: Brown Razor Foam
Thorax: Peacock herl
Gills: White ostrich herl

Barbed Wire (Black)

Originator: Mark Boname
Tier: Stone Creek

Hook: #18-22 Dai-Riki 235
Bead: Black glass
Thread: Black 8/0 Uni
Rib: Silver Lagartun wire (extra fine)
Body: Tying thread
Gills: White Z-lon

Barbed Wire (Root Beer)

Originator: Mark Boname
Tier: Stone Creek

Hook:	#18-22 Dai-Riki 235
Bead:	Root beer glass
Thread:	Tan 8/0 Uni
Rib:	Silver Lagartun wire (extra fine)
Body:	Tying thread
Gills:	White Z-lon

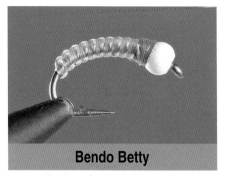

Bendo Betty

Originator: Bruce Smith
Tier: Bruce Smith

Hook:	#14 Tiemco 2457
Bead:	White metal
Thread:	Light olive 8/0 Uni
Body:	Tying thread
Rib:	Clear .7mm Stretch Magic
Collar:	Orange 6/0 Uni

Bionic Midge (Black/Gold)

Originator: Mark Boname
Tier: Stone Creek

Hook:	#18-22 Dai-Riki 135
Thread:	Black 70-denier UTC
Tail:	Root beer Krystal Flash
Body:	Black 70-denier UTC
Rib:	Gold Ultra Wire (extra small)
Thorax:	Black Fine and Dry
Wing buds:	Pearl Krystal Flash

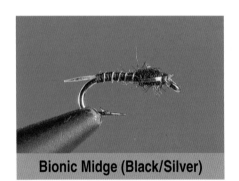

Bionic Midge (Black/Silver)

Originator: Mark Boname
Tier: Stone Creek

Hook:	#18-22 Dai-Riki 060
Thread:	Black 8/0 Uni
Tail:	Pearl Krystal Flash
Body:	Tying thread
Rib:	Silver Lagartun wire (extra fine)
Thorax:	Black Fine and Dry
Wing buds:	Pearl Krystal Flash

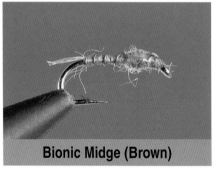

Bionic Midge (Brown)

Originator: Mark Boname
Tier: Stone Creek

Hook:	#18-22 Dai-Riki 060
Thread:	Brown 70-denier UTC
Tail:	Root beer Krystal Flash
Body:	Tying thread
Rib:	Gold Lagartun wire (extra fine)
Thorax:	March Brown Fine and Dry
Wing buds:	Root beer Krystal Flash

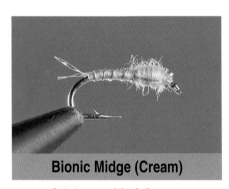

Bionic Midge (Cream)

Originator: Mark Boname
Tier: Stone Creek

Hook:	#18-22 Dai-Riki 060
Thread:	Cream 70-denier UTC
Tail:	Pearl Krystal Flash
Body:	Cream 70-denier UTC
Rib:	Gold Lagartun wire (extra fine)
Thorax:	Cream Fine and Dry
Wing buds:	Pearl Krystal Flash

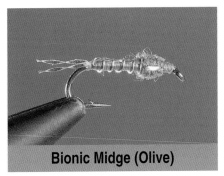

Bionic Midge (Olive)

Originator: Mark Boname
Tier: Stone Creek

Hook: #18-22 Dai-Riki 060
Thread: Olive 70-denier UTC
Tail: Pearl Krystal Flash
Body: Tying thread
Rib: Gold Lagartun wire (extra fine)
Thorax: Gray Fine and Dry
Wing buds: Pearl Krystal Flash

Black Sally Pyramid Style

Originator: Bruce Smith
Tier: Bruce Smith

Hook: #16-20 Tiemco 200R
Bead: Black nickel metal
Thread: Black 3/0 Danville Monocord
Trailing shuck: Pearl Krystal Flash
Body: Silver Ultra Wire (small)
Rib: Black Super Floss
Thorax: Peacock Ice Dub
Gills: White Antron
Note: We came up with this midge while fishing Pyramid Lake, Nevada. The cutthroat's large teeth tear up midges constructed of standard materials.

Flashback Midge

Originator: John Nichols
Tier: John Nichols

Hook: #14-20 Tiemco 2457
Bead: Silver tungsten
Thread: Black 8/0 Uni
Tail: Antron
Rib: Red Ultra Wire (fine)
Body: Tying thread
Wing case: Pearl Mylar tinsel coated with epoxy
Thorax: Green and gray rabbit

Glasshead Gillie

Originator: Bruce Smith
Tier: Bruce Smith

Hook: #16-20 Tiemco 200R
Bead: Pearl glass
Thread: Gray 8/0 Uni
Tail: Pearl Krystal Flash
Gills: White Z-lon
Rib: Silver Ultra Wire (small)
Body: 50% Hareline dubbing Adams gray #3, 50% Arizona Crystal Rabbit Adams gray
Wing buds: Brown goose biot
Thorax: Peacock Ice Dub

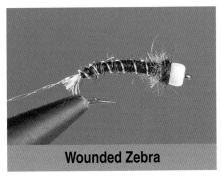

Wounded Zebra

Originator: Bruce Smith
Tier: Bruce Smith

Hook: #18 Tiemco 200R
Bead: White glass
Thread: Black 8/0 Uni
Tail: Pearl Krystal Flash
Gills: White Antron
Abdomen: Black Arizona Crystal Rabbit
Rib: Silver Ultra Wire (small)
Wing buds: Hot orange dubbing

Marsh's Midge Pupa

Originator: John Nichols
Tier: John Nichols

Hook: #16-18 Tiemco 2457
Thread: Black 8/0 Uni
Tail/Gills: White Antron
Body: Green seal fur
Rib: Gold Ultra Wire (small)
Thorax: Rabbit underfur

Northern Bomber

Originator: Bruce Smith
Tier: Bruce Smith

Hook:	#12 Tiemco 200R
Thread:	Black 8/0 Uni
Body:	Red Holographic Flashabou
Rib 1:	Black V Rib (small)
Rib 2:	Red Ultra Wire (small)
Thorax:	Peacock herl
Wing case:	Pearl UTC flat tinsel (large)
Gills:	White Z-lon
Wing pads:	Orange Flex Floss

Pheasant Tail Midge

Originator: John Nichols
Tier: John Nichols

Hook:	#14-20 Tiemco 2457
Thread:	Black 8/0 Uni
Tail:	White Antron
Rib:	Copper Ultra Wire (extra small)
Body:	Green pheasant tail
Wing case:	Black Thin Skin, pearl Mylar tinsel coated with epoxy
Thorax:	Green Ultra Wire (small)

Riwaka Brassie

Originator: John Nichols
Tier: John Nichols

Hook:	#14-20 Tiemco 2457
Thread:	Black 8/0 Uni
Body:	Red and green Ultra Wire (small)
Wing:	White Z-lon
Thorax:	Dark rabbit mixed with green

Standard Black Midge

Originator: Unknown
Tier: John Nichols

Hook:	#16-22 Kamasan B405
Thread:	Black 8/0 Uni
Tail:	White Antron
Rib:	Silver Ultra Wire (extra small)
Body:	Black thread
Thorax:	Peacock herl
Gills:	White Antron

Standard Green Midge

Originator: Unknown
Tier: John Nichols

Hook:	#16-22 Kamasan B405
Thread:	Black 8/0 Uni
Tail:	White Antron
Rib:	Gold Ultra Wire (extra small)
Body:	Olive 8/0 Uni
Thorax:	Peacock herl
Gills:	White Antron

TIM (The Irwell Midge)

Originator: John Nichols
Tier: John Nichols

Hook:	#16-20 Kamasan B405
Thread:	Red 8/0 Uni
Tail:	White Antron
Rib:	Stripped peacock herl
Body:	Red 8/0 Uni
Thorax:	Black Super Fine
Gills:	White Antron

Bengal Tiger

Originator: Bruce Smith
Tier: Bruce Smith

Hook: #14 Tiemco 2312
Bead: Black nickel metal
Thread: Red 8/0 Uni
Shuck: Pearl Krystal Flash
Tail: White Antron
Body: Tying thread
Rib: Black Ultra Wire (small)
Thorax: Peacock Ice Dub
Gills: White Antron

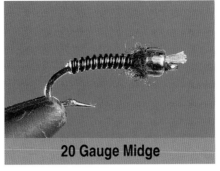

20 Gauge Midge

Originator: Bob Dye
Tier: Bob Dye

Hook: #22-24 Dai-Riki 270
Bead: Gunmetal glass
Thread: Black 8/0 Uni
Body: Gunmetal blue Ultra Wire (small)
Rib: Silver Ultra Wire (extra small)
Gills: White Flouro Fibre
Thorax: Black Super Fine

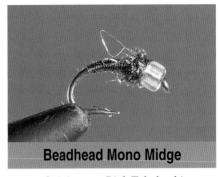

Beadhead Mono Midge

Originator: Rick Takahashi
Tier: Rick Takahashi

Hook: #18-24 Tiemco 2487
Bead: Clear glass
Thread: White 17/0 Uni
Body: Monofilament thread
Collar: Olive brown Ice Dub

Beadhead Thread Pupa

Originator: Rick Takahashi
Tier: Rick Takahashi

Hook: #18-24 Tiemco 2487
Bead: Brown matte
Thread: White 17/0 Uni
Body: Summer brown (54A) Coats & Clark
Collar: Brown olive Ice Dub

Buckskin Flash Pupa

Originator: Rick Takahashi
Tier: Rick Takahashi

Hook: #20-24 Tiemco 2488
Thread: White 17/0 Uni
Body: Buckskin Micro Tubing
Collar: Pearl Krystal Flash
Head: Tying thread
Note: Color the thread with tan Chartpak marker to form the head.

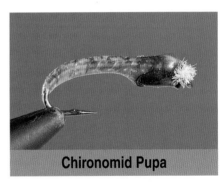

Chironomid Pupa

Originator: Brian Yamauchi
Tier: Brian Yamauchi

Hook: #14-16 Tiemco 2302
Thread: White 17/0 Uni
Body: Cream latex
Rib: Tying thread
Wing buds: Black Microfibetts
Gills: Oral-B Ultra Floss
Note: Two spools of thread are attached to the hook, one behind the eye and the other at the rear. Wrap the thread when you wrap the latex and color it with a marker. To form the wing buds, burn the Microfibetts on the ends and pull them over. Coat body and thorax with Loon UV Knot Sense.

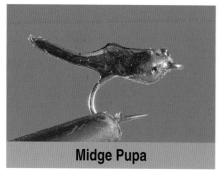

Midge Pupa

Originator: Brian Yamauchi
Tier: Brian Yamauchi

Hook: #18-24 Tiemco 2488
Thread: White 17/0 Uni
Body: Brown UTC Vinyl D Rib
Wing buds: Black Microfibetts
Note: Color the hemostats with black marker then heat the hemostats and crimp the D Rib to form the body. Coat the body and thorax with Loon UV Knot Sense. To form the wing buds, burn the Microfibetts on the ends and pull them over.

Tan Midge

Originator: Russell Ellis
Tier: Russell Ellis

Hook: #20-22 Tiemco 2487
Bead: Gunmetal Hi-Lite
Thread: Rusty dun 8/0 Uni
Tail: Hungarian partridge
Body: Tying thread

Olive Midge

Originator: Russell Ellis
Tier: Russell Ellis

Hook: #20-22 Tiemco 2487
Bead: Copper Hi-Lite
Thread: Olive 8/0 Uni
Tail: Olive Hungarian partridge
Body: Tying thread

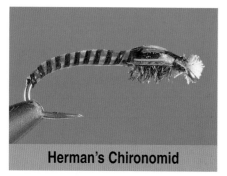

Herman's Chironomid

Originator: Herman deGala
Tier: Herman deGala

Hook: #16-20 Targus 2302
Thread: White 17/0 Uni
Body: Tying thread
Rib: Stripped red peacock herl
Thorax: Peacock herl
Wing case: Medallion Sheeting
Wing buds: Turkey quill
Gills: White CDC
Note: Color the thread with red Chartpak marker for the body. The entire fly except for the gills are covered with Clear Loon UV Knot Sense.

Deep Buzzer

Originator: Henk Verhaar
Tier: Henk Verhaar

Hook: #10-16 Tiemco 2457
Thread: Black 8/0 Uni
Body: Tying thread
Rib: Silver Holographic Tinsel
Thorax: Tying thread over lead wire
Wing case: Gray Swiss Straw
Gills: White Z-lon
Note: Cover entire fly with nail polish except for gills. This pattern was inspired by Han Weilenmann's CDC & Elk.

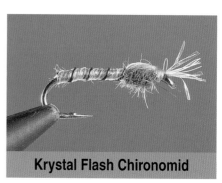

Krystal Flash Chironomid

Originator: Austin Haacke
Tier: Austin Haacke

Hook: #18-24 Tiemco 3761
Thread: Gray 8/0 Uni
Body: Pearl Krystal Flash
Rib: Copper Lagartun wire (fine)
Gills: White Antron and Crystal Splash
Thorax: Brown Super Fine

Stupid Midge

Originator: Unknown
Tier: Gordon Waldmier

Hook: #16-24 Tiemco 2487
Thread: Black 8/0 Uni
Body: Stripped peacock herl
Collar: Peacock herl

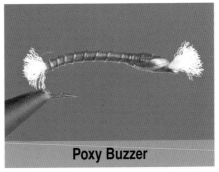

Poxy Buzzer

Originator: Henk Verhaar
Tier: Henk Verhaar

Hook: #10-14 Tiemco 200R
Thread: Olive 8/0 Uni
Tail: White Antron
Body: Tying thread
Rib: Copper Ultra Wire (small)
Thorax: Tying thread over lead wire
Wing case: Gold Swiss Straw
Gills: White Antron
Note: Cover entire fly with nail polish except for gills.

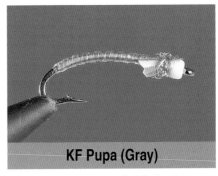

KF Pupa (Gray)

Originator: Rick Takahashi
Tier: Rick Takahashi

Hook: #18-22 Tiemco 200R
Bead: Flat white glass
Thread: White 17/0 Uni
Body: Tying thread
Rib: Pearl Krystal Flash
Collar: Olive brown Ice Dub
Wing buds: Cream goose biot
Note: Color the tying thread with light gray Chartpak marker.

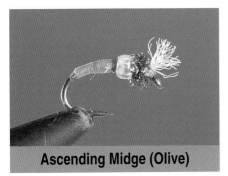

Ascending Midge (Olive)

Originator: Rick Takahashi
Tier: Rick Takahashi

Hook: #18-24 Tiemco 2457
Bead: Clear (with white center) glass
Thread: White 8/0 Uni
Body: Latex
Collar: Peacock Ice Dub
Gills: White poly yarn
Note: Color the latex with olive Chartpak marker.

Ascending Midge (Tan)

Originator: Rick Takahashi
Tier: Rick Takahashi

Hook: #18-24 Tiemco 2457
Bead: Clear (with white center) glass
Thread: White 8/0 Uni
Body: Latex
Collar: Rust Ice Dub
Gills: White poly yarn
Note: Color the latex with sand Chartpak marker.

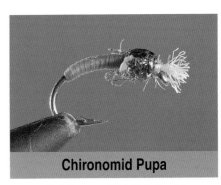

Chironomid Pupa

Originator: Rick Takahashi
Tier: Rick Takahashi

Hook: #14-18 Tiemco 2457
Thread: White 8/0 Uni
Body: Latex
Collar: Peacock Ice Dub
Gills: White poly yarn
Wing buds: Rust goose biot
Wing case: Dark dun Medallion Sheeting
Note: Color the latex with sepia Chartpak marker.

Crystal Chironomid (Olive)

Originator: Rick Takahashi
Tier: Rick Takahashi

Hook:	#14-18 Tiemco 200R
Thread:	White 8/0 Uni
Tail/Gills:	Oral-B Ultra Floss
Body:	Olive latex
Rib:	Silver Holographic Tinsel
Wing buds:	Brown Stretch Floss
Gills:	White poly yarn

Note: Cover entire fly with Loon UV Knot Sense.

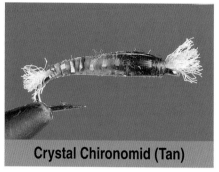

Crystal Chironomid (Tan)

Originator: Rick Takahashi
Tier: Rick Takahashi

Hook:	#12-22 Tiemco 200R
Thread:	White 17/0 Uni
Tail/Gills:	Oral-B Ultra Floss
Body:	1/8-inch latex strip
Rib:	Gold Holographic Tinsel
Thorax:	Tying thread
Wing buds:	Brown Flexi Floss

Note: Color the latex and tying thread for the thorax with tan Pantone marker. Coat fly with Loon UV Knot Sense.

Imposter Pupa

Originator: Rick Takahashi
Tier: Rick Takahashi

Hook:	#14-18 Tiemco 200R
Bead:	Flat white glass
Thread:	White 8/0 Uni
Tail:	White poly yarn
Body:	Olive Krystal Flash
Rib:	Olive Lagartun wire (fine)
Wing buds:	Rust goose biot
Wing case:	Brown Stretch Floss
Thorax:	Peacock Ice Dub

Red Hot Variant

Originator: John Mundinger
Tier: John Mundinger

Hook:	#18 Mustad 3906
Bead:	Red glass
Thread:	Olive 8/0 Uni
Body:	Peacock herl
Rib:	Red Ultra Wire (Brassie)

Brassie Variant

Originator: John Mundinger
Tier: John Mundinger

Hook:	#18 Mustad 3906
Thread:	Olive 8/0 Uni
Body:	Copper, gold, and chartreuse Ultra Wire (small) twisted together
Thorax:	Peacock herl

Henk's Zebra Midge

Originator: Jeff Henkemeyer
Tier: Jeff Henkemeyer

Hook:	#18-22 Tiemco 2487
Thread:	Black 70-denier UTC
Rib:	Copper Lagartun wire (fine)
Body:	Black thread
Thorax:	Peacock Ice Dub

Note: Before tying in the thorax, use the copper wire from the rib as added weight under the thorax.

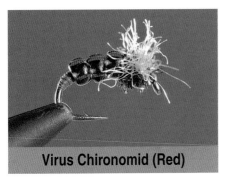

Virus Chironomid (Red)

Originator: Rainy Riding
Tier: Rainy's Fly Company

Hook: #16-20 Tiemco 2487
Thread: Red 8/0 Uni
Butt: Tying thread
Body: Three red glass beads
Thorax: Peacock herl
Gills: White Antron

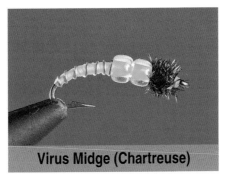

Virus Midge (Chartreuse)

Originator: Rainy Riding
Tier: Rainy's Fly Company

Hook: #18-22 Tiemco 200R
Bead: Chartreuse glass
Thread: Chartreuse 6/0 Uni
Body: Tying thread
Rib: Silver Ultra Wire (fine)
Thorax: Peacock herl

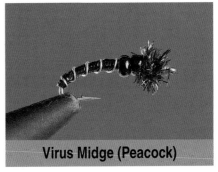

Virus Midge (Peacock)

Originator: Rainy Riding
Tier: Rainy's Fly Company

Hook: #18-22 Tiemco 200R
Bead: Two gunmetal glass
Thread: Black 8/0 Uni
Body: Pearl Krystal Flash dyed purple
Rib: Silver Ultra Wire (small)
Thorax: Peacock herl

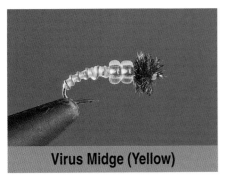

Virus Midge (Yellow)

Originator: Rainy Riding
Tier: Rainy's Fly Company

Hook: #18-22 Tiemco 200R
Bead: Two yellow glass
Thread: Yellow 8/0 Uni
Body: Tying thread
Rib: Silver Ultra Wire (small)
Thorax: Peacock herl

Virus Midge (Pearl)

Originator: Rainy Riding
Tier: Rainy's Fly Company

Hook: #18-22 Tiemco 200R
Bead: Two pearl glass
Thread: White 8/0 Uni
Body: Pearl Krystal Flash
Rib: Silver Ultra Wire (extra small)
Thorax: Peacock herl

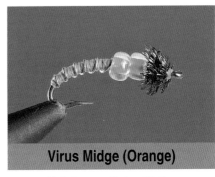

Virus Midge (Orange)

Originator: Rainy Riding
Tier: Rainy's Fly Company

Hook: #18-22 Tiemco 200R
Bead: Two hot orange glass
Thread: Hot orange 6/0 Uni
Body: Orange Krystal Flash
Rib: Silver Lagartun wire (fine)
Thorax: Peacock herl

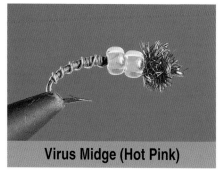

Virus Midge (Hot Pink)

Originator: Rainy Riding
Tier: Rainy's Fly Company

Hook:	#18-22 Tiemco 200R
Bead:	Two hot pink glass
Thread:	Hot pink 6/0 Uni
Body:	Hot pink Krystal Flash
Rib:	Silver Ultra Wire (small)
Thorax:	Peacock herl

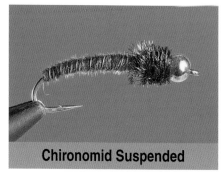

Chironomid Suspended

Originator: John Shewey
Tier: Rainy's Fly Company

Hook:	#12-16 Tiemco 200R
Bead:	Gold metal
Thread:	Black 8/0 Uni
Body:	Pheasant tail
Rib:	Gold Lagartun wire (fine)
Thorax:	Peacock herl

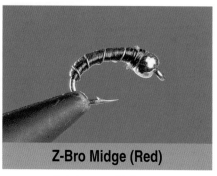

Z-Bro Midge (Red)

Originator: Unknown
Tier: Rainy's Fly Company

Hook:	#16-22 Tiemco 2457
Bead:	Nickel metal
Thread:	Red 8/0 Uni
Body:	Tying thread
Rib:	Gold Lagartun wire (fine)

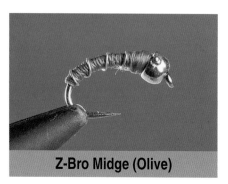

Z-Bro Midge (Olive)

Originator: Unknown
Tier: Rainy's Fly Company

Hook:	#16-22 Tiemco 2487
Bead:	Nickel metal
Thread:	Olive 8/0 Uni
Body:	Tying thread
Rib:	Silver Lagartun wire (fine)

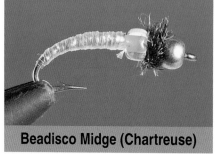

Beadisco Midge (Chartreuse)

Originator: Rainy Riding
Tier: Rainy's Fly Company

Hook:	#18-22 Tiemco 200R
Bead:	Gold metal
Thread:	Chartreuse 8/0 Uni
Body:	Chartreuse Krystal Flash
Thorax:	Chartreuse glass bead and peacock herl

Beadisco Midge (Peacock)

Originator: Rainy Riding
Tier: Rainy's Fly Company

Hook:	#18-22 Tiemco 200R
Bead:	Gold metal
Thread:	Black 8/0 Uni
Body:	Pearl Krystal Flash dyed purple
Thorax:	Gunmetal glass bead and peacock herl

Beadisco Midge (Pearl)

Originator: Rainy Riding
Tier: Rainy's Fly Company

Hook:	#18-22 Tiemco 200R
Bead:	Gold metal
Thread:	White 8/0 Uni
Body:	Pearl Krystal Flash
Thorax:	Pearl glass bead and peacock herl

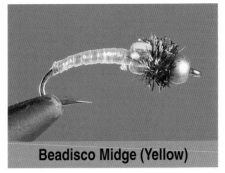

Beadisco Midge (Yellow)

Originator: Rainy Riding
Tier: Rainy's Fly Company

Hook:	#18-22 Tiemco 200R
Thread:	Yellow 8/0 Uni
Bead:	Gold metal
Body:	Yellow Krystal Flash
Thorax:	Yellow glass bead and peacock herl

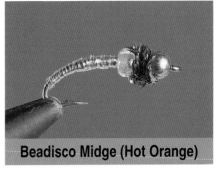

Beadisco Midge (Hot Orange)

Originator: Rainy Riding
Tier: Rainy's Fly Company

Hook:	#18-22 Tiemco 200R
Bead:	Gold metal
Thread:	Hot orange 8/0 Uni
Body:	Orange Krystal Flash
Thorax:	Hot orange glass bead and peacock herl

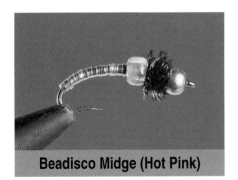

Beadisco Midge (Hot Pink)

Originator: Rainy Riding
Tier: Rainy's Fly Company

Hook:	#18-22 Tiemco 200R
Bead:	Gold metal
Thread:	Hot pink 6/0 Uni
Body:	Hot pink Krystal Flash
Thorax:	Hot pink glass bead and peacock herl

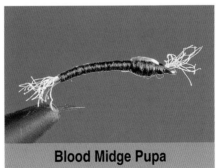

Blood Midge Pupa

Originator: Jason Haslam
Tier: Rainy's Fly Company

Hook:	#18-22 Tiemco 200R
Thread:	Red 8/0 Uni
Tail:	White Z-lon
Body:	Tying thread
Gills:	White Z-lon
Wing case:	White Z-lon
Thorax:	Tying thread

Zebra Midge Pupa

Originator: Jason Haslam
Tier: Rainy's Fly Company

Hook:	#18-22 Tiemco 200R
Tail:	White CDC
Thread:	Black 14/0 Gordon Griffiths
Body:	Tying thread
Rib:	Gold Ultra Wire (small)
Wing case:	White CDC
Gills:	White CDC
Thorax:	Tying thread

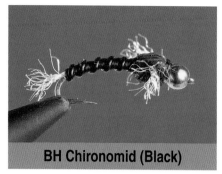

BH Chironomid (Black)

Originator: Rainy Riding
Tier: Rainy's Fly Company

Hook:	#10-18 Tiemco 2302
Bead:	Gold metal
Thread:	Clear 8/0 Uni
Shuck:	White Antron
Body:	Black Danville floss
Rib:	Red D Rib
Wing case:	Black duck quill
Thorax:	Peacock herl
Tail/Gills:	White Antron

BH Chironomid (Olive)

Originator: Rainy Riding
Tier: Rainy's Fly Company

Hook:	#10-18 Tiemco 2302
Shuck:	White Antron
Bead:	Gold metal
Thread:	Clear 8/0 Uni
Body:	Olive UTC Vinyl D Rib
Wing case:	Olive duck quill
Thorax:	Peacock herl
Tail/Gills:	White Antron

Marc-O-Midge (Olive)

Originator: Rainy Riding
Tier: Rainy's Fly Company

Hook:	#18-22 Tiemco 2487
Bead:	Gold metal
Thread:	Olive 8/0 Uni
Body:	Tying thread
Rib:	Copper Ultra Wire (small)
Gills:	White Antron

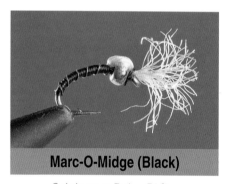

Marc-O-Midge (Black)

Originator: Rainy Riding
Tier: Rainy's Fly Company

Hook:	#18-22 Tiemco 2487
Bead:	Gold metal
Thread:	Black 6/0 Uni
Body:	Tying thread
Rib:	Gold Ultra Wire (small)
Gills:	White Antron

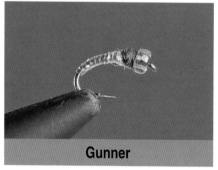

Gunner

Originator: John Gordon
Tier: John Gordon

Hook:	#24-26 Tiemco 2487
Bead:	Clear glass
Thread:	Fire orange 8/0 Uni
Body:	Pearl Krystal Flash
Thorax:	Tying thread

Duran's WD-40

Originator: Unknown
Tier: John Gordon

Hook:	#22 Tiemco 2488
Thread:	Gray 8/0 Uni
Tail:	Medium dun hackle
Body:	Tying thread
Thorax:	Gray Super Fine
Wing case:	Open cell foam; pearl Krystal Flash

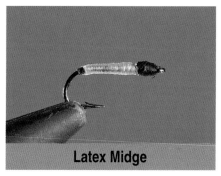

Latex Midge

Originator: John Gordon
Tier: John Gordon

Hook: #22-24 Tiemco 101
Thread: Black 8/0 Uni
Body: Latex strip
Head: Tying thread

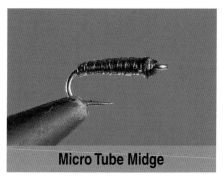

Micro Tube Midge

Originator: John Gordon
Tier: John Gordon

Hook: #20-22 Tiemco 101
Thread: Olive 8/0 Uni
Body: Olive Micro Tubing
Head: Black 8/0 Uni

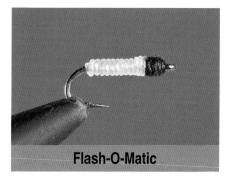

Flash-O-Matic

Originator: John Gordon
Tier: John Gordon

Hook: #20-22 Tiemco 101
Thread: Brown 8/0 Uni
Body: Gudebrod "A" HT thread
Head: Tying thread

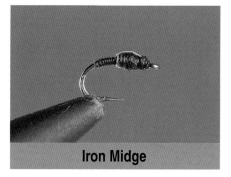

Iron Midge

Originator: John Gordon
Tier: John Gordon

Hook: #24-26 Tiemco 2488
Thread: Iron gray 8/0 Uni
Body: Tying thread
Thorax: Tying thread
Wing case: Pearl Krystal Flash
Head: Tying thread

Near Perfect Buzzer

Originator: Stanley Headly
Tier: Dennis Shaw

Hook: #10-20 K14ST
Thread: Black 8/0 Uni
Body: Stripped peacock herl,
              varnished
Thorax: Peacock herl
Wing buds: Orange Datam Glo-Brite
              floss
Collar: Gray dun hen

Blushing Midge

Originator: Stanley Headly
Tier: Dennis Shaw

Hook: #10-20 K14ST
Thread: Black 8/0 Uni
Body: Tying thread, varnished
Thorax: Peacock herl
Wing buds: Orange Datam Glo-Brite
              floss
Collar: Black dun hen

Video Buzzer

Originator: Nigel Stallard and Barrie Cook
Tier: Dennis Shaw

Hook:	#12-18 Kamasan B160
Thread:	Black 8/0 Uni
Tail:	White Multiyarn
Body:	VHS video cassette tape cut 1½ to 2mm strip
Rib:	Silver Lagartun wire (fine)
Thorax:	Peacock herl
Gills:	White Multiyarn

Grey Boy Buzzer

Originator: Alex Ferguson
Tier: Alex Ferguson

Hook:	#10 Hyabusa 384
Thread:	Black 8/0 Uni
Body:	Aluminum tin foil
Rib:	Stripped peacock quill dyed olive
Thorax:	Brown tying thread
Thorax cover:	Pearl UTC Mylar
Wing buds:	Brown raffia

Note: Tie the tin foil in dull side up and coat with Super Glue and Sally Hansen Hard As Nails.

Olive Quill Buzzer

Originator: Alex Ferguson
Tier: Alex Ferguson

Hook:	#10-16 Hyabusa 384
Thread:	Red Power Silk
Body:	Tying thread
Rib 1:	Stripped peacock quill dyed crimson
Rib 2:	Black tying thread
Thorax:	Tying thread
Thorax cover:	Pearl UTC Mylar
Wing buds:	Orange raffia tinted with red alcohol based marker

Note: Coat the body with Super Glue and Sally Hansen Hard As Nails.

Straight Brown Buzzer

Originator: Alex Ferguson
Tier: Alex Ferguson

Hook:	#10-14 Hyabusa 384
Thread:	Medium brown 6/0 Uni
Body:	Tying thread
Rib 1:	Pearl UTC Mylar (fine)
Rib 2:	Copper Lagartun wire (extra fine)
Wing buds:	Split jungle cock nail

Note: Coat the body and rib with Super Glue and Sally Hansen Hard As Nails.

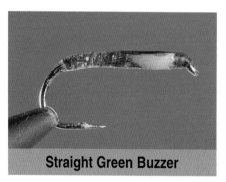

Straight Green Buzzer

Originator: Alex Ferguson
Tier: Alex Ferguson

Hook:	#10-14 Hyabusa 752
Thread:	Medium olive 6/0 Uni
Body:	Tying thread
Rib 1:	Pearl UTC Mylar (fine)
Rib 2:	Fine copper wire
Wing buds:	Split jungle cock nail

Note: This particular pattern closely mirrors a fly given to me by Mr. Ian Ritchie. Ian's fly has a holographic gold cheek as apposed to the split jungle cock. Coat the body and rib with Super Glue and Sally Hansen Hard As Nails.

Black and Red Buzzer

Originator: Alex Ferguson
Tier: Alex Ferguson

Hook:	#10-16 Hyabusa 384
Thread:	Black 6/0 Uni
Body:	Black 10/0 Power Silk
Rib:	Stripped peacock quill, dyed crimson
Thorax:	Tying thread and pearl UTC Mylar
Wing buds:	Red UTC Holographic Tinsel

Note: The whole fly is given one coat of super glue and two coats of Sally Hansen Hard As Nails. This pattern looks very similar to Basil Sheild's Claret and Black Buzzer. Other hook(s): Tiemco 2487.

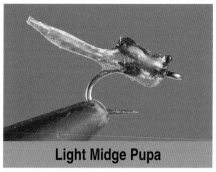

Light Midge Pupa

Originator: Brian Yamauchi
Tier: Brian Yamauchi

Hook: #18-24 Tiemco 2488
Thread: White 17/0 Uni
Body: UTC Vinyl D Rib
Wing buds: Black Microfibetts
Eyes: Burnt end of Microfibetts
Thorax: Tying thread
Note: Crimp the D Rib with hemostats and coat entire fly with Loon UV Knot Sense.

Dark Midge Pupa

Originator: Brian Yamauchi
Tier: Brian Yamauchi

Hook: #18-26 Tiemco 2488
Thread: White 17/0 Uni
Body: UTC Vinyl D Rib
Wing buds: Black Microfibetts
Eyes: Burnt end of Microfibetts
Thorax: Tying thread

Purple Hazard

Originator: Chad Gauerke
Tier: Chad Gauerke

Hook: #18 Mustad C53S
Bead: Purple/aqua Czech
Thread: Purple 8/0 Uni
Body: Tying thread
Rib: Silver Lagartun wire (fine)
Wing case: UTC Mirage Tinsel (medium)
Thorax: Hot purple Prism SLF

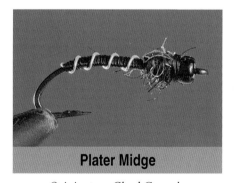

Plater Midge

Originator: Chad Gauerke
Tier: Chad Gauerke

Hook: #18 Tiemco 200R or Dai-Riki 270
Bead: Ruby red glass
Thread: Black 8/0 Uni
Body: Tying thread
Rib: Chartreuse Ultra Wire (small)
Wing case: UTC Mirage Tinsel (medium)
Thorax: Mix of different black dubbing material

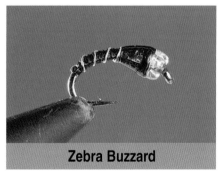

Zebra Buzzard

Originator: Chad Gauerke
Tier: Chad Gauerke

Hook: #20 Dai-Riki 135
Bead: Silver Hi-Lite
Thread: Black 8/0 Uni
Body: Tying thread
Rib: Silver Lagartun wire (fine)
Wing buds: UTC Mirage Tinsel

Black Magic

Originator: Chad Gauerke
Tier: Chad Gauerke

Hook: #20 Dai-Riki 270
Thread: Black 8/0 Uni
Body: Tying thread
Rib: Silver Mirage Tinsel

Rainbow Snack

Originator: Chad Gauerke
Tier: Chad Gauerke

Hook: #20 Dai-Riki 135
Thread: Black 8/0 Uni
Body: Tying thread
Rib: Silver Lagartun wire (fine)
Head: Red 8/0 Uni covered with high gloss nail polish

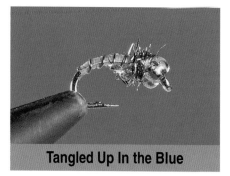

Tangled Up In the Blue

Originator: Chad Gauerke
Tier: Chad Gauerke

Hook: #20 Dai-Riki 135
Bead: Blue luster Czech
Thread: White10/0 Gudebrod
Body: Tying thread
Rib: Blue Lagartun wire (fine)
Thorax: Blue Ice Dub

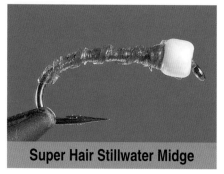

Super Hair Stillwater Midge

Originator: Mark Schoenbaum
Tier: Mark Schoenbaum

Hook: #12-14 Mustad 3399A
Bead: White glass
Thread: Olive 8/0 Uni
Body: Olive Super Hair, twisted
Rib: Olive UTC Vinyl D Rib
Note: Two coats Sally Hansen Hard as Nails.

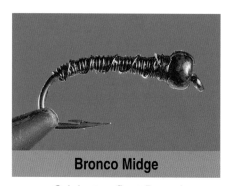

Bronco Midge

Originator: Scott Patton/
Mark Schoenbaum
Tier: Mark Schoenbaum

Hook: #12 Mustad 3399A
Bead: Brown Hi-Lite
Thread: Copper/rust 6/0 Uni
Body: Gunmetal blue Ultra Wire (extra small)
Rib: Red Ultra Wire (small)

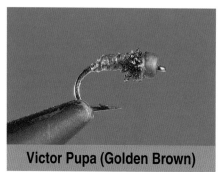

Victor Pupa (Golden Brown)

Originator: Rick Takahashi
Tier: Rick Takahashi

Hook: #18-24 Tiemco 2488
Bead: Olive glass
Thread: White 17/0 Uni
Body: Golden brown Glitter Thread
Rib: Clear .5mm Stretch Magic
Collar: Black peacock Ice Dub
Note: In memory of my friend Victor Dennis Watson Feeny III. Other hook(s): Dai-Riki 125.

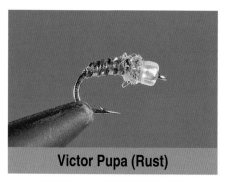

Victor Pupa (Rust)

Originator: Rick Takahashi
Tier: Rick Takahashi

Hook: #18-24 Tiemco 2488
Bead: Clear glass
Thread: White 17/0 Uni
Body: Rust Glitter Thread
Rib: Clear .5mm Stretch Magic
Collar: Rust peacock Ice Dub
Note: Other hook(s): Dai-Riki 125.

Victor Pupa (White and Black)

Originator: Rick Takahashi
Tier: Rick Takahashi

Hook: #18-24 Tiemco 2488
Bead: Pewter glass
Thread: White 17/0 Uni
Body: Pearl Glitter Thread
Rib: Clear .5mm Stretch Magic
Collar: Black peacock Ice Dub
Note: Other hook(s): Dai-Riki 125.

Victor Pupa (Golden Olive)

Originator: Rick Takahashi
Tier: Rick Takahashi

Hook: #18-24 Tiemco 2488
Bead: Root beer glass
Thread: White 17/0 Uni
Body: Golden olive Glitter Thread
Rib: Clear .5mm Stretch Magic
Collar: Rust peacock Ice Dub
Note: Other hook(s): Dai-Riki 125.

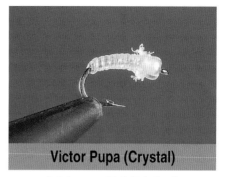

Victor Pupa (Crystal)

Originator: Rick Takahashi
Tier: Rick Takahashi

Hook: #18-24 Tiemco 2488
Bead: Clear glass with white center
Thread: White 17/0 Uni
Body: Pearl Glitter Thread
Rib: Clear .5mm Stretch Magic
Collar: White peacock Ice Dub
Note: Other hook(s): Dai-Riki 125.

Psych Midge (Rust)

Originator: Rick Takahashi
Tier: Rick Takahashi

Hook: #18-24 Tiemco 2488
Thread: White 17/0 Uni
Underbody: Rust Glitter Thread
Body: Clear .5mm Stretch Magic
Gills: Oral-B Ultra Floss
Head: Tying thread
Note: Color tying thread with black Sharpie to form the head. Other hook(s): Dai-Riki 125.

Psych Midge (Golden Olive)

Originator: Rick Takahashi
Tier: Rick Takahashi

Hook: #18-24 Tiemco 2488
Thread: White 17/0 Uni
Underbody: Golden olive Glitter Thread
Body: Clear .5mm Stretch Magic
Gills: Oral-B Ultra Floss
Head: Tying thread
Note: Color tying thread with black Sharpie to form the head. Other hook(s): Dai-Riki 125.

Psych Midge (Pewter)

Originator: Rick Takahashi
Tier: Rick Takahashi

Hook: #18-24 Tiemco 2488
Thread: White 17/0 Uni
Underbody: Pewter Glitter Thread
Body: Clear .5mm Stretch Magic
Gills: Oral-B Ultra Floss
Head: Tying thread
Note: Color tying thread with black Sharpie to form the head. Other hook(s): Dai-Riki 125.

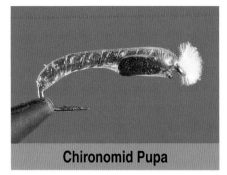

Chironomid Pupa

Originator: Brian Yamauchi
Tier: Brian Yamauchi

Hook: #12-16 Tiemco 2302
Thread: White 17/0 Uni
Body: Latex
Rib: Tying thread
Wing buds: Black Microfibetts
Eyes: Burnt end of Microfibetts
Thorax: Tying thread
Gills: White CDC
Note: Entire fly except for gills is covered with UV Knot Sense.

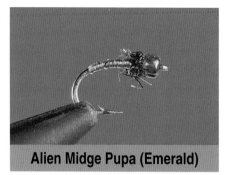

Alien Midge Pupa (Emerald)

Originator: Rick Takahashi
Tier: Rick Takahashi

Hook: #18-24 Tiemco 2488
Bead: Root beer glass
Thread: White 17/0 Uni
Body: Golden olive Glitter Thread
Collar: Peacock Ice Dub
Note: Other hook(s): Dai-Riki 125.

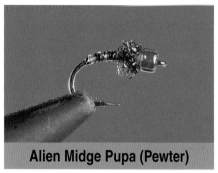

Alien Midge Pupa (Pewter)

Originator: Rick Takahashi
Tier: Rick Takahashi

Hook: #18-24 Tiemco 2488
Bead: Root beer glass
Thread: White 17/0 Uni
Body: Pewter Glitter Thread
Collar: Peacock Ice Dub
Note: Other hook(s): Dai-Riki 125.

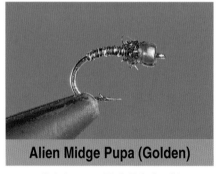

Alien Midge Pupa (Golden)

Originator: Rick Takahashi
Tier: Rick Takahashi

Hook: #18-24 Tiemco 2488
Bead: Root beer glass
Thread: White 17/0 Uni
Body: Golden brown Glitter Thread
Collar: Peacock Ice Dub
Note: Other hook(s): Dai-Riki 125.

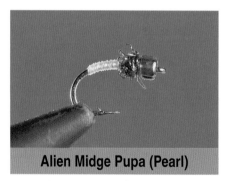

Alien Midge Pupa (Pearl)

Originator: Rick Takahashi
Tier: Rick Takahashi

Hook: #18-24 Tiemco 2488
Bead: Root beer glass
Thread: White 17/0 Uni
Body: Pearl Glitter Thread
Collar: Peacock Ice Dub
Note: Other hook(s): Dai-Riki 125.

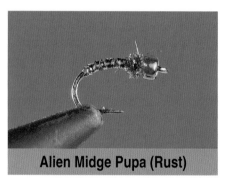

Alien Midge Pupa (Rust)

Originator: Rick Takahashi
Tier: Rick Takahashi

Hook: #18-24 Tiemco 2488
Bead: Root beer glass
Thread: White 17/0 Uni
Body: Rust Glitter Thread
Collar: Peacock Ice Dub
Note: Other hook(s): Dai-Riki 125.

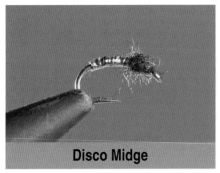

Disco Midge

Originator: Unknown
Tier: Russell Stanton

Hook:	#22 Tiemco 2487
Thread:	Black 10/0 Gudebrod
Body:	Flashabou
Thorax:	Black beaver

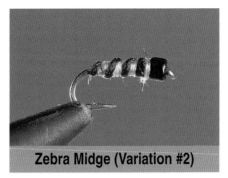

Zebra Midge (Variation #2)

Originator: Unknown
Tier: Russell Stanton

Hook:	#22 Tiemco 100
Bead:	Black glass
Thread:	White 10/0 Gudebrod
Body:	White Pearsall's silk
Rib:	Black Coats & Clark

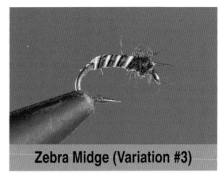

Zebra Midge (Variation #3)

Originator: Russell Stanton
Tier: Russell Stanton

Hook:	#22 Tiemco 2487
Thread:	White 10/0 Gudebrod
Body:	White stripped quill
Rib:	Black stripped quill
Thorax:	Black beaver

Zebra Midge (Variation #4)

Originator: Russell Stanton
Tier: Russell Stanton

Hook:	#22 Tiemco 200R
Thread:	White 10/0 Gudebrod
Body:	White goose biot
Rib:	Black Coats & Clark
Thorax:	Black beaver

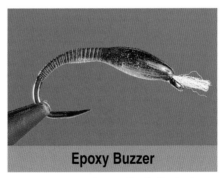

Epoxy Buzzer

Originator: Brian Healy/Padraig
Costello
Tier: Marvin Nolte

Hook:	#12-14 Partridge SHR
Gills:	White Antron
Thread:	Yellow-olive and medium brown 70-denier UTC
Body:	Stripped peacock quill
Thorax:	Red, olive, and orange Flex-Floss

Note: Coat fly with 5-minute epoxy.
Other hook(s): #8-10 Mustad C49S.

Punk Rojo

Originator: Kelli Sandoval
Tier: Kelli Sandoval

Hook:	#18-22 Daiichi 1273
Thread:	Red 70-denier UTC
Body:	Tying thread
Rib:	Black Ultra Wire (extra small)
Collar:	Peacock herl

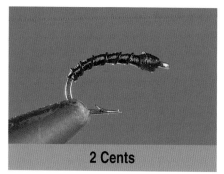

2 Cents

Originator: Kelli Sandoval
Tier: Kelli Sandoval

Hook:	#22-26 Tiemco 2488
Thread:	Red 70-denier UTC
Body:	Tying thread
Rib:	Black Lagartun wire (extra fine)
Head:	Tying thread colored black

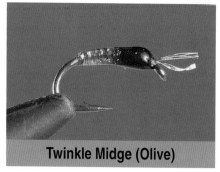

Twinkle Midge (Olive)

Originator: Rick Takahashi
Tier: Rick Takahashi

Hook:	#18-24 Tiemco 2487
Thread:	White 8/0 Uni
Body:	Golden olive Glitter Thread
Gills:	Pearl Glitter Thread
Head:	Tying thread

Note: Color the tying thread with dark brown Chartpak marker to form the head. Cover thread with Loon UV Knot Sense.

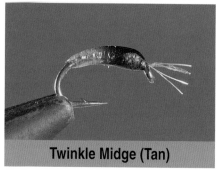

Twinkle Midge (Tan)

Originator: Rick Takahashi
Tier: Rick Takahashi

Hook:	#18-24 Tiemco 2487
Thread:	White 8/0 Uni
Body:	Pearl Glitter Thread
Gills:	Pearl Glitter Thread
Head:	Tying thread

Note: Color the Glitter Thread on the body with sand Chartpak marker and the tying thread with dark brown Chartpak marker to form the head. Cover thread with Loon UV Knot Sense.

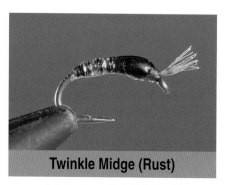

Twinkle Midge (Rust)

Originator: Rick Takahashi
Tier: Rick Takahashi

Hook:	#18-24 Tiemco 2487
Thread:	White 8/0 Uni
Body:	Rust Glitter Thread
Gills:	Pearl Glitter Thread
Head:	Tying thread

Note: Color the tying thread with dark brown Chartpak marker to form the head. Cover thread with Loon UV Knot Sense.

Twinkle Midge (Rust)

Originator: Rick Takahashi
Tier: Rick Takahashi

Hook:	#18-24 Tiemco 2487
Thread:	White 8/0 Uni
Body:	Golden brown Glitter Thread
Gills:	Pearl Glitter Thread
Head:	Tying thread

Note: Color the tying thread with dark brown Chartpak marker to form the head. Cover thread with Loon UV Knot Sense.

Twinkle Midge (Black)

Originator: Rick Takahashi
Tier: Rick Takahashi

Hook:	#18-24 Tiemco 2487
Thread:	White 8/0 Uni
Body:	Black Glitter Thread
Gills:	Pearl Glitter Thread
Head:	Tying thread

Note: Color the tying thread with dark brown Chartpak marker to form the head. Cover thread with Loon UV Knot Sense.

Ice Cream Cone (Tan)

Originator: Spirit River
Tier: Spirit River

Hook:	#10-16 Spear-It CS048
Bead:	White Hot Bead
Thread:	Tan 6/0 Uni
Body:	Tan Flex-Floss
Rib:	Silver Lagartun wire (fine)
Thorax:	Black 8/0 Uni

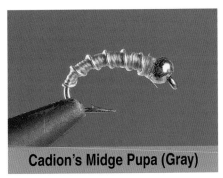

Cadion's Midge Pupa (Gray)

Originator: Bryce Cadion
Tier: Spirit River

Hook:	#16-20 Spear-It CS048
Bead:	Silver metal
Thread:	Gray 140-denier UTC
Body:	Tying thread
Rib:	Silver Lagartun wire (fine)

Note: Other hook(s): Daiichi 1130.

Cadion's Midge Pupa (Olive)

Originator: Bryce Cadion
Tier: Spirit River

Hook:	#16-20 Spear-It CS048
Bead:	Gold metal
Thread:	Olive 140-denier UTC
Body:	Tying thread
Rib:	Red Lagartun wire (fine)

Note: Other hook(s): Daiichi 1130.

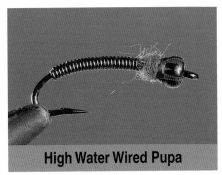

High Water Wired Pupa

Originator: Jerry Saiz
Tier: Jerry Saiz

Hook:	#18-22 Daiichi 1273
Bead:	Red glass
Thread:	Red 8/0 Uni
Body:	Red Ultra Wire (small)
Thorax:	Red Super Fine

Hump-Bak Midge (Olive)

Originator: Spirit River
Tier: Spirit River

Hook:	#12-18 Spear-It CS048
Thread:	Olive 8/0 Uni
Body:	Pearl Mirror Flash
Rib:	Clear .5mm Stretch Magic
Thorax:	Peacock herl and Hump-Bak bead

Note: Other hook(s): Daiichi 1130.

Hump-Bak Midge (Brown)

Originator: Spirit River
Tier: Spirit River

Hook:	#12-18 Spear-It CS048
Thread:	Brown 8/0 Uni
Body:	Pearl Mirror Flash
Rib:	Clear .5mm Stretch Magic
Thorax:	Peacock herl and Hump-Bak bead

Note: Other hook(s): Daiichi 1130.

Quick Silver Blood Midge

Originator: Spirit River
Tier: Spirit River

Hook:	#18-22 Spear-It CS200
Bead:	Mercury glass
Thread:	Red 8/0 Uni
Body:	Tying thread
Rib:	Gold Lagartun wire (fine)
Thorax:	Peacock herl

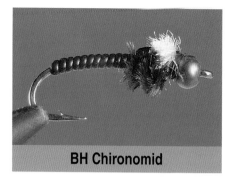

BH Chironomid

Originator: Bill Black
Tier: Spirit River

Hook:	#12-18 Spear-It D312
Thread:	Black 8/0 Uni
Bead:	Black metal
Body:	Black Vinyl D Rib
Thorax:	Peacock herl
Gills:	White Antron
Wing case:	Swiss Straw
Note:	Other hook(s): Daiichi 1260.

Olive Bomber

Originator: Unknown
Tier: Chad Gauerke

Hook:	#22 Dai-Riki 270
Bead:	Red Hi-Lite
Thread:	Black 8/0 Uni
Body:	Olive Ultra Wire (small)
Collar:	Olive Life Cycle dubbing

Psychopath

Originator: Unknown
Tier: Chad Gauerke

Hook:	#14 Dai-Riki 270
Bead:	Silver octagon tungsten
Thread:	Black 8/0 Uni
Body:	Peacock MFC Phoenix dubbing
Collar:	Peacock MFC Phoenix dubbing

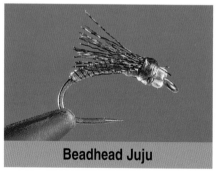

Beadhead Juju

Originator: Charlie Craven (variation)
Tier: Chad Gauerke

Hook:	#18 Skalka P Midge Hook
Bead:	Silver Hi-Lite
Thread:	White 10/0 Bennechi
Body:	Olive Super Hair
Rib:	Black Super Hair
Wing:	Black Fluoro Fibre
Head:	Black Power Silk

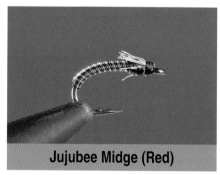

Jujubee Midge (Red)

Originator: Charlie Craven
Tier: Charlie Craven

Hook:	#18-22 Tiemco 2488
Thread:	White 10/0 Gudebrod
Body:	Super Hair, two red and one white strand
Wing buds:	White Fluoro Fibre
Thorax:	Red 8/0 Uni

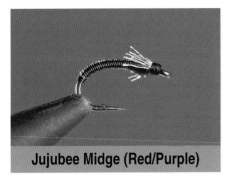

Jujubee Midge (Red/Purple)

Originator: Charlie Craven
Tier: Charlie Craven

Hook:	#18-22 Tiemco 2488
Thread:	White 10/0 Gudebrod
Body:	Super Hair, two purple and one red strand
Wing buds:	White Fluoro Fibre
Thorax:	Black 8/0 Uni

Jujubee Midge (Tiger)

Originator: Charlie Craven
Tier: Charlie Craven

Hook:	#18-22 Tiemco 2488
Thread:	White 10/0 Gudebrod
Body:	Super Hair, two black and one orange strand
Wing buds:	White Fluoro Fibre
Thorax:	Black 8/0 Uni

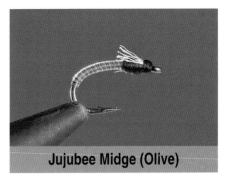

Jujubee Midge (Olive)

Originator: Charlie Craven
Tier: Charlie Craven

Hook:	#18-22 Tiemco 2488
Thread:	White 10/0 Gudebrod
Body:	Super Hair, two chartreuse and one olive strand
Wing buds:	White Fluoro Fibre
Thorax:	Black 8/0 Uni

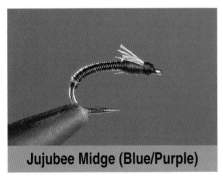

Jujubee Midge (Blue/Purple)

Originator: Charlie Craven
Tier: Charlie Craven

Hook:	#18-22 Tiemco 2488
Thread:	White 10/0 Gudebrod
Body:	Super Hair, two purple and one blue strand
Wing buds:	White Fluoro Fibre
Thorax:	Black 8/0 Uni

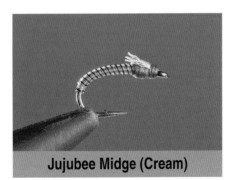

Jujubee Midge (Cream)

Originator: Charlie Craven
Tier: Charlie Craven

Hook:	#18-22 Tiemco 2488
Thread:	White 10/0 Gudebrod
Body:	Super Hair, two tan and one dark brown strand
Wing buds:	White Fluoro Fibre
Thorax:	Tan 8/0 Uni

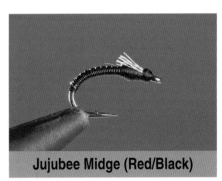

Jujubee Midge (Red/Black)

Originator: Charlie Craven
Tier: Charlie Craven

Hook:	#18-22 Tiemco 2488
Thread:	White 10/0 Gudebrod
Body:	Super Hair, two black and one red strand
Wing buds:	White Fluoro Fibre
Thorax:	Black 8/0 Uni

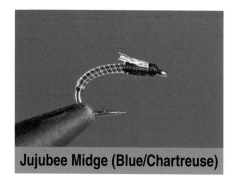

Jujubee Midge (Blue/Chartreuse)

Originator: Charlie Craven
Tier: Charlie Craven

Hook: #18-22 Tiemco 2488
Thread: White 10/0 Gudebrod
Body: Super Hair, two blue and one chartreuse strand
Wing buds: White Fluoro Fibre
Thorax: Black 8/0 Uni

Jujubee Midge (Olive)

Originator: Charlie Craven
Tier: Charlie Craven

Hook: #18-22 Tiemco 2488
Thread: White 10/0 Gudebrod
Body: Super Hair, two olive and one black strand
Wing buds: White Fluoro Fibre
Thorax: Black 8/0 Uni

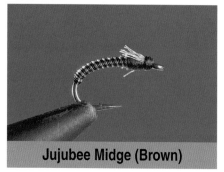

Jujubee Midge (Brown)

Originator: Charlie Craven
Tier: Charlie Craven

Hook: #18-22 Tiemco 2488
Thread: White 10/0 Gudebrod
Body: Super Hair, two brown and one white strand
Wing buds: White Fluoro Fibre
Thorax: Dark brown 8/0 Uni

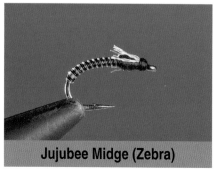

Jujubee Midge (Zebra)

Originator: Charlie Craven
Tier: Charlie Craven

Hook: #18-22 Tiemco 2488
Thread: White 10/0 Gudebrod
Body: Super Hair, two black and one white strand
Wing buds: White Fluoro Fibre
Thorax: Black 8/0 Uni

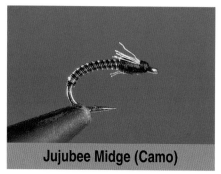

Jujubee Midge (Camo)

Originator: Charlie Craven
Tier: Charlie Craven

Hook: #18-22 Tiemco 2488
Thread: White 10/0 Gudebrod
Body: Super Hair, strand of olive, dark brown, and black
Wing buds: White Fluoro Fibre
Thorax: Black 8/0 Uni

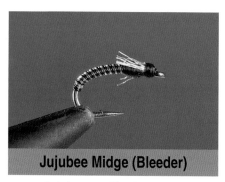

Jujubee Midge (Bleeder)

Originator: Charlie Craven
Tier: Charlie Craven

Hook: #18-22 Tiemco 2488
Thread: White 10/0 Gudebrod
Body: Super Hair, strand of black, red, and white
Wing buds: White Fluoro Fibre
Thorax: Black 8/0 Uni

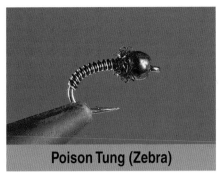

Poison Tung (Zebra)

Originator: Charlie Craven
Tier: Charlie Craven

Hook:	#16-22 Tiemco 2488
Bead:	Black tungsten
Thread:	Black 10/0 Gudebrod
Body:	Black (brassie) and silver Ultra Wire (extra small)
Thorax:	Black peacock Ice Dub

Poison Tung (Chartreuse)

Originator: Charlie Craven
Tier: Charlie Craven

Hook:	#16-22 Tiemco 2488
Bead:	Black tungsten
Thread:	Black 10/0 Gudebrod
Body:	Chartreuse Ultra Wire (extra small)
Thorax:	Black peacock Ice Dub

Poison Tung (Olive and Black)

Originator: Charlie Craven
Tier: Charlie Craven

Hook:	#16-22 Tiemco 2488
Bead:	Black tungsten
Thread:	Black 10/0 Gudebrod
Body:	Olive (brassie) and black (small) Ultra Wire
Thorax:	Black peacock Ice Dub

Poison Tung (Wine and Silver)

Originator: Charlie Craven
Tier: Charlie Craven

Hook:	#16-22 Tiemco 2488
Bead:	Black tungsten
Thread:	Black 10/0 Gudebrod
Body:	Wine (brassie) and silver (small) Ultra Wire
Thorax:	Black peacock Ice Dub

Poison Tung (Deep Purple)

Originator: Charlie Craven
Tier: Charlie Craven

Hook:	#16-22 Tiemco 2488
Bead:	Black tungsten
Thread:	Purple 10/0 Gudebrod
Body:	Tying thread
Rib:	Peacock blue Lagartun wire (fine)
Thorax:	Holographic purple Ice Dub

Poison Tung (Black)

Originator: Charlie Craven
Tier: Charlie Craven

Hook:	#16-22 Tiemco 2488
Bead:	Black tungsten
Body:	Black Ultra Wire (small)
Thorax:	Black peacock Ice Dub

Gordo's Fuzzy Navel Pupa

Originator: Gordon Waldmier
Tier: Gordon Waldmier

Hook:	#16-22 Tiemco 2488
Thread:	Black 10/0 Gudebrod
Body:	Rust micro peacock herl
Head:	Red and black 8/0 Uni, mixed

Golden Jubilation

Originator: Deward Yocum
Tier: Deward Yocum

Hook:	#18-22 Tiemco 200R
Bead:	Gold glass
Thread:	Light cahill 8/0 Uni
Body:	Tying thread
Rib:	Silver Lagartun wire (fine)
Thorax:	Peacock herl
Gills:	White Z-lon

Bush Master

Originator: Deward Yocum
Tier: Deward Yocum

Hook:	#18-22 Tiemco 200R
Bead:	Black glass
Thread:	Olive dun 8/0 Uni
Tail:	Black Antron
Body:	Tying thread
Rib:	Copper Lagartun wire (fine)
Thorax:	Peacock herl

Wannabe

Originator: Deward Yocum
Tier: Deward Yocum

Hook:	#18-22 Tiemco 200R
Bead:	Clear glass
Thread:	Iron gray 8/0 Uni
Body:	Tying thread
Rib:	Pearl Flashabou
Gills:	White Antron
Wing:	Pearl Krystal Flash

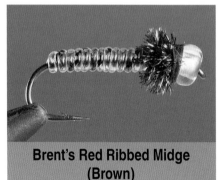

Brent's Red Ribbed Midge (Brown)

Originator: Brent Schlenker
Tier: Pacific Fly Group

Hook:	#10-14 Daiichi 1280
Bead:	Pearl glass
Thread:	Brown 6/0 Uni
Underbody:	Tying thread
Rib:	Red Krystal Flash
Body:	Clear UTC Vinyl D Rib
Collar:	Peacock herl

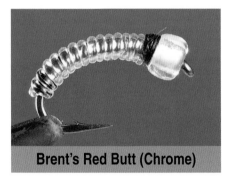

Brent's Red Butt (Chrome)

Originator: Brent Schlenker
Tier: Pacific Fly Group

Hook:	#10-14 Daiichi 1120
Bead:	Pearl glass
Thread:	Black 6/0 Uni
Tag:	Red Krystal Flash
Underbody:	Pearl Krystal Flash
Body:	Clear UTC Vinyl D Rib

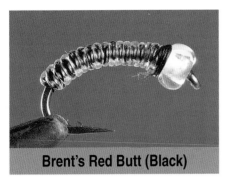

Brent's Red Butt (Black)

Originator: Brent Schlenker
Tier: Pacific Fly Group

Hook: #10-14 Daiichi 1120
Bead: Pearl glass
Thread: Black 6/0 Uni
Tag: Red Krystal Flash
Underbody: Tying thread
Body: Clear UTC Vinyl D Rib

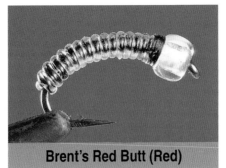

Brent's Red Butt (Red)

Originator: Brent Schlenker
Tier: Pacific Fly Group

Hook: #10-14 Daiichi 1120
Bead: Pearl glass
Thread: Red 6/0 Uni
Underbody: Red Krystal Flash
Body: Clear UTC Vinyl D Rib

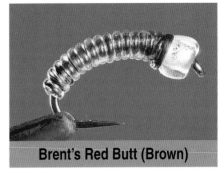

Brent's Red Butt (Brown)

Originator: Brent Schlenker
Tier: Pacific Fly Group

Hook: #10-14 Daiichi 1120
Bead: Pearl glass
Thread: Brown 6/0 Uni
Tag: Red Krystal Flash
Underbody: Tying thread
Body: Clear UTC Vinyl D Rib

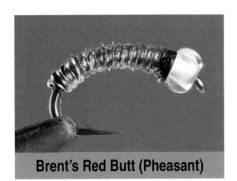

Brent's Red Butt (Pheasant)

Originator: Brent Schlenker
Tier: Pacific Fly Group

Hook: #10-14 Daiichi 1120
Bead: Pearl glass
Thread: Black 6/0 Uni
Tag: Red Krystal Flash
Underbody: Pheasant tail
Body: Clear UTC Vinyl D Rib

Brent's Magic Midge (Black)

Originator: Brent Schlenker
Tier: Pacific Fly Group

Hook: #10-14 Daiichi 1270
Bead: Pearl glass
Thread: Black 6/0 Uni
Body: Black UTC Vinyl D Rib
Thorax: Peacock herl

Brent's Magic Midge (Peacock)

Originator: Brent Schlenker
Tier: Pacific Fly Group

Hook: #10-14 Daiichi 1270
Bead: Pearl glass
Thread: Black 6/0 Uni
Underbody: Green Krystal Flash
Body: Clear UTC Vinyl D Rib
Thorax: Peacock herl

Brent's Magic Midge (Pearl)

Originator: Brent Schlenker
Tier: Pacific Fly Group

Hook:	#10-14 Daiichi 1270
Bead:	Pearl glass
Thread:	Black 6/0 Uni
Underbody:	Pearl Krystal Flash
Body:	Clear UTC Vinyl D Rib
Thorax:	Peacock herl

Brent's Magic Midge (Red)

Originator: Brent Schlenker
Tier: Pacific Fly Group

Hook:	#10-14 Daiichi 1270
Bead:	Pearl glass
Thread:	Black 6/0 Uni
Body:	Red UTC Vinyl D Rib
Thorax:	Peacock herl

Brent's Magic Midge (Root Beer)

Originator: Brent Schlenker
Tier: Pacific Fly Group

Hook:	#10-14 Daiichi 1270
Bead:	Pearl glass
Thread:	Black 6/0 Uni
Body:	Tan UTC Vinyl D Rib
Thorax:	Peacock herl

Chironomid Pupa (Black)

Originator: Dennis Komatsu
Tier: Pacific Fly Group

Hook:	#18-20 Daiichi 1130
Bead:	Black Killer Caddis
Thread:	Black 8/0 Uni
Body:	Black Krystal Flash
Thorax:	Black Super Fine

Chironomid Pupa (Green)

Originator: Dennis Komatsu
Tier: Pacific Fly Group

Hook:	#18-20 Daiichi 1130
Bead:	Green Killer Caddis
Thread:	Light olive 6/0 Uni
Body:	Green Krystal Flash
Thorax:	Light olive Super Fine

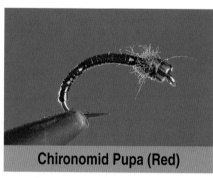

Chironomid Pupa (Red)

Originator: Dennis Komatsu
Tier: Pacific Fly Group

Hook:	#18-20 Daiichi 1130
Bead:	Red Killer Caddis
Thread:	Red 8/0 Uni
Body:	Red Krystal Flash
Thorax:	Red dubbing

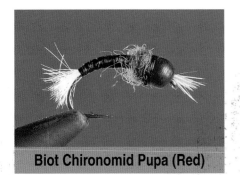

Biot Chironomid Pupa (Red)

Originator: Dennis Komatsu
Tier: Pacific Fly Group

Hook: #18-24 Daiichi 1130
Bead: Black Cyclops
Thread: Red 8/0 Uni
Gills: White ostrich herl
Body: Red goose biot
Thorax: Red Super Fine

Biot Chironomid Pupa (Brown)

Originator: Dennis Komatsu
Tier: Pacific Fly Group

Hook: #18-24 Daiichi 1130
Bead: Black Cyclops
Thread: Black 8/0 Uni
Gills: White ostrich herl
Body: Brown goose biot
Thorax: Black Super Fine

Biot Chironomid Pupa (Olive)

Originator: Dennis Komatsu
Tier: Pacific Fly Group

Hook: #18-24 Daiichi 1130
Bead: Black Cyclops
Thread: Light olive 8/0 Uni
Gills: White ostrich herl
Body: Light olive goose biot
Thorax: Light olive Super Fine

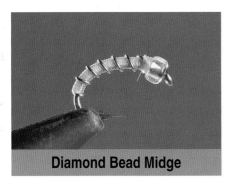

Diamond Bead Midge

Originator: Unknown
Tier: Pacific Fly Group

Hook: #20-24 Daiichi 1130
Bead: Diamond Killer Caddis
Thread: Tan 8/0 Uni
Body: Tying thread
Rib: Copper Lagartun wire (fine)

Glass Bead Black Beauty

Originator: Unknown
Tier: Pacific Fly Group

Hook: #20-24 Daiichi 1130
Bead: Diamond Killer Caddis
Thread: Black 8/0 Uni
Body: Tying thread
Rib: Copper Lagartun wire (fine)
Thorax: Black Super Fine

Tav's Big Mac Pupa (Iron Gray)

Originator: John Tavenner
Tier: Pacific Fly Group

Hook: #18-22 Daiichi 1270
Bead: Gunmetal glass
Thread: Iron gray 6/0 Uni
Underbody: Tying thread
Body: Clear Micro Tubing

Tav's Big Mac Pupa (Olive Yellow)

Originator: John Tavenner
Tier: Pacific Fly Group

Hook:	#18-22 Daiichi 1270
Bead:	Gunmetal glass
Thread:	Light olive 8/0 Uni
Underbody:	Tying thread
Body:	Clear Micro Tubing

Tav's Big Mac Pupa (Olive)

Originator: John Tavenner
Tier: Pacific Fly Group

Hook:	#18-22 Daiichi 1270
Bead:	Gunmetal glass
Thread:	Olive 8/0 Uni
Underbody:	Tying thread
Body:	Clear Micro Tubing

Tav's Big Mac Pupa (Iron Gray)

Originator: John Tavenner
Tier: Pacific Fly Group

Hook:	#18-22 Daiichi 1270
Thread:	Iron gray 8/0 Uni
Underbody:	Tying thread
Body:	Clear Micro Tubing
Thorax:	Black Super Fine

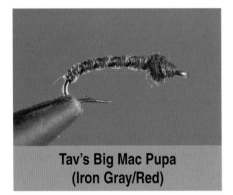

**Tav's Big Mac Pupa
(Iron Gray/Red)**

Originator: John Tavenner
Tier: Pacific Fly Group

Hook:	#18-22 Daiichi 1270
Thread:	Tan 8/0 Uni
Body:	Tying thread
Rib 1:	Clear Micro Tubing
Rib 2:	Red tying thread
Thorax:	Black Super Fine

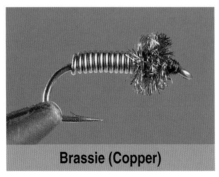

Brassie (Copper)

Originator: Unknown
Tier: Pacific Fly Group

Hook:	#14-22 Daiichi 1560
Thread:	Black 6/0 Uni
Body:	Copper wire
Thorax:	Peacock herl

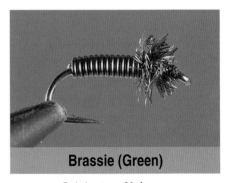

Brassie (Green)

Originator: Unknown
Tier: Pacific Fly Group

Hook:	#14-22 Daiichi 1560
Thread:	Black 6/0 Uni
Body:	Green Ultra Wire (extra small)
Thorax:	Peacock herl

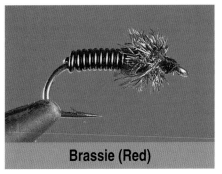

Brassie (Red)

Originator: Unknown
Tier: Pacific Fly Group

Hook: #14-22 Daiichi 1560
Thread: Black 6/0 Uni
Body: Red Ultra Wire (small)
Thorax: Peacock herl

Bead Brassie (Copper)

Originator: Unknown
Tier: Pacific Fly Group

Hook: #14-18 Daiichi 1560
Bead: Gold Cyclops
Thread: Black 6/0 Uni
Body: Copper Ultra Wire (extra small)
Thorax: Peacock herl

Bead Brassie (Green)

Originator: Unknown
Tier: Pacific Fly Group

Hook: #14-18 Daiichi 1560
Bead: Gold Cyclops
Thread: Black 6/0 Uni
Body: Green Ultra Wire (extra small)
Thorax: Peacock herl

Bead Brassie (Red)

Originator: Unknown
Tier: Pacific Fly Group

Hook: #14-18 Daiichi 1560
Bead: Gold Cyclops
Thread: Black 6/0 Uni
Body: Red Ultra Wire (extra small)
Thorax: Peacock herl

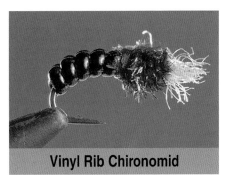

Vinyl Rib Chironomid

Originator: Dennis Komatsu
Tier: Pacific Fly Group

Hook: #14-20 Daiichi 1150
Thread: Black 6/0 Uni
Gills: White Antron
Body: Red UTC Vinyl D Rib
Wing case: Turkey tail
Thorax: Peacock herl

Vinyl Rib Chironomid (Black)

Originator: Unknown
Tier: Pacific Fly Group

Hook: #14-20 Daiichi 1150
Thread: Black 6/0 Uni
Gills: White Antron
Body: Black UTC Vinyl D Rib
Wing case: Turkey tail
Thorax: Peacock herl

X-Mas Tree

Originator: Tom Whitly
Tier: Pacific Fly Group

Hook:	#18-22 Daiichi 1273
Thread:	Gray 8/0 Uni
Body:	Green Ultra Wire (small)
Thorax:	Peacock herl

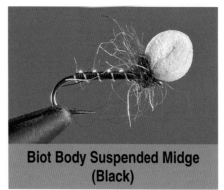

Biot Body Suspended Midge (Black)

Originator: Unknown
Tier: Pacific Fly Group

Hook:	#18-22 Daiichi 1180
Thread:	Black 8/0 Uni
Body:	Tying thread
Rib:	Silver Ultra Wire (extra small)
Post:	Gray 2mm foam
Thorax:	Black rabbit dubbing

Allen's Golden Flashback Chironomid

Originator: Allen Peterson
Tier: Pacific Fly Group

Hook:	#12-16 Daiichi 1260
Thread:	Brown 6/0 Uni
Body:	Pheasant tail
Rib:	Copper Ultra Wire (small)
Wing case:	Pearl Flashabou
Thorax:	Peacock herl
Gills:	White Antron

Brent's Bomber

Originator: Brent Schlenker
Tier: Pacific Fly Group

Hook:	#12-16 Daiichi 1260
Thread:	Black 6/0 Uni
Underbody:	Tying thread
Body:	Clear UTC Vinyl D Rib
Wing case:	Pheasant tail
Thorax:	Peacock herl
Gills:	White ostrich

Black Sally

Originator: Phil Rowley
Tier: Phil Rowley

Hook:	#8-16 Mustad C49S
Bead:	Gold metal
Thread:	Black 8/0 Uni
Butt/Rib:	Red Holographic Tinsel
Body:	Black Flashabou
Thorax:	Peacock herl
Gills:	Stillwater Solutions Midge Gill

Green and Copper

Originator: Phil Rowley
Tier: Phil Rowley

Hook:	#8-16 Mustad C49S
Bead:	Copper metal
Thread:	Olive 8/0 Uni
Butt/Rib:	Copper Lagartun wire (fine)
Body:	Green Holographic Tinsel
Thorax:	Peacock herl
Gills:	Stillwater Solutions Midge Gill

Red Back Pheasant

Originator: Phil Rowley
Tier: Phil Rowley

Hook:	#8-16 Mustad C49S
Bead:	Gold metal
Thread:	Brown 8/0 Uni
Rib:	Gold Lagartun wire (fine)
Body:	Claret pheasant tail
Thorax:	Peacock herl
Gills:	Stillwater Solutions Midge Gill

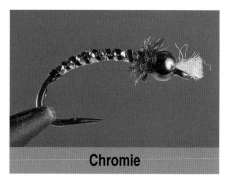

Chromie

Originator: Phil Rowley
Tier: Phil Rowley

Hook:	#8-16 Mustad C49S
Bead:	Black metal
Thread:	Black 8/0 Uni
Butt/Rib:	Red Holographic Tinsel
Body:	Silver Flashabou
Thorax:	Peacock herl
Gills:	Stillwater Solutions Midge Gill

Clearwater Pupa

Originator: Phil Rowley
Tier: Phil Rowley

Hook:	#8-16 Mustad C49S
Thread:	Olive 8/0 Uni
Butt/Rib:	Silver Lagartun wire (fine)
Body:	Black Stillwater Solutions Midge Braid
Back:	Uni Pearlescent Mylar
Wing buds:	Peacock/orange Uni Mylar
Thorax:	Tying thread
Gills:	Stillwater Solutions Midge Gill

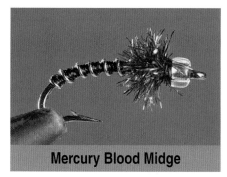

Mercury Blood Midge

Originator: Pat Dorsey
Tier: Pat Dorsey

Hook:	#18-22 Tiemco 200R
Bead:	Mercury glass
Thread:	Red 8/0 Uni
Abdomen:	Tying thread
Rib:	Gold Lagartun wire (fine)
Thorax:	Peacock herl

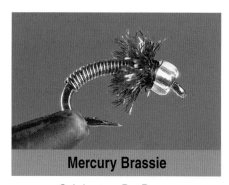

Mercury Brassie

Originator: Pat Dorsey
Tier: Pat Dorsey

Hook:	#18-24 Tiemco 2487
Bead:	Mercury glass
Thread:	Black 8/0 Uni
Body:	Copper Lagartun wire (fine)
Thorax:	Peacock herl

Note: Other hook(s): Dai-Riki 135.

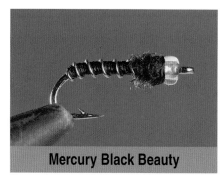

Mercury Black Beauty

Originator: Pat Dorsey
Tier: Phil Rowley

Hook:	#18-24 Tiemco 101
Bead:	Mercury glass
Thread:	Black 8/0 Uni
Body:	Copper Lagartun wire (fine)
Thorax:	Black Fine and Dry

Note: Other hook(s): Dai-Riki 301.

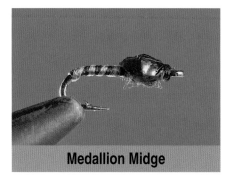

Medallion Midge

Originator: Pat Dorsey
Tier: Pat Dorsey

Hook: #18-22 Tiemco 101
Thread: Dark brown 8/0 Uni
Abdomen: Tying thread
Rib: White 6/0 Uni
Thorax: Brown Super Fine
Wing buds: Medium dun Medallion Sheeting

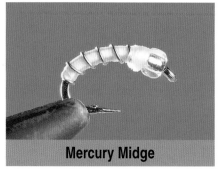

Mercury Midge

Originator: Pat Dorsey
Tier: Pat Dorsey

Hook: #18-24 Tiemco 2487
Bead: Mercury glass
Thread: White 8/0 Uni
Abdomen: Tying thread
Rib: Copper Lagartun wire (fine)
Thorax: Tying thread

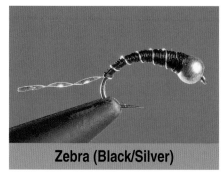

Zebra (Black/Silver)

Originator: Unknown
Tier: Pacific Fly Group

Hook: #16-22 Daiichi 1130
Tail: Pearl Krystal Flash
Bead: Silver Cyclops
Thread: Black 6/0 Uni
Body: Tying thread
Rib: Silver Ultra Wire (small)

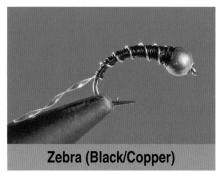

Zebra (Black/Copper)

Originator: Unknown
Tier: Pacific Fly Group

Hook: #16-22 Daiichi 1130
Bead: Copper Cyclops
Thread: Black 6/0 Uni
Tail: Pearl Krystal Flash
Body: Tying thread
Rib: Copper Ultra Wire (small)

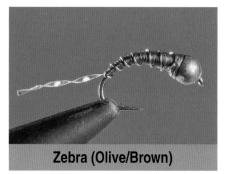

Zebra (Olive/Brown)

Originator: Unknown
Tier: Pacific Fly Group

Hook: #16-22 Daiichi 1130
Bead: Copper Cyclops
Thread: Olive brown 6/0 Uni
Tail: Pearl Krystal Flash
Body: Tying thread
Rib: Copper Ultra Wire (small)

Beadhead Chironomid (Black)

Originator: Unknown
Tier: Pacific Fly Group

Hook: #10-16 Daiichi 1130
Bead: Gold Cyclops
Thread: Black 6/0 Uni
Tail: Black turkey marabou
Body: Tying thread
Rib: Silver Ultra Wire (small)
Thorax: Black Super Fine

Beadhead Chironomid (Red)

Originator: Unknown
Tier: Pacific Fly Group

Hook:	#10-16 Daiichi 1130
Bead:	Gold Cyclops
Thread:	Red 6/0 Uni
Tail:	Red turkey marabou
Body:	Tying thread
Rib:	Silver Ultra Wire (small)
Thorax:	Red Super Fine

Red Brown Chironomid

Originator: Brian Chan
Tier: Brian Chan

Hook:	#10-14 Mustad C49S
Thread:	Maroon 8/0 Uni
Body:	Dark red brown Stretch Flex
Rib:	Red Ultra Wire (small)
Gills:	Stillwater Solutions Midge Gill
Back:	Cock pheasant tail
Thorax:	Peacock herl

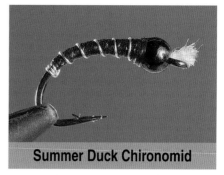

Summer Duck Chironomid

Originator: Brian Chan
Tier: Brian Chan

Hook:	#10-14 Mustad C59S
Bead:	Black metal
Thread:	Light brown 8/0 Uni
Body:	Summer duck Midge Flex
Overbody:	Red Stretch Floss
Rib:	Silver Ultra Wire (small)
Gills:	Stillwater Solutions Midge Gill

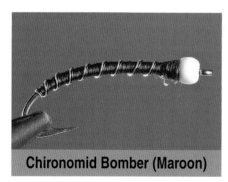

Chironomid Bomber (Maroon)

Originator: Brian Chan
Tier: Brian Chan

Hook:	#10-12 Mustad C53S or Tiemco 2302
Bead:	White metal
Thread:	Dark brown 8/0 Uni
Body:	Maroon Stretch Flex
Rib:	Red and silver Ultra Wire (small)

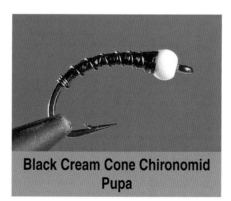

Black Cream Cone Chironomid Pupa

Originator: Brian Chan
Tier: Brian Chan

Hook:	#16-18 Mustad C49S
Bead:	White metal
Thread:	Black 8/0 Uni
Body:	Black Stretch Flex
Rib:	Red Ultra Wire (small)

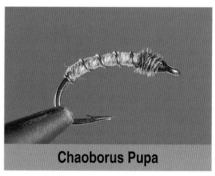

Chaoborus Pupa

Originator: Brian Chan
Tier: Brian Chan

Hook:	#14-16 Mustad C49S
Thread:	Bright green 8/0 Uni
Body:	Lime green Lagartun Mini Flat Braid
Rib:	Copper Ultra Wire (small)
Thorax:	Pheasant tail

Pheasant Tail Chironomid Pupa

Originator: Brian Chan
Tier: Brian Chan

Hook:	#12-16 Mustad C53S or Tiemco 2302
Thread:	Dark brown 8/0 Uni
Body:	Ringneck pheasant tail
Rib:	Red Ultra Wire (small)
Back:	Pheasant tail
Thorax:	Peacock herl
Gills:	Stillwater Solutions Midge Gill

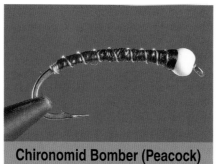

Chironomid Bomber (Peacock)

Originator: Brian Chan
Tier: Brian Chan

Hook:	#10-12 Mustad C53S or Tiemco 2302
Bead:	White metal
Thread:	Black 8/0 Uni
Body:	Green/bronze Lagartun Mini Flat Braid
Rib:	Gold Ultra Wire (medium)

Rojo Midge (Light Olive)

Originator: Greg Garcia
Tier: Greg Garcia

Hook:	#16-22 Tiemco 200R
Thread:	Light olive 8/0 Uni
Bead:	Red glass
Body:	Tying thread
Rib:	Chartreuse Lagartun wire (fine)
Collar:	Peacock herl
Gills:	Oral-B Ultra Floss

Rojo Midge (Purple)

Originator: Greg Garcia
Tier: Greg Garcia

Hook:	#16-22 Tiemco 200R
Thread:	Purple 8/0 Uni
Bead:	Red glass
Body:	Tying thread
Rib:	Blue Lagartun wire (fine)
Collar:	Peacock herl
Gills:	Oral-B Ultra Floss

Rojo Midge (Red)

Originator: Greg Garcia
Tier: Greg Garcia

Hook:	#16-22 Tiemco 200R
Thread:	Red 8/0 Uni
Bead:	Red glass
Body:	Tying thread
Rib:	Red Lagartun wire (fine)
Collar:	Peacock herl
Gills:	Oral-B Ultra Floss

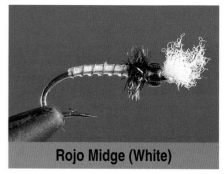

Rojo Midge (White)

Originator: Greg Garcia
Tier: Greg Garcia

Hook:	#16-22 Tiemco 200R
Thread:	White 8/0 Uni
Bead:	Red glass
Body:	Tying thread
Rib:	Gold Lagartun wire (fine)
Collar:	Peacock herl
Gills:	Oral-B Ultra Floss

Tungsten Rojo Midge (Black)

Originator: Greg Garcia
Tier: Greg Garcia

Hook:	#16-22 Tiemco 200R
Thread:	Black 8/0 Uni
Bead 1:	Red glass
Bead 2:	Black tungsten, reversed
Body:	Tying thread
Rib:	Copper Lagartun wire (fine)
Collar:	Peacock herl
Gills:	Oral-B Ultra Floss

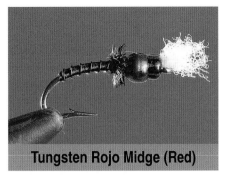

Tungsten Rojo Midge (Red)

Originator: Greg Garcia
Tier: Greg Garcia

Hook:	#16-22 Tiemco 200R
Thread:	Red 8/0 Uni
Bead 1:	Red glass
Bead 2:	Black tungsten, reversed
Body:	Tying thread
Rib:	Red Lagartun wire (fine)
Collar:	Peacock herl
Gills:	Oral-B Ultra Floss

Tungsten Rojo Midge (White)

Originator: Greg Garcia
Tier: Greg Garcia

Hook:	#16-22 Tiemco 200R
Thread:	White 8/0 Uni
Bead 1:	Red glass
Bead 2:	Black tungsten, reversed
Body:	Tying thread
Rib:	Gold Lagartun wire (fine)
Collar:	Peacock herl
Gills:	Oral-B Ultra Floss

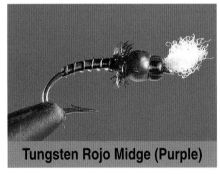

Tungsten Rojo Midge (Purple)

Originator: Greg Garcia
Tier: Greg Garcia

Hook:	#16-22 Tiemco 200R
Thread:	Purple 8/0 Uni
Bead 1:	Red glass
Bead 2:	Black tungsten, reversed
Body:	Tying thread
Rib:	Blue Lagartun wire (fine)
Collar:	Peacock herl
Gills:	Oral-B Ultra Floss

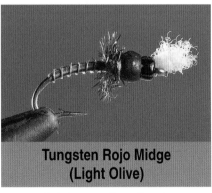

Tungsten Rojo Midge (Light Olive)

Originator: Greg Garcia
Tier: Greg Garcia

Hook:	#16-22 Tiemco 200R
Thread:	Light olive 8/0 Uni
Bead 1:	Red glass
Bead 2:	Black tungsten, reversed
Body:	Tying thread
Rib:	Gold Lagartun wire (fine)
Collar:	Peacock herl
Gills:	Oral-B Ultra Floss

NPA Chironomid (White)

Originator: North Park Anglers
Tier: North Park Anglers

Hook:	#12-16 Tiemco 5212
Thread:	White 6/0 Uni
Body:	White Antron
Rib:	Silver Lagartun wire (fine)
Thorax:	Peacock herl
Gills:	White Antron

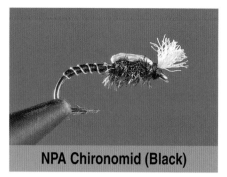

NPA Chironomid (Black)

Originator: North Park Anglers
Tier: North Park Anglers

Hook:	#12-16 Tiemco 5212
Thread:	Black 6/0 Uni
Body:	Tying thread
Rib:	Silver Lagartun wire (fine)
Thorax:	Peacock herl
Gills:	White Antron

NPA Chironomid (Olive)

Originator: North Park Anglers
Tier: North Park Anglers

Hook:	#12-16 Tiemco 5212
Thread:	Olive 6/0 Uni
Body:	Tying thread
Rib:	Silver Lagartun wire (fine)
Thorax:	Peacock herl
Gills:	White Antron

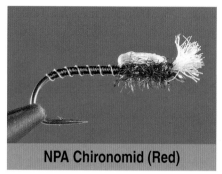

NPA Chironomid (Red)

Originator: North Park Anglers
Tier: North Park Anglers

Hook:	#12-16 Tiemco 5212
Thread:	Red 6/0 Uni
Body:	Tying thread
Rib:	Silver Lagartun wire (fine)
Thorax:	Peacock herl
Gills:	White Antron

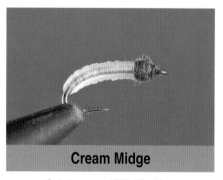

Cream Midge

Originator: ATF Fly Shop
Tier: Tim Mack

Hook:	#20-24 Tiemco 200R
Thread:	Brown 8/0 Uni
Body:	White Flex-Floss
Head:	Brown Super Fine

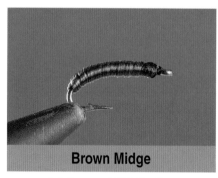

Brown Midge

Originator: ATF Fly Shop
Tier: Tim Mack

Hook:	#20-24 Daiichi 1273
Thread:	Black 8/0 Uni
Body:	Brown Flex-Floss
Head:	Tying thread

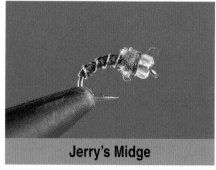

Jerry's Midge

Originator: Jerry Saiz
Tier: Tim Mack

Hook:	#22 Tiemco 2487
Bead:	Clear glass
Thread:	Iron gray 8/0 Uni
Body:	Tying thread
Rib:	Silver Lagartun wire (fine)
Thorax:	Gray muskrat dubbing

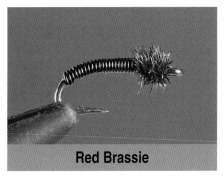

Red Brassie

Originator: Unknown
Tier: Duranglers Fly Shop

Hook:	#18-22 Tiemco 200R
Thread:	Black 8/0 Uni
Body:	Red Ultra Wire (small)
Thorax:	Peacock herl
Head:	Tying thread

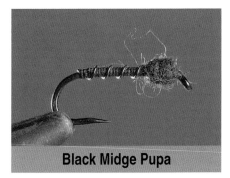

Black Midge Pupa

Originator: Unknown
Tier: Duranglers Fly Shop

Hook:	#18-24 Tiemco 100BL
Thread:	Black 8/0 Uni
Body:	Tying thread
Rib:	Copper Lagartun wire (fine)
Thorax:	Black Super Fine

Gray Midge Pupa

Originator: Unknown
Tier: Duranglers Fly Shop

Hook:	#18-22 Tiemco 2487
Thread:	Light gray 8/0 Uni
Body:	Clear Micro Tubing
Thorax:	Dark gray dubbing

Gray San Juan Midge Pupa

Originator: Unknown
Tier: Duranglers Fly Shop

Hook:	#18-24 Tiemco 501
Thread:	Black 14/0 Gordon Griffiths
Body:	Olive Tier's Lace
Thorax:	Dark gray Super Fine

Tung Zebra Brassie (Brown)

Originator: Unknown
Tier: Montana Fly Company

Hook:	#14-22 MFC 7045
Bead:	Gold tungsten
Thread:	Black 8/0 Uni
Body:	Brown and white Ultra Wire (extra small)
Thorax:	Peacock

Tung Zebra Brassie (Red)

Originator: Unknown
Tier: Montana Fly Company

Hook:	#14-22 MFC 7045
Bead:	Gold tungsten
Thread:	Black 8/0 Uni
Body:	Red and white Ultra Wire (extra small)
Thorax:	Peacock

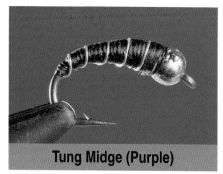

Tung Midge (Purple)

Originator: Unknown
Tier: Montana Fly Company

Hook:	#14-22 MFC 7045
Bead:	Gold tungsten
Thread:	Purple 8/0 Uni
Body:	Tying thread
Rib:	Silver Ultra Wire
	(extra small)

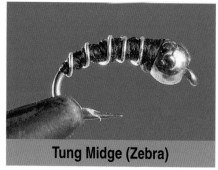

Tung Midge (Zebra)

Originator: Unknown
Tier: Montana Fly Company

Hook:	#14-22 MFC 7045
Bead:	Gold tungsten
Thread:	Black 8/0 Uni
Body:	Tying thread
Rib:	Silver Ultra Wire
	(extra small)

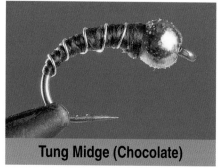

Tung Midge (Chocolate)

Originator: Unknown
Tier: Montana Fly Company

Hook:	#14-22 MFC 7045
Bead:	Gold tungsten
Thread:	Dark brown 8/0 Uni
Body:	Tying thread
Rib:	Silver Ultra Wire
	(extra small)

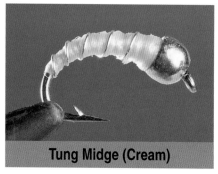

Tung Midge (Cream)

Originator: Unknown
Tier: Montana Fly Company

Hook:	#14-22 MFC 7045
Bead:	Gold tungsten
Thread:	White 8/0 Uni
Body:	Tying thread
Rib:	Silver Ultra Wire
	(extra small)

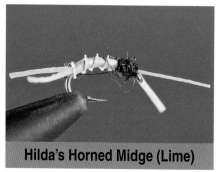

Hilda's Horned Midge (Lime)

Originator: Hilda Herrera
Tier: Montana Fly Company

Hook:	#18-22 MFC 7045
Thread:	Black 8/0 Uni
Tail/gills:	Chartreuse Tentacles
Body:	Lime turkey biot
Head:	Black Wing N' Flash

Hilda's Horned Midge (Red)

Originator: Hilda Herrera
Tier: Montana Fly Company

Hook:	#18-22 MFC 7045
Thread:	Black 8/0 Uni
Tail/gills:	Red Tentacles
Body:	Red turkey biot
Head:	Black Wing N' Flash

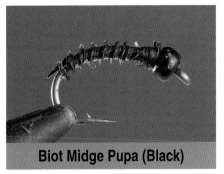

Biot Midge Pupa (Black)

Originator: Unknown
Tier: Montana Fly Company

Hook:	#14-22 MFC 7045
Bead:	Black glass
Thread:	Black 8/0 Uni
Body:	Black turkey biot
Rib:	Pearl Flashabou Accent

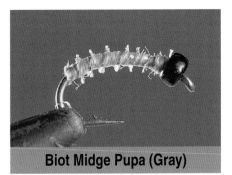

Biot Midge Pupa (Gray)

Originator: Unknown
Tier: Montana Fly Company

Hook:	#18-22 MFC 7045
Bead:	Black glass
Thread:	Gray 8/0 Uni
Body:	Gray turkey biot
Rib:	Pearl Flashabou Accent

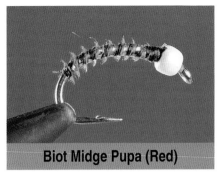

Biot Midge Pupa (Red)

Originator: Unknown
Tier: Montana Fly Company

Hook:	#18-22 MFC 7045
Bead:	White glass
Thread:	Red 8/0 Uni
Body:	Red turkey biot
Rib:	Pearl Flashabou Accent

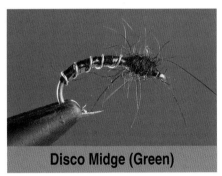

Disco Midge (Green)

Originator: Unknown
Tier: Montana Fly Company

Hook:	#18-22 MFC 7045
Thread:	Black 8/0 Uni
Body:	Kelly green High Voltage
Rib:	Silver Ultra Wire
Head:	Black Wabbit dubbing

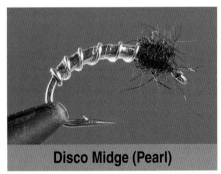

Disco Midge (Pearl)

Originator: Unknown
Tier: Montana Fly Company

Hook:	#18-22 MFC 7045
Thread:	Black 8/0 Uni
Body:	Pearl Mylar tinsel (flat)
Rib:	Silver Ultra Wire
Head:	Black Wabbit dubbing

Palomino Midge (Black)

Originator: Unknown
Tier: Montana Fly Company

Hook:	#18-22 MFC 7045
Thread:	Black 8/0 Uni
Body:	Black Ultra Chenille
Wing case:	White Gator Hair
Thorax:	Black Wabbit dubbing

Palomino Midge (Olive)

Originator: Unknown
Tier: Montana Fly Company

Hook: #18-22 MFC 7045
Thread: Black 8/0 Uni
Body: Olive Ultra Chenille
Wing case: White Gator Hair
Thorax: Light olive Wabbit dubbing

Palomino Midge (Tan)

Originator: Unknown
Tier: Montana Fly Company

Hook: #18-22 MFC 7045
Thread: Tan 8/0 Uni
Body: Tan Ultra Chenille
Wing case: White Gator Hair
Thorax: Hare's ear Wabbit dubbing

Kelly's Ice Cream Cone (Tan)

Originator: Kelly Davidson
Tier: Montana Fly Company

Hook: #10-14 MFC 7026
Bead: White metal
Thread: Black 6/0 Uni
Underbody: Gold Mylar tinsel (flat)
Body: Tan Wonderwrap
Rib: Copper Ultra Wire

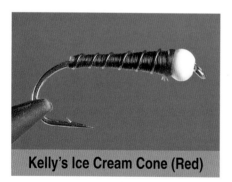

Kelly's Ice Cream Cone (Red)

Originator: Kelly Davidson
Tier: Montana Fly Company

Hook: #10-14 MFC 7026
Bead: White metal
Thread: Red 6/0 Uni
Underbody: Gold Mylar tinsel (flat)
Body: Red Wonderwrap
Rib: Copper Ultra Wire

Kelly's Ice Cream Cone (Black)

Originator: Kelly Davidson
Tier: Montana Fly Company

Hook: #10-14 MFC 7026
Bead: White metal
Thread: Black 6/0 Uni
Underbody: Pearl Mylar tinsel (flat)
Body: Black Wonderwrap
Rib: Copper Ultra Wire

Morrison's Tartan (Olive)

Originator: Peter Morrison
Tier: Montana Fly Company

Hook: #10-14 MFC 7045
Bead: Black metal
Thread: Black 8/0 Uni
Body: Golden olive Gator Hair
Rib 1: Black UTC Vinyl D Rib
Rib 2: Red Ultra Wire
Wing case: Silver Holographic High Voltage
Thorax: Natural peacock herl
Gills: White marabou blood quill

Morrison's Tartan (Silver)

Originator: Peter Morrison
Tier: Montana Fly Company

Hook:	#10-14 MFC 7045
Bead:	Black glass
Thread:	Black 8/0 Uni
Body:	Silver Mylar tinsel (flat)
Rib 1:	Black UTC Vinyl D Rib
Rib 2:	Red Ultra Wire
Wing case:	Red High Voltage
Thorax:	Natural peacock herl
Gills:	White marabou blood quill

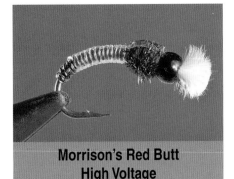

Morrison's Red Butt High Voltage

Originator: Peter Morrison
Tier: Montana Fly Company

Hook:	#10-14 MFC 7045
Bead:	Black glass
Thread:	Black 8/0 Uni
Tag:	Red High Voltage
Body:	Opal Mirage
Rib:	Clear UTC Vinyl D Rib
Wing case:	Opal Mirage
Thorax:	Natural peacock herl
Gills:	White marabou blood quill

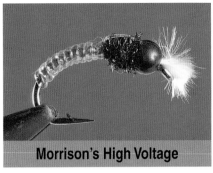

Morrison's High Voltage

Originator: Peter Morrison
Tier: Montana Fly Company

Hook:	#10-14 MFC 7045
Bead:	Black glass
Thread:	Black 8/0 Uni
Body:	Opal Mirage
Rib:	Clear UTC Vinyl D Rib
Wing case:	Opal Mirage
Thorax:	Natural peacock herl
Gills:	White marabou blood quill

Gebhart's Gen-X Brassie (Copper)

Originator: Karl Gebhart
Tier: Montana Fly Company

Hook:	#10-14 MFC 7045
Bead:	Gold metal
Thread:	Black 8/0 Uni
Body:	Copper Ultra Wire
Wing case:	Opal Mirage
Thorax:	Mixture of black Tentacles, brown and golden amber Wabbit Dubbing, and copper Wing N' Flash

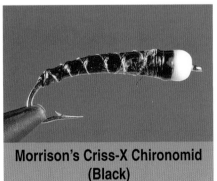

Morrison's Criss-X Chironomid (Black)

Originator: Peter Morrison
Tier: Montana Fly Company

Hook:	#10-12 MFC 7002
Bead:	White metal
Thread:	Black 6/0 Uni
Body:	Black 6/0 Uni
Rib:	Red and silver Ultra Wire

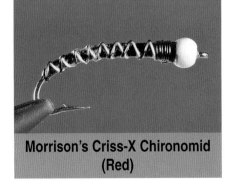

Morrison's Criss-X Chironomid (Red)

Originator: Peter Morrison
Tier: Montana Fly Company

Hook:	#10-12 MFC 7002
Bead:	White metal
Thread:	Black 6/0 Uni
Body:	Red tying thread
Rib:	Red and white Ultra Wire

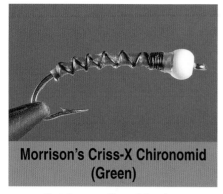

Morrison's Criss-X Chironomid (Green)

Originator: Peter Morrison
Tier: Montana Fly Company

Hook:	#10-12 MFC 7002
Bead:	White metal
Thread:	Light olive 6/0 Uni
Body:	Tying thread
Rib:	Red and green Ultra Wire

Silverman's Mongo Lake (Tan)

Originator: Joel Silverman
Tier: Montana Fly Company

Hook:	#10-14 MFC 7002
Thread:	Black 6/0 Uni
Tail:	Black Wing N' Flash
Body:	Black and tan tying thread
Thorax:	Peacock Wing N' Flash
Gills:	Pearl Wing N' Flash

Silverman's Mongo Lake (Olive)

Originator: Joel Silverman
Tier: Montana Fly Company

Hook:	#10-14 MFC 7002
Thread:	Black 6/0 Uni
Tail:	Black Wing N' Flash
Body:	Olive and black tying thread
Thorax:	Peacock Wing N' Flash
Gills:	Pearl Wing N' Flash

Sparkle Green Soft Hackle

Originator: Yancey Cox
Tier: Yancey Cox

Hook:	#19-21 Tiemco 103BL
Thread:	Olive 14/0 Gordon Griffiths
Body:	Tying thread
Overbody:	Pearl Krystal Flash
Rib:	Tying thread, twisted
Hackle:	Starling

Red Sparkle Bead Soft Hackle

Originator: Yancey Cox
Tier: Yancey Cox

Hook:	#19-21 Tiemco 103BL
Bead:	Red glass
Thread:	Red 14/0 Gordon Griffiths
Body:	Tying thread
Rib:	Twisted tying thread
Thorax:	Tying thread and pearl Flashabou
Hackle:	Starling

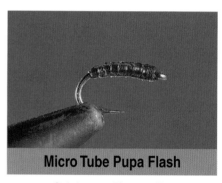

Micro Tube Pupa Flash

Originator: Yancey Cox
Tier: Yancey Cox

Hook:	#18-24 Tiemco 2488
Thread:	Brown 14/0 Gordon Griffiths
Underbody:	Tying thread
Flash:	Pearl Krystal Flash
Body:	Brown Micro Tubing

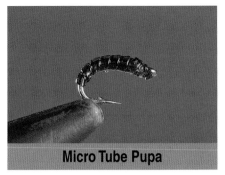

Micro Tube Pupa

Originator: Yancey Cox
Tier: Yancey Cox

Hook: #18-24 Tiemco 2488
Thread: Brown 14/0 Gordon Griffiths
Underbody: Tying thread
Body: Root beer Micro Tubing

Micro Tube Wet

Originator: Yancey Cox
Tier: Yancey Cox

Hook: #18-24 Tiemco 2488
Thread: Olive 14/0 Gordon Griffiths
Underbody: Tying thread
Body: Olive Micro Tubing
Hackle: Starling

Red Hairy Midge

Originator: Yancey Cox
Tier: Yancey Cox

Hook: #18-24 Tiemco 103BL
Thread: Red 14/0 Gordon Griffiths
Underbody: Tying thread
Rib: Twisted tying thread
Collar: Hare's ear dubbing

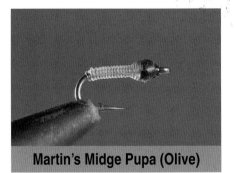

Martin's Midge Pupa (Olive)

Originator: Jason Goodale
Tier: Jason Goodale

Hook: #16-24 Tiemco 101
Thread: Olive 10/0 Bennechi
Underbody: Tying thread
Body: .005 clear mono
Head: Black 10/0 covered with Loon UV Knot Sense

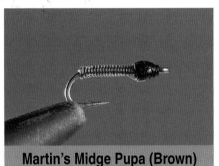

Martin's Midge Pupa (Brown)

Originator: Jason Goodale
Tier: Jason Goodale

Hook: #16-24 Tiemco 101
Thread: Brown 10/0 Bennechi
Underbody: Tying thread
Body: .005 clear mono
Head: Black 10/0 covered with Loon UV Knot Sense

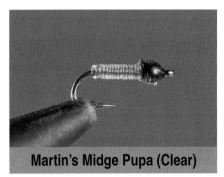

Martin's Midge Pupa (Clear)

Originator: Jason Goodale
Tier: Jason Goodale

Hook: #16-24 Tiemco 101
Thread: White 10/0 Bennechi
Underbody: Tying thread
Body: .005 clear mono
Head: Black 10/0 covered with Loon UV Knot Sense

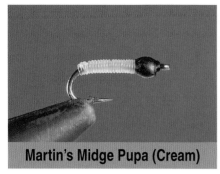

Martin's Midge Pupa (Cream)

Originator: Jason Goodale
Tier: Jason Goodale

Hook: #16-24 Tiemco 101
Thread: Cream 10/0 Bennechi
Underbody: Tying thread
Body: .005 clear mono
Head: Black 10/0 covered with
Loon UV Knot Sense

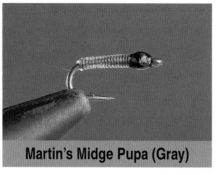

Martin's Midge Pupa (Gray)

Originator: Jason Goodale
Tier: Jason Goodale

Hook: #16-24 Tiemco 101
Thread: Black 10/0 Bennechi
Underbody: Tying thread
Body: .005 clear mono
Head: Black 10/0 covered with
Loon UV Knot Sense

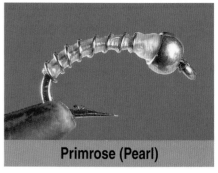

Primrose (Pearl)

Originator: Mike Kruise
Tier: Laughing Grizzly Fly Shop

Hook: #18-22 Dai-Riki 135
Bead: Copper metal
Thread: Yellow 70-denier UTC
Body: Yellow Glitter Thread
Rib: Copper Ultra Wire
(extra small)
Collar: Tying thread

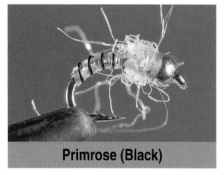

Primrose (Black)

Originator: Mike Kruise
Tier: Laughing Grizzly Fly Shop

Hook: #18-22 Dai-Riki 135
Bead: Copper metal
Thread: Yellow 70-denier UTC
Body: Yellow Glitter Thread
Rib: Black Ultra Wire
(extra small)
Collar: UV light yellow Ice Dub

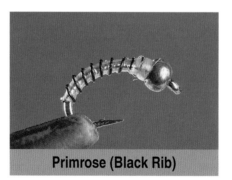

Primrose (Black Rib)

Originator: Mike Kruise
Tier: Laughing Grizzly Fly Shop

Hook: #18-22 Dai-Riki 135
Bead: Copper metal
Thread: Yellow 70-denier UTC
Body: Yellow Glitter Thread
Rib: Black Ultra Wire
(extra small)
Collar: Tying thread

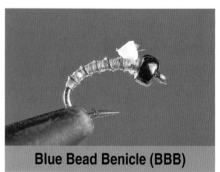

Blue Bead Benicle (BBB)

Originator: Jim Auman
Tier: Jim Auman

Hook: #18-24 Tiemco 2487
Bead: Blue gunmetal glass
Thread: Dun 8/0 Uni
Body: Pearl Krystal Flash
Rib: Copper Lagartun wire
(extra fine)
Wing: White foam

Green Giant

Originator: Jim Auman
Tier: Jim Auman

Hook:	#18-24 Tiemco 100
Thread:	Olive 10/0 Gudebrod
Tail:	Olive hackle
Body:	Tying thread
Rib:	Copper Lagartun wire (extra fine)
Thorax:	Peacock herl
Wing case:	Medallion Sheeting

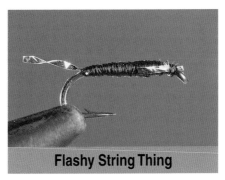

Flashy String Thing

Originator: Jim Auman
Tier: Jim Auman

Hook:	#20-26 Tiemco 100
Thread:	Black 10/0 Bennechi
Shuck:	Pearl Krystal Flash
Body:	Tying thread
Wing buds:	Pearl Krystal Flash
Head:	Black 10/0 Bennechi

Pink Bead Wing

Originator: Ron Donahue
Tier: Ron Donahue

Hook:	#22-26 Tiemco 2488
Bead:	Black glass
Thread:	White 14/0 Gordon Griffiths
Body:	Pink Krystal Flash

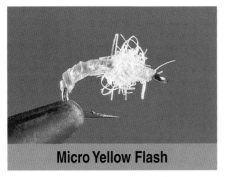

Micro Yellow Flash

Originator: Ron Donahue
Tier: Ron Donahue

Hook:	#22-26 Tiemco 2488
Thread:	Yellow 14/0 Gordon Griffiths
Body:	Yellow Krystal Flash
Thorax:	Yellow Ice Dub
Head:	Tying thread

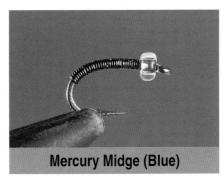

Mercury Midge (Blue)

Originator: Ron Donahue
Tier: Ron Donahue

Hook:	#22-24 Tiemco 2488
Bead:	Mercury glass
Body:	Gunmetal blue Ultra Wire

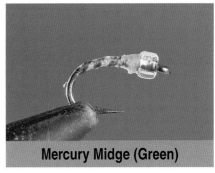

Mercury Midge (Green)

Originator: Ron Donahue
Tier: Ron Donahue

Hook:	#22-26 Tiemco 2488
Bead:	Mercury glass
Thread:	Fl. green 70-denier UTC
Body:	Tying thread
Rib:	Black thread

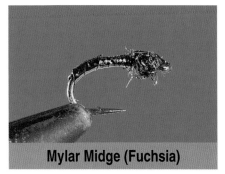

Mylar Midge (Fuchsia)

Originator: Ron Donahue
Tier: Ron Donahue

Hook: #24-26 Tiemco 2488
Thread: White 17/0 Uni
Body: Fuchsia Mylar
Thorax: Red Ice Dub

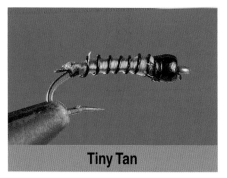

Tiny Tan

Originator: Ron Donahue
Tier: Ron Donahue

Hook: #20-22 Tiemco 200R
Bead: Black glass
Thread: Dark tan 70-denier UTC
Body: Tying thread
Rib: Black Lagartun wire
             (extra fine)

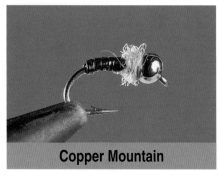

Copper Mountain

Originator: Stan Benton
Tier: Stan Benton

Hook: #18-22 Tiemco 2487
Bead: Copper metal
Thread: Rust brown 8/0 Uni
Body: Pheasant tail Micro Tubing
Collar: Ginger Life Cycle caddis
             dubbing

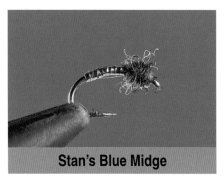

Stan's Blue Midge

Originator: Stan Benton
Tier: Stan Benton

Hook: #20-22 Tiemco 2487
Thread: Gray 8/0 Uni
Body: Blue Krystal Flash
Collar: Stalcup's Trico Dry Fly
             Dub

Red Bird

Originator: Stan Benton
Tier: Stan Benton

Hook: #18-20 Tiemco 2487
Bead: Black metal
Thread: Black 8/0 Uni
Body: Red Micro Tubing
Collar: Peacock Ice Dub

Pearl's Revenge

Originator: David Carpenter
Tier: Rick Takahashi

Hook: #18-22 Tiemco 2488
Thread: Black 8/0 Uni
Body: Scarlet macaw tail fibers
Thorax: Gray muskrat

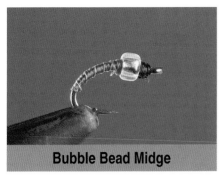

Bubble Bead Midge

Originator: Rob Jiron
Tier: Rob Jiron

Hook: #20-24 Daiichi 1140
Bead: Clear glass
Body: Olive 8/0 Uni
Rib: Silver Lagartun wire (fine)
Head: Black 8/0 Uni

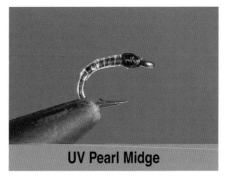

UV Pearl Midge

Originator: Juan Ramirez
Tier: Juan Ramirez

Hook: #20-24 Tiemco 2488 or Dai-Riki 125
Thread: Black 14/0 Gordon Griffiths
Body: Pearl UV Krystal Flash
Thorax: Black thread

Black Cherry Midge

Originator: Juan Ramirez
Tier: Juan Ramirez

Hook: #20-24 Tiemco 2488 or Dai-Riki 270
Thread: Gray 14/0 Gordon Griffiths
Body: Pearl Krystal Flash dyed red
Thorax: Black thread
Note: Coat body with Loon Hard Head.

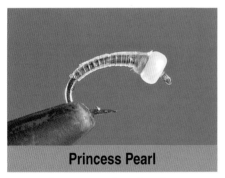

Princess Pearl

Originator: Juan Ramirez
Tier: Juan Ramirez

Hook: #20-24 Tiemco 2457 or Dai-Riki 135
Bead: Pearl glass
Thread: Fire orange 8/0 Gordon Griffiths
Body: Pearl Krystal Flash
Thorax: Tying thread
Note: Coat body with Loon Hard Head.

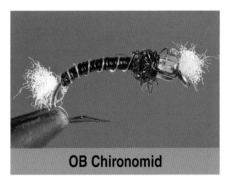

OB Chironomid

Originator: Steve Thrapp
Tier: Steve Thrapp

Hook: #12-14 Mustad 3399A
Bead: Orange glass
Thread: Black 70-denier UTC
Body: Tying thread
Rib: Silver Ultra Wire (extra small)
Gills: White McFly Foam
Thorax: Black Ice Dub

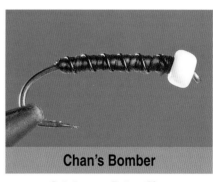

Chan's Bomber

Originator: Brian Chan
Tier: Peter Koga

Hook: #12 Tiemco 2302
Bead: White plastic
Thread: Black 8/0 Uni
Body: Black Flexi Floss
Rib: Red Lagartun wire (fine)

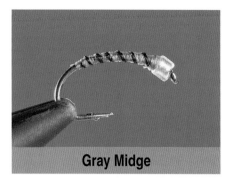

Gray Midge

Originator: Peter Koga
Tier: Peter Koga

Hook:	#14 Tiemco 2457
Bead:	Clear white glass
Thread:	Cream 8/0 Uni
Body:	Tying thread
Rib:	Black 8/0 Uni

Black Midge

Originator: Peter Koga
Tier: Peter Koga

Hook:	#16 Tiemco 2487
Bead:	Black Brite Bead
Thread:	Black 8/0 Uni
Body:	Tying thread
Rib:	White 8/0 Uni
Gills:	White poly yarn

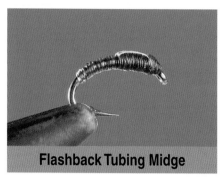

Flashback Tubing Midge

Originator: Jude Duran
Tier: Jude Duran

Hook:	#18-24 Daiichi 1130
Thread:	Iron gray 8/0 Uni
Rib:	Clear Micro Tubing
Thorax:	Tying thread
Body:	Black Flexi Floss
Wing case:	Pearl Flashabou

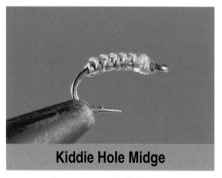

Kiddie Hole Midge

Originator: Jude Duran
Tier: Jude Duran

Hook:	#18-24 Tiemco 2488
Thread:	Brown gray 70-denier UTC
Rib:	Clear UTC Vinyl D Rib
Head:	Tying thread

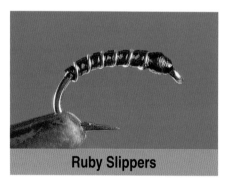

Ruby Slippers

Originator: Jude Duran
Tier: Jude Duran

Hook:	#18-24 Daiichi 1130
Thread:	Red 70-denier UTC
Body:	Red Krystal Flash
Rib 1:	Gold Lagartun wire (fine)
Rib 2:	Red Micro Tubing
Head:	Tying thread coated with Sally Hansen Hard As Nails

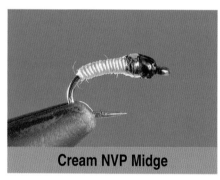

Cream NVP Midge

Originator: Jude Duran
Tier: Jude Duran

Hook:	#18-24 Tiemco 2488
Thread:	Cream A Belding Corticelli silk, spun
Thorax:	Black 12/0 Bennechi
Flash:	Pearl Krystal Flash
Head:	Thread coated with Sally Hansen Hard As Nails

Black Buzzer

Originator: Peter Durisik
Tier: Peter Durisik

Hook: #10-12 Dohiku G 644BL
Thread: Black 70-denier UTC
Abdomen: Black Flexi Floss with black (rear) and red (front) tying thread
Rib: Silver Lagartun wire (fine)
Wing buds: Bronze cheek
Thorax: Tying thread
Gills: White CDC
Note: Coat entire fly except gills with Sally Hansen Hard As Nails.

MF&PD Red Buzzer

Originator: Peter Durisik
Tier: Peter Durisik

Hook: #10-12 Dohiku G 644BL
Thread: Red 70-denier UTC
Abdomen: Red Flexi Floss
Rib: Fine silver wire and black Hends Fine Hair
Thorax: Black 70-denier UTC
Note: Coat entire fly with Sally Hansen Hard As Nails.

Olive Buzzer

Originator: Peter Durisik
Tier: Peter Durisik

Hook: #10-12 Dohiku G 644BL
Thread: Olive 70-denier
Abdomen: Light gray Flexi Floss
Rib: Silver Lagartun wire (fine)
Collar: Fl. orange 70-denier UTC
Thorax: Black 70-denier UTC
Gills: White CDC
Note: Coat entire fly except gills with Sally Hansen Hard As Nails.

Olive Buzzer 1

Originator: Peter Durisik
Tier: Peter Durisik

Hook: #10-12 Dohiku G 644BL
Thread: Yellow olive 70-denier UTC
Abdomen: Black Flexi Floss with yellow (rear) and red (front) tying thread
Rib: Silver Lagartun wire (fine)
Thorax: Tying thread
Gills: White CDC
Note: Coat entire fly except gills with Sally Hansen Hard As Nails.

Frying Pan Midge

Originator: Jude Duran
Tier: Jude Duran

Hook: #16-22 Tiemco 200R
Bead: Mercury glass
Thread: Olive brown 70-denier UTC
Rib: Clear Midge Tubing
Thorax: Small natural ostrich herl

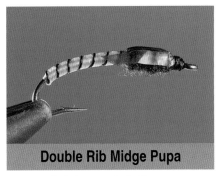

Double Rib Midge Pupa

Originator: Jude Duran
Tier: Jude Duran

Hook: #16-22 Tiemco 200R
Thread: Cream 70-denier UTC
Rib 1: Black Ultra Wire (small)
Rib 2: Clear Midge Tubing
Wing case: Mottled brown Medallion Sheeting
Thorax: Mahogany Super Fine
Wing buds: Medallion Sheeting

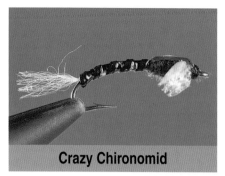

Crazy Chironomid

Originator: Jude Duran
Tier: Jude Duran

Hook: #16-18 Tiemco 200R
Thread: Olive brown 70-denier UTC
Tail: White Darlon
Rib 1: Blue Mylar tinsel
Rib 2: Brown Midge Tubing
Wing case: Green pearl Mylar
Thorax: Mahogany Super Fine
Wing buds: Open cell foam

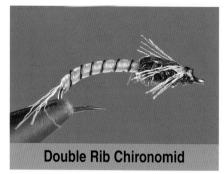

Double Rib Chironomid

Originator: Jude Duran
Tier: Jude Duran

Hook: #10-18 Tiemco 200R
Tail: White Fluoro Fibre
Thread: Cream 70-denier UTC
Rib 1: Black Ultra Wire (small)
Rib 2: Clear Midge Tubing
Wing case: Blue Mylar
Thorax: Black Ice Dub
Wing buds: White Flouro Fibre

Fire Midge

Originator: Mark McMillan
Tier: Mark McMillan

Hook: #18-26 Tiemco 2487
Thread: Fl. orange 70-denier
Rib: Gold Ultra Wire (extra small)
Abdomen: Orange plastic craft garland
Thorax/collar: Peacock herl

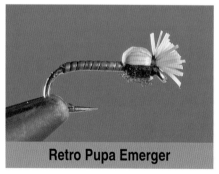

Retro Pupa Emerger

Originator: Mark McMillan
Tier: Mark McMillan

Hook: #18-26 Tiemco 100
Thread: Olive 70-denier UTC
Abdomen: Gray Midge Tubing
Back/gills: Fine deer hair
Thorax: Brown beaver

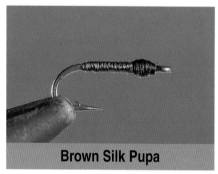

Brown Silk Pupa

Originator: Charles Vestal
Tier: Charles Vestal

Hook: #18-26 Tiemco 101
Thread: Black 8/0 Uni
Body: Brown Pearsall's silk
Head: Tying thread

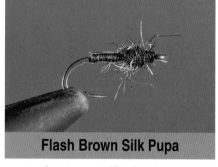

Flash Brown Silk Pupa

Originator: Charles Vestal
Tier: Charles Vestal

Hook: #18-26 Tiemco 101
Thread: Black 8/0 Uni
Body: Brown Pearsall's silk
Flash: Pearl Flashabou
Head: Tying thread

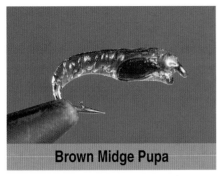

Brown Midge Pupa

Originator: Brian Yamauchi
Tier: Brian Yamauchi

Hook: #18-24 Tiemco 100
Thread: White 17/0 Uni
Body: Latex strip
Rib: Tying thread
Thorax: Tying thread colored with marker
Eyes/Wing buds: Black Microfibetts
Note: Coat entire body with Loon UV Knot Sense.

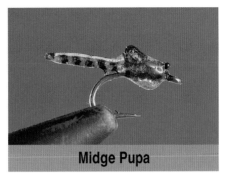

Midge Pupa

Originator: Brian Yamauchi
Tier: Brian Yamauchi

Hook: #18-24 Tiemco 2488
Thread: White 17/0 Uni
Body: UTC Vinyl D Rib
Wing buds: Black Microfibetts
Note: Color the teeth of the forceps with dark brown marker before crimping D Rib. Burn the ends of the Microfibetts to form the eye and bend them forward to create the wing buds. Coat the body with Loon UV Knot Sense.

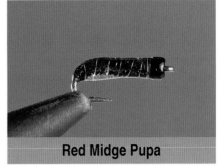

Red Midge Pupa

Originator: Brian Yamauchi
Tier: Brian Yamauchi

Hook: #20-24 Tiemco 101
Bead: Black glass
Thread: White 17/0 Uni
Body: Latex colored with red marker
Rib: Tying thread
Thorax: Tying thread
Note: Cover entire fly with Loon UV Knot Sense.

Olive Brown Chironomid Pupa

Originator: Brian Yamauchi
Tier: Brian Yamauchi

Hook: #10-16 Tiemco 2302
Thread: White 17/0 Uni
Body: Latex strip
Rib: Gold Lagartun wire (extra fine)
Thorax: Tying thread colored with marker
Eyes/Wing buds: Black Microfibetts
Gills: White CDC
Note: Coat entire body with Loon UV Knot Sense.

Cream Midge Pupa

Originator: Brian Yamauchi
Tier: Brian Yamauchi

Hook: #10-16 Tiemco 100
Thread: White 17/0 Uni
Body: Latex strip
Rib: Tying thread
Thorax: Tying thread colored with tan marker
Eyes/Wing buds: Black Microfibetts
Note: Coat entire body with Loon UV Knot Sense.

Olive Tyvek Pupa

Originator: Steve Thrapp
Tier: Steve Thrapp

Hook: #18-24 Tiemco 2487
Thread: Black 8/0 Uni
Body: Strip of Tyvek colored with olive Chartpak marker
Wing: White Antron
Thorax: Tying thread

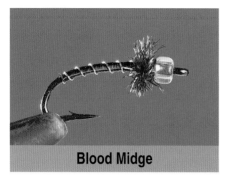

Blood Midge

Originator: Jeremy Berela
Tier: Jeremy Berela

Hook:	#18-22 Daiichi 1273
Bead:	Mercury glass
Thread:	Red 8/0 Uni
Rib:	Silver Lagartun wire (extra fine)
Body:	Tying thread
Thorax:	Peacock herl

BK Midge

Originator: Jeremy Berela
Tier: Jeremy Berela

Hook:	#18-22 Daiichi 1130
Bead:	Copper metal
Thread:	Black 12/0 Bennechi
Shuck:	Pearl Krystal Flash
Rib:	Copper Lagartun wire (extra fine)
Body:	Pearl and black Krystal Flash
Thorax:	Black thread

Beadhead BK Midge

Originator: Jeremy Berela
Tier: Jeremy Berela

Hook:	#18-22 Daiichi 1130
Bead:	Copper metal
Thread:	Tan 8/0 Uni
Rib:	Red Ultra Wire (small)
Body:	Tying thread
Thorax:	Peacock herl
Gills:	White Z-lon

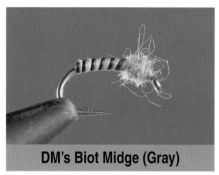

DM's Biot Midge (Gray)

Originator: Dennis Martin
Tier: Dennis Martin

Hook:	#18-24 Tiemco 2487
Thread:	Dun 14/0 Gordon Griffiths
Body:	Natural Canada goose biot
Thorax:	Adams gray Super Fine

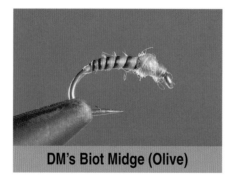

DM's Biot Midge (Olive)

Originator: Dennis Martin
Tier: Dennis Martin

Hook:	#18-24 Tiemco 2487
Thread:	Olive 14/0 Gordon Griffiths
Body:	Canada goose biot dyed olive
Thorax:	Olive Super Fine

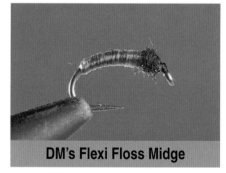

DM's Flexi Floss Midge

Originator: Dennis Martin
Tier: Dennis Martin

Hook:	#18-24 Tiemco 2487
Thread:	Black 14/0 Gordon Griffiths
Body:	Chartreuse Flexi Floss
Thorax:	Black Super Fine

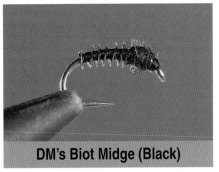

DM's Biot Midge (Black)

Originator: Dennis Martin
Tier: Dennis Martin

Hook: #18-24 Tiemco 2487
Thread: Black 14/0 Gordon Griffiths
Body: Black goose biot
Thorax: Black Super Fine

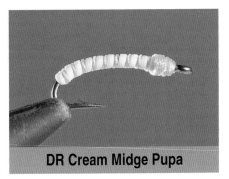

DR Cream Midge Pupa

Originator: Jude Duran
Tier: Jude Duran

Hook: #18-24 Tiemco 200R
Thread: Cream 8/0 Uni
Body: White Micro Tubing
Rib: Tying thread, twisted
Thorax: Tying thread

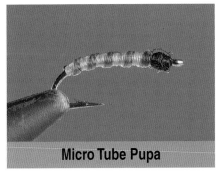

Micro Tube Pupa

Originator: Unknown
Tier: Jerry Saiz

Hook: #18-24 Tiemco 200R
Thread: Light cahill 8/0 Uni
Body: Tying thread
Rib: Pheasant tail Micro Tubing
Head: Black 8/0 Uni

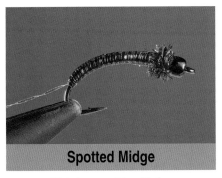

Spotted Midge

Originator: Alex Malvo
Tier: Alex Malvo

Hook: #18 Partridge Klinkhammer 15BN
Bead: Brown metallic Killer Caddis
Thread: Black 6/0 Uni
Tail: Pearl Krystal Flash
Body: Black and pearl Krystal Flash
Rib: Pumpkin seed Liquid Lace
Wing case: Silver Holographic Tinsel
Thorax: Peacock herl
Note: Liquid Lace is injected with baby oil to add volume and shimmer. This technique was developed by Mike Tucker and shown to me by Ed Smith of B.C., Canada.

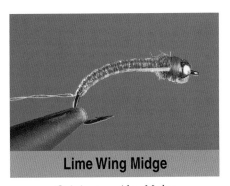

Lime Wing Midge

Originator: Alex Malvo
Tier: Alex Malvo

Hook: #18 Partridge Klinkhammer 15BN
Bead: Copper
Thread: Olive green 140-denier UTC
Body: Tying thread spiraled with Opal Tinsel
Tail: Pearl Krystal Flash
Rib: Clear Liquid Lace
Wing case: Silver Holographic Tinsel
Thorax: Dark olive dubbing
Wing buds: White turkey biots
Note: Liquid Lace is injected with baby oil to add volume and shimmer. This technique was developed by Mike Tucker and shown to me by Ed Smith of B.C., Canada.

Christmas Midge

Originator: Alex Malvo
Tier: Alex Malvo

Hook: #18 Partridge Klinkhammer 15BN
Bead: Gunmetal Killer Caddis
Thread: Black 6/0 Uni
Body: Black Krystal Flash with small red Holographic Tinsel (small)
Tail: Pearl Krystal Flash
Rib: Pumpkin seed Liquid Lace
Wing case: Peacock herl
Thorax: Black dubbing
Wing buds: Rusty Spinner turkey biots
Note: Liquid Lace is injected with baby oil to add volume and shimmer. This technique was developed by Mike Tucker and shown to me by Ed Smith of B.C., Canada.

Pearl Midge Pupa

Originator: Unknown
Tier: Jerry Saiz

Hook: #18-24 Tiemco 2487
Thread: Black 8/0 Uni
Body: Pearl Krystal Flash
Rib: Clear Micro Tubing
Head: Tying thread

Bubble Smut

Originator: Darrel Martin
Tier: Kevin Compton

Hook: #20 Partridge K14ST
Bead: Orangish red glass
Thread: White 10/0 Gudebrod
Tail: Pearl Tiewell Sparkleflash
Body: Silver Ultra Wire (small)
Thorax: Black Super Fine
Gills: White CDC

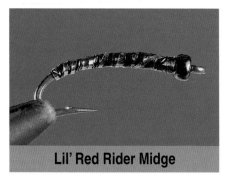

Lil' Red Rider Midge

Originator: Jerry Hubka
Tier: Jerry Hubka

Hook: #16-20 Tiemco 200R
Bead: Peacock glass
Thread: Red 8/0 Uni
Body: Red Tiewell Sparkleflash
Note: Coat entire fly with Griff's Thin Head Cement.

Black Beauty Buzzer

Originator: Unknown
Tier: Bubba Smith

Hook: #18-24 Tiemco 200R
Thread: Black 8/0 Uni
Body: Holographic Tinsel
Thorax: Muskrat dubbing
Gills: White Fluoro Fibre

Bubba's Bubble Head (Black)

Originator: Unknown
Tier: Bubba Smith

Hook: #18-24 Tiemco 2487
Bead: Clear glass with black center
Thread: Black 8/0 Uni
Body: Tying thread
Rib: Red Ultra Wire (extra small)
Thorax: Muskrat dubbing

Bubba's Bubble Head (Olive)

Originator: Unknown
Tier: Bubba Smith

Hook: #18-24 Tiemco 2487
Bead: Clear glass with black center
Thread: Olive 8/0 Uni
Body: Tying thread
Rib: Yellow Ultra Wire (extra small)
Thorax: Muskrat dubbing

Trout Crack II

Originator: Unknown
Tier: Bubba Smith

Hook:	#18-24 Tiemco 2487
Bead:	Amber glass
Thread:	Black 8/0 Uni
Body:	Tying thread
Rib:	Copper Ultra Wire (extra small)
Wings:	Pearl UV Krystal Flash
Thorax:	Tying thread

Red Buzzer

Originator: Unknown
Tier: Bubba Smith

Hook:	#18-24 Tiemco 200R
Thread:	Red 8/0 Uni
Body:	Red Midge Lace
Wing:	White Fluoro Fibre
Thorax:	Peacock herl
Head:	Tying thread

Biot Pupa

Originator: Unknown
Tier: Bubba Smith

Hook:	#18-24 Tiemco 200R
Thread:	Olive 8/0 Uni
Body:	Olive turkey biot
Wing:	Pearl Krystal Flash
Thorax:	Peacock herl

Renke's Black Pupa

Originator: Larry Renke
Tier: Larry Renke

Hook:	#18-24 Tiemco 2488
Thread:	Black 8/0 Uni
Bead:	Gunmetal glass
Body:	Black Micro Tubing
Gills:	White Antron

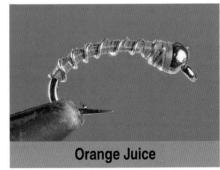

Orange Juice

Originator: Unknown
Tier: Bruce Hopper

Hook:	#20 Tiemco 2487
Bead:	Gold metal
Thread:	Hot orange 70-denier UTC
Rib:	Gold Ultra Wire (extra small)

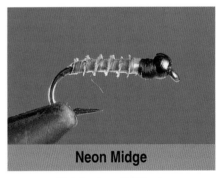

Neon Midge

Originator: Ed Engle
Tier: Ed Engle

Hook:	#18-24 Tiemco 100
Bead:	Black metal
Thread:	Black 8/0 Uni
Body:	Olive goose biot
Rib:	Pearlescent Mylar

Black Soft Hackle Midge

Originator: Carl Pennington
Tier: Carl Pennington

Hook: #18-24 Dai-Riki 125
Thread: Black 8/0 Uni
Body: Tying thread
Rib: Copper Lagartun wire (fine)
Thorax: Black Super Fine
Hackle: Grizzly hen cape

White Soft Hackle Midge

Originator: Carl Pennington
Tier: Carl Pennington

Hook: #18-24 Dai-Riki 125
Thread: White 8/0 Uni
Body: Tying thread
Rib: Copper Lagartun wire (fine)
Thorax: Black Super Fine
Hackle: Grizzly hen cape

Three Pete Black Beauty

Originator: Gary Okazaki
Tier: Gary Okazaki

Hook: #8-16 Tiemco 400T
Thread: Black 8/0 Uni
Head: Tying thread
Body: Tying thread
Rib: Copper Lagartun wire (fine)
Note: Other hook(s): Dai-Riki 1770.

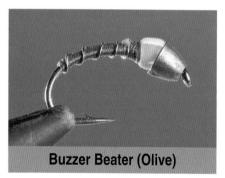

Buzzer Beater (Olive)

Originator: Nick Jones
Tier: Nick Jones

Hook: #10-14 Tiemco 2487
Bead: Copper conehead
Thorax: Clear glass bead with orange center
Thread: Olive 8/0 Uni
Abdomen: Tying thread
Rib: Copper Lagartun wire (small)

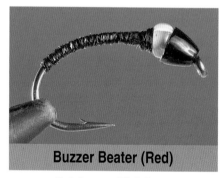

Buzzer Beater (Red)

Originator: Nick Jones
Tier: Nick Jones

Hook: #10-14 Tiemco 2487
Bead: Black conehead
Thorax: Clear glass bead with orange center
Thread: Olive 8/0 Uni
Abdomen: Red Glitter Thread

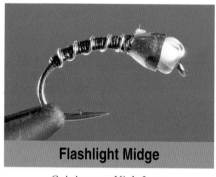

Flashlight Midge

Originator: Nick Jones
Tier: Nick Jones

Hook: #10-14 Tiemco 2487
Thorax: Gold conehead, reversed
Bead: Clear glass with white painted center
Thread: Red 8/0 Uni
Abdomen: Tying thread
Rib: Silver Lagartun wire (small)

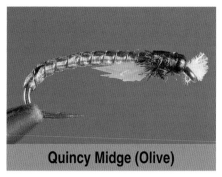

Quincy Midge (Olive)

Originator: Herman deGala
Tier: Herman deGala

Hook: #14-16 Tiemco 2302
Bead: Black tungsten
Thread: White 17/0 Uni
Gills: Dun CDC
Thorax: Peacock herl
Abdomen: Clear UTC Vinyl D Rib
Body: Olive 12/0 Bennechi
Rib: Gold Ultra Wire (fine)
Back: Mottled brown Medallion Sheeting
Wing buds: Copper Swiss Straw

Quincy Midge (Black)

Originator: Herman deGala
Tier: Herman deGala

Hook: #14-16 Tiemco 2302
Bead: Black tungsten
Thread: White 17/0 Uni
Gills: Dun CDC
Thorax: Peacock herl
Abdomen: Clear UTC Vinyl D Rib
Body: Black 12/0 Bennechi
Rib: Silver Ultra Wire (fine)
Back: Mottled brown Medallion Sheeting
Wing buds: Copper Swiss Straw

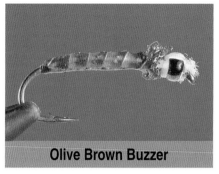

Olive Brown Buzzer

Originator: Rick Takahashi
Tier: Rick Takahashi

Hook: #10-16 Tiemco 2302
Bead: Clear glass with black painted center
Thread: Fl. yellow 6/0 Uni
Gills: Oral-B Ultra Floss
Body: Tying thread
Thorax: Olive brown Ice Dub
Rib 1: Brown Flex-Floss
Rib 2: Gold Lagartun wire (fine)
Note: Coat abdomen with Loon UV Knot Sense.

Dark Olive and Brown Buzzer

Originator: Rick Takahashi
Tier: Rick Takahashi

Hook: #10-16 Tiemco 2302
Bead: Clear glass with black painted center
Thread: Olive dun 6/0 Uni
Gills: Oral-B Ultra Floss
Body: Tying thread
Thorax: Tying thread
Rib 1: Brown Flex-Floss
Rib 2: Gold Lagartun wire (fine)
Note: Coat abdomen with Loon UV Knot Sense.

Copper Barb

Originator: Steve Thrapp
Tier: Steve Thrapp

Hook: #18-22 Tiemco 2487
Bead: Copper
Thread: Olive dun 8/0 Uni
Gills: White organza
Thorax: Peacock Ice Dub
Body: Tying thread
Rib: Gold Lagartun wire (extra fine)

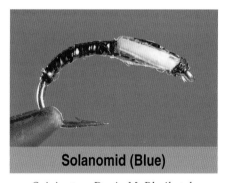

Solanomid (Blue)

Originator: Davie McPhail style
Tier: Steve Solano

Hook: #18-22 Tiemco 2487
Thread: Black 140-denier UTC
Thorax: Tying thread
Wing buds: White goose biot
Wing case: Pearl Mylar
Body: Tying thread
Rib: Blue Holographic Flashabou
Note: Cover with Loon UV Knot Sense.

Solanomid (Copper)

Originator: Davie McPhail style
Tier: Steve Solano

Hook: #18-22 Tiemco 2487
Thread: Black 140-denier UTC
Thorax: Tying thread
Wing buds: White goose biot
Wing case: Pearl Mylar
Body: Tying thread
Rib: Copper Flashabou
Note: Cover with Loon UV Knot Sense.

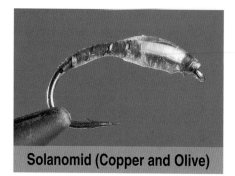

Solanomid (Copper and Olive)

Originator: Davie McPhail style
Tier: Steve Solano

Hook: #18-22 Tiemco 2487
Thread: Olive 140-denier UTC
Thorax: Tying thread
Wing buds: White goose biot
Wing case: Pearl Mylar
Body: Tying thread
Rib: Copper Flashabou
Note: Cover with Loon UV Knot Sense.

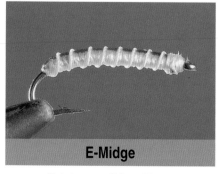

E-Midge

Originator: Ethan Emery
Tier: Ethan Emery

Hook: #18-22 Tiemco 2302
Thread: White 140-denier UTC
Body: Tying thread
Back: Pearl Mylar
Rib: Tying thread

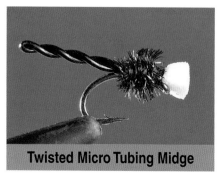

Twisted Micro Tubing Midge

Originator: Pat Murphy
Tier: Pat Murphy

Hook: #20 Daiichi 1120
Thread: Black 8/0 Uni
Thorax: Peacock herl
Gills: White foam
Body: Brown Micro Tubing

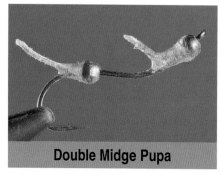

Double Midge Pupa

Originator: Gary Okazaki
Tier: Gary Okazaki

Hook: #8-16 Tiemco 400T
Thread: White 17/0 Uni
Bead: Copper metal
Body: Clear UTC Vinyl D Rib
Note: Crimp the D Rib with pliers and cover fly with UV Knot Sense. Other hook(s): Dai-Riki 1770.

Tak's Two Tone Beadhead Pupa

Originator: Rick Takahashi
Tier: Rick Takahashi

Hook: #18-22 Tiemco 2487
Bead: Black brass
Thread: White 70-denier UTC
Body: Tying thread
Dorsal line: Latex strip
Rib: Gold Lagartun wire (fine)
Collar: Light olive brown Targus SST dubbing
Note: Create the underbody by coloring the tying thread with a sand Chartpak marker and the dorsal line by coloring the latex with brown Chartpak marker.

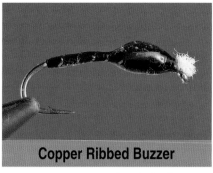

Copper Ribbed Buzzer

Originator: Rick Takahashi
Tier: Rick Takahashi

Hook: #12-16 Tiemco 2302
Thread: Black 140-denier UTC
Thorax: Tying thread
Gills: Oral-B Ultra Floss
Body: Tying thread
Rib: Copper Flashabou
Note: Cover body with Loon UV Knot Sense.

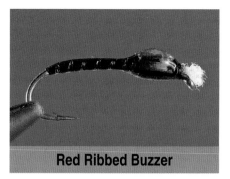

Red Ribbed Buzzer

Originator: Rick Takahashi
Tier: Rick Takahashi

Hook: #12-16 Tiemco 2302
Thread: Black 140-denier UTC
Thorax: Tying thread
Gills: Oral-B Ultra Floss
Body: Tying thread
Rib: Red Holographic Flashabou
Note: Cover body with Loon UV Knot Sense.

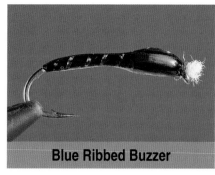

Blue Ribbed Buzzer

Originator: Rick Takahashi
Tier: Rick Takahashi

Hook: #12-16 Tiemco 2302
Thread: Black 140-denier UTC
Thorax: Tying thread
Gills: Oral-B Ultra Floss
Body: Tying thread
Rib: Blue Holographic Flashabou
Note: Cover body with Loon UV Knot Sense.

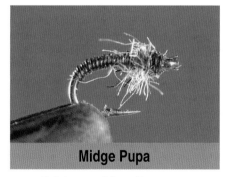

Midge Pupa

Originator: Masa Katsumata
Tier: Masa Katsumata

Hook: #32 Tiemco 518
Thread: Gray Tiemco mono
Body: Tying thread
Thorax: Gray Trouthunter CEN dubbing

Standard Buzzer

Originator: Unknown
Tier: Roy Christie

Hook: #10 Partridge 15BNV
Thread: Orange Pearsall's silk
Gills: White CDC
Body: Mother of pearl Mylar, lacquered
Rib: Peacock herl
Thorax: Red and rust brown Super Fine, mixed

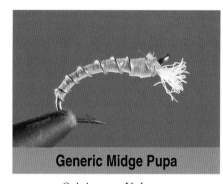

Generic Midge Pupa

Originator: Unknown
Tier: Roy Christie

Hook: #16-20 Drennan Sedge
Gills: White Antron
Thread: Antique gold Pearsall's silk
Body: Mother of pearl Mylar
Rib: Copper Lagartun wire (fine)

Green UV Flash Pupa

Originator: John Larson
Tier: John Larson

Hook: #22-24 Tiemco 101
Thread: Black 14/0 Gordon Griffiths
Body: Chartreuse Glo Flash
Rib: Black Krystal Flash
Thorax: UV black Ice Dub
Note: Coat the body with Wet and Wild Rock Solid Nail Polish.

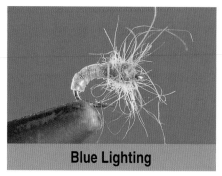

Blue Lighting

Originator: John Larson
Tier: John Larson

Hook: #32 Tiemco 518
Thread: White Spiderweb
Body: Blue UV Krystal Flash
Thorax: Blue Damsel dubbing
Note: Coat the body with Wet and Wild Rock Solid Nail Polish.

Pupa #1

Originator: Prof. J. R. Harris
Tier: Roy Christie

Hook: #12 Kamasan B160
Thread: Yellow Pearsall's silk
Tag: Silver tinsel
Body: Yellow-olive Swannundaze
Wing case: Jungle cock eye
Thorax: Light brown turkey herl
Hackle: Jungle cock

Pupa #2

Originator: Prof. J. R. Harris
Tier: Roy Christie

Hook: #12 Kamasan B160
Thread: Orange Pearsall's silk
Tag: Silver tinsel
Body: Tan Swannundaze
Wing case: Jungle cock eye
Thorax: Dark brown turkey herl
Hackle: Jungle cock

Pupa #3

Originator: Roy Christie
Tier: Roy Christie

Hook: #12 Drennan Sedge
Thread: Orange silk
Gills: Clear Antron
Body: Mother of pearl Lurex and orange and lime Krystal Flash
Rib: Blue eared pheasant herl
Wing buds: Red goose biots
Thorax: Black hare's ear
Tail/Gills: White Z-lon

Diamond Midge (Purple)

Originator: Rick Takahashi
Tier: Rick Takahashi

Hook: #12-24 Tiemco 2457
Thread: Black 8/0 Uni
Body: Tying thread
Rib: Purple tinsel
Wing buds: Orange Flexi Floss
Wing case: Pearl UTC Tinsel (medium)
Gills: Oral-B Ultra Floss
Note: Tinsel comes from a Christmas wreath. Coat entire fly with Sally Hansen Hard As Nails then coat top half with Wet and Wild Diamond Nail Polish.

Diamond Midge (Copper)

Originator: Rick Takahashi
Tier: Rick Takahashi

Hook: #12-24 Tiemco 2457
Thread: Black 8/0 Uni
Body: Tying thread
Rib: Copper tinsel
Wing buds: Orange Flexi Floss
Wing case: Pearl UTC Tinsel (medium)
Gills: Oral-B Ultra Floss
Note: Tinsel comes from a Christmas wreath. Coat entire fly with Sally Hansen Hard As Nails then coat top half with Wet and Wild Diamond Nail Polish.

Diamond Midge (Red)

Originator: Rick Takahashi
Tier: Rick Takahashi

Hook: #12-24 Tiemco 2457
Thread: Black 8/0 Uni
Body: Tying thread
Rib: Red tinsel
Wing buds: Orange Flexi Floss
Wing case: Pearl UTC Tinsel (medium)
Gills: Oral-B Ultra Floss
Note: Tinsel comes from a Christmas wreath. Coat entire fly with Sally Hansen Hard As Nails then coat top half with Wet and Wild Diamond Nail Polish.

Diamond Midge (Pink Pearl)

Originator: Rick Takahashi
Tier: Rick Takahashi

Hook: #12-24 Tiemco 2457
Thread: White 8/0 Uni
Body: Tying thread
Rib: Pearl Targus Liquid Flash
Wing buds: Brown biot
Wing case: Pearl UTC Tinsel (medium)
Gills: Oral-B Ultra Floss
Note: Coat entire fly with Sally Hansen Hard As Nails then coat top half with Wet and Wild Diamond Nail Polish.

Magic Pearl Midge

Originator: Rick Takahashi
Tier: Rick Takahashi

Hook: #12-24 Tiemco 2457
Thread: White 8/0 Uni, colored
Body: Tying thread
Rib: Clear .5mm Stretch Magic
Collar: Fl. orange 70-denier UTC
Thorax: Tying thread
Note: Color the tying thread with tan Chartpak marker to form the thorax.Coat entire fly with Sally Hansen Hard As Nails then coat top half with Wet and Wild Diamond Nail Polish.

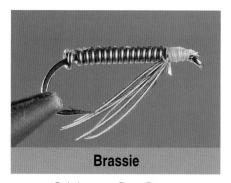

Brassie

Originator: Gary Borger
Tier: Gary Borger

Hook: #14-18 TAR 100 or 3769
Thread: Fl. red 8/0 Uni
Body: 28-gauge copper wire
Throat: Pheasant tail
Head: Tying thread
Note: The original South Platte Brassie was a scud imitation. Ed Marsh wrote about it in *Outdoor Life* in 1971. Do not tie in the wire. Simply wrap it from bend to head as a single layer, and cut off the excess. Crimp the trimmed ends against the hook with your thumbnail or a small pair of flat-jawed pliers. Coat the wire with head cement to keep it bright.

Sparkle Midge Pupa

Originator: Gary Borger
Tier: Gary Borger

Hook: #14-28 TAR 100 or 3769
Thread: Gray 8/0 Uni
Abdomen: Gray Targus SuperDry
Thorax: Targus SST dubbing cut to twice the length of the hook and brushed

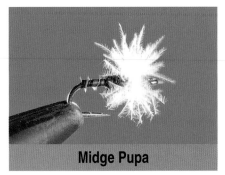

Midge Pupa

Originator: Mike Heck
Tier: Mike Heck

Hook:	18-24 Tiemco 101
Thread:	Black 8/0 Uni
Body:	Olive biot
Thorax:	Tying thread
Gills:	White CDC

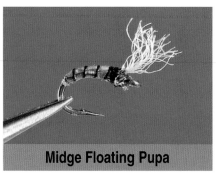

Midge Floating Pupa

Originator: Noritaka Osada
Tier: Noritaka Osada

Hook:	#30 Tiemco 2488
Thread:	Black 16/0 Tiemco
Abdomen:	Tan 16/0 Tiemco
Rib:	Black Danville 3/0 Monocord
Thorax:	Black 16/0
Wing:	Ram's wool

Bow Tie Buzzer

Originator: Unknown
Tier: Rick Takahashi

Hook:	#10-16 Mustad 9672
Thread:	Black Danville 6/0
Tail:	White poly yarn
Abdomen:	Tying thread
Rib:	Silver Lagartun wire (extra fine)
Thorax:	Peacock herl
Gills:	White poly yarn

Palomino Midge

Originator: Brett Smith
Tier: Rick Takahashi

Hook:	#18-24 Tiemco 2487
Thread:	Black 8/0 Uni
Abdomen:	Rust EZ Magic Dub
Wing case/Gills:	Mallard fibers
Thorax:	Gray Super Fine

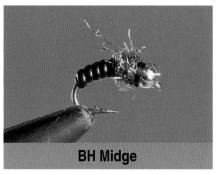

BH Midge

Originator: Jeff Henkemeyer
Tier: Jeff Henkemeyer

Hook:	#18-22 Tiemco 2487
Bead:	Gold metal
Thread:	Black 8/0 Uni
Body:	Black Micro Tubing
Thorax:	Peacock Ice Dub

Tungsten Cluster Black Beauty

Originator: Gary Okazaki
Tier: Gary Okazaki

Hook:	#8-16 Tiemco 400T
Thread:	Black 8/0 Uni
Body:	Tying thread
Rib:	Copper Lagartun wire (fine)
Head:	Black metal

Note: Other hook(s): Dai-Riki 1770.

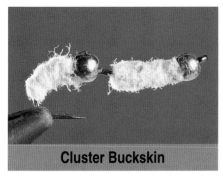

Cluster Buckskin

Originator: Gary Okazaki
Tier: Gary Okazaki

Hook: #8-16 Tiemco 400T
Thread: Black 8/0 Uni
Bead: Gold tungsten
Body: Chamois
Note: Other hook(s): Dai-Riki 1770.

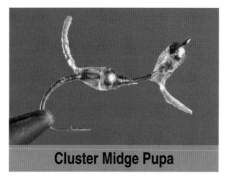

Cluster Midge Pupa

Originator: Gary Okazaki
Tier: Gary Okazaki

Hook: #8-16 Tiemco 400T
Thread: White 17/0 Uni
Bead: Copper
Body: Clear UTC Vinyl D Rib
Thorax: Latex
Note: Coat fly with Loon UV Knot Sense or Sally Hansen Hard As Nails. Other hook(s): Dai-Riki 1770.

Cluster Partridge Delight

Originator: Gary Okazaki
Tier: Gary Okazaki

Hook: #8-16 Tiemco 400T
Thread: Tan Pearsall's silk
Head: Tying thread
Body: Tying thread
Hackle: Partridge
Note: Other hook(s): Dai-Riki 1770.

Cluster Miracle

Originator: Gary Okazaki
Tier: Gary Okazaki

Hook: #8-16 Tiemco 400T
Thread: Black 8/0 Uni
Head: Black rabbit dubbing
Body: White goose biot
Note: Other hook(s): Dai-Riki 1770.

Tying the Emerger

THE EMERGING PHASE of the midge is a transitional stage between the pupal and the adult stages. Though it is not a scientifically recognized life-cycle stage, it is important for anglers to imitate. During this stage of the midge life cycle, the pupa travels from its home on or near the bottom to just under the water's surface, where trout feed heavily on them.

We've had great success fishing emerging midges as they ascend and prepare to hatch into adults. Flash or glass beads can simulate the gaseous bubble under the exoskeleton that is shiny, and even represent the wings pads on the sides of the thorax.

Midge pupae wiggle to the water's surface, break through the surface film, and emerge into adults.

Pupal shucks on the surface of a lake are a sure sign of a midge hatch.

Olive and Gray Glitter Wing Emerger

This first midge emerger pattern uses pearl Glitter Thread to simulate the gas bubble the pupa uses to ascend to the surface. Canadian Llama Company's Glitter Thread is made up of a strand of Krystal Flash with several strands of Antron fiber intertwined along its length. This product comes in several colors and can be used to create bodies, thoraxes, wingcases, and wing buds.

Materials

Hook:	#18 Tiemco 2488
Thread:	Olive 8/0 Uni
Rib:	Gold Lagartun wire (fine)
Thorax:	Gray Super Fine
Flash:	Pearl Glitter Thread

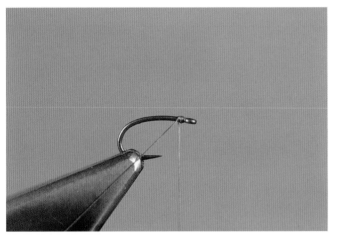

1. Attach the thread at the hook eye and wrap back to the two-thirds point on the shank.

2. Trim the tag end of the tying thread. Tie in the wire with a few wraps of thread, allowing a small tag of wire to extend past the thread wraps. This makes it easier to tie in the wire.

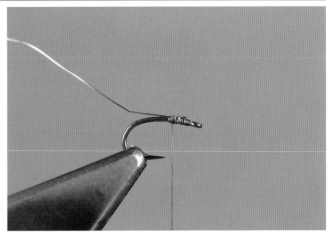

3. Pull the wire so that the tag end slips under the tying thread.

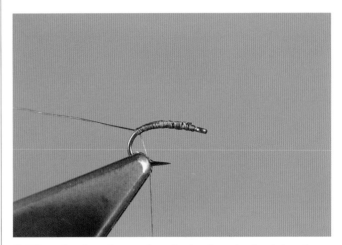

4. Wrap the thread over the wire back to the hook bend to a point just above the barb.

5. Wrap the tying thread forward to about one-third the distance of the hook shank back from the hook eye. Begin wrapping the wire forward in evenly spaced wraps.

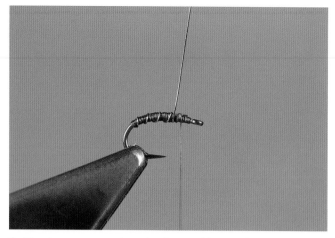

6. Continue to wrap the wire forward in evenly spaced wraps until you reach the one-third position.

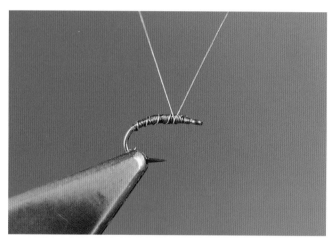

7. Tie off the wire with two turns of tying thread.

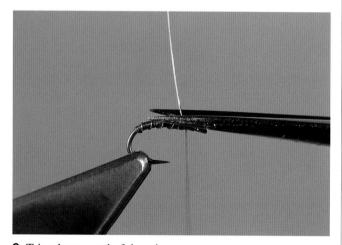

8. Trim the tag end of the wire.

9. Tie in one strand of pearl Glitter Thread with two wraps of tying thread.

10. Fold the front piece of Glitter Thread back toward the rear of the hook, and take a wrap or two of tying thread over it so that both strands face toward the rear.

11. Trim both ends of Glitter Thread to about half the length of the body.

12. The trimmed Glitter Thread.

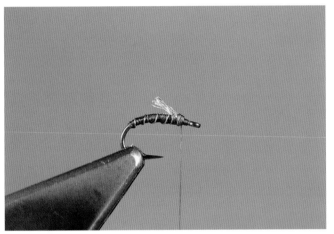

13. Wrap the thread over the Glitter Thread, forcing the fibers to bend toward the rear of the hook.

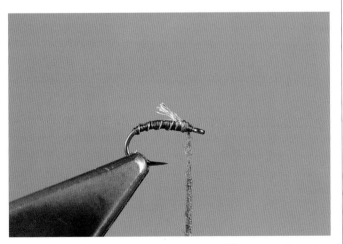

14. Dub a small amount of gray Super Fine onto the tying thread.

15. Wrap the dubbing, starting at the base of the wing tapering forward to the hook eye.

16. Whip-finish the head.

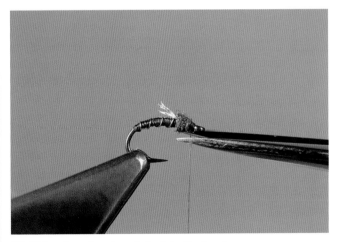

17. Trim the tying thread flush to the hook.

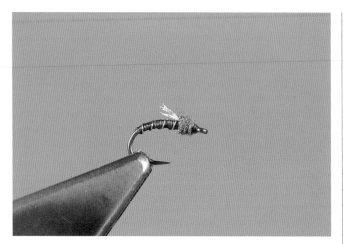

18. Completed Olive and Gray Glitter Wing Emerger.

Foam Wing Emerger

Foam is a versatile material for various types of midge patterns. In patterns like this Foam Wing Emerger, the foam may represent the gaseous bubble in the thorax of a midge pupa, its emerging wings, or simply act as an attractant. Open-cell foam absorbs water, so it is more appropriate for sinking patterns. Closed-cell foam is sealed and float the fly, making it ideal for dry-fly patterns.

Materials

Hook:	#16-24 Tiemco 2488
Thread:	White 70-denier UTC
Abdomen:	Tying thread colored with light gray permanent marker
Rib:	Tying thread colored with dark brown permanent marker
Thorax:	Adams gray Super Fine
Wing:	White closed-cell foam

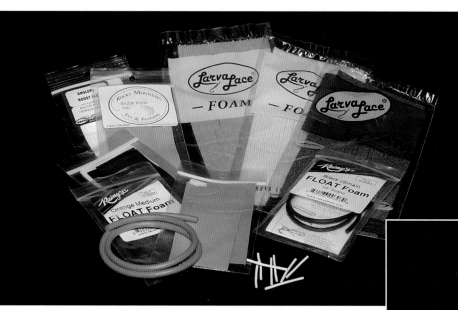

Foam comes in many types, colors, shapes, and sizes, including cylinders and sheets. You can also use the protective foam that comes with most electronic equipment. Foam is mostly used for floating patterns, and its applications are only limited by your imagination.

Permanent markers such as Pantone, Chartpak, and Sharpies can be used to color threads or any part of the flies. These markers usually don't require a coating to preserve the color; however, we've often used the solvent in head cements as a blending medium. Nonpermanent markers require a protective coating of head cement, fingernail polish, or UV Knot Sense.

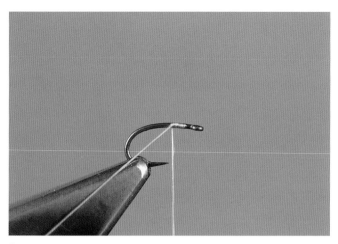

1. Attach the thread behind the hook eye.

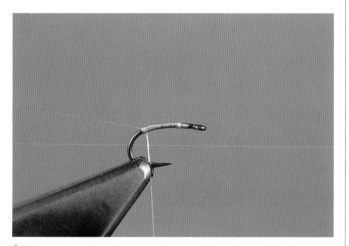

2. Wrap the tying thread to the hook bend opposite the barb.

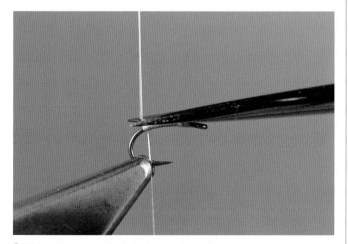

3. Trim the tag end of the tying thread.

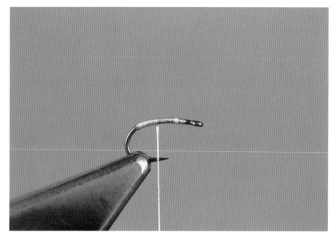

4. Wrap the tying thread forward in touching wraps to the hook eye. This helps to make a slightly thicker abdomen.

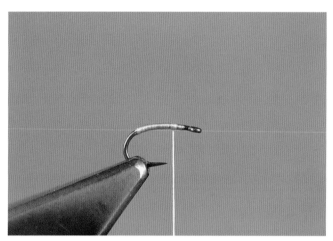

5. Continue wrapping the tying thread forward in touching wraps to a point one eye width behind the hook eye.

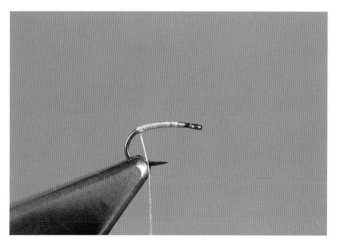

6. Wrap the tying thread with touching wraps back to the hook bend opposite the barb.

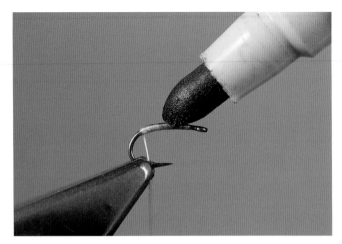

7. Color the thread body with light gray permanent marker

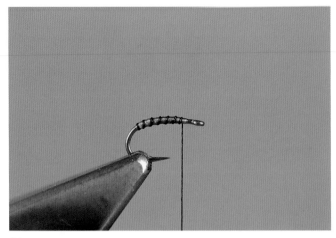

10. Continue to wrap the tying thread forward in evenly spaced wraps to a point one eye width behind the hook eye.

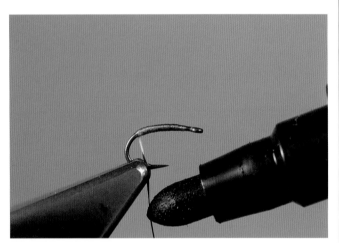

8. Color the tying thread with a dark brown permanent marker.

11. Cut a point in a ¹⁄₁₆-inch-square piece of white foam. Tie in the foam at the tip with several wraps to secure it to the hook.

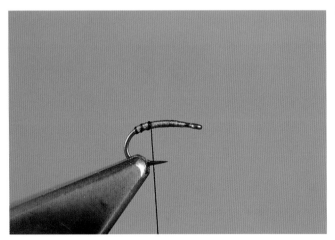

9. Spin the bobbin clockwise to tighten the tying thread; this is then used as the rib. Begin wrapping the tying thread forward in evenly spaced wraps.

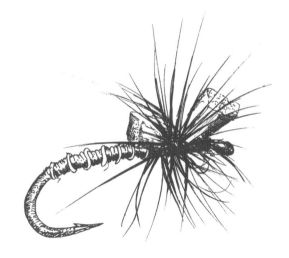

Puff Emerger

12. Dub a small amount of gray Super Fine onto the tying thread.

13. Wrap the dubbing behind the foam.

14. Continue to wrap dubbing in front of the wing.

15. Trim the foam close to the body.

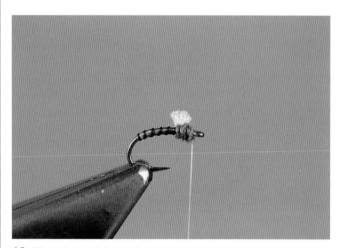

16. The trimmed foam should look like this.

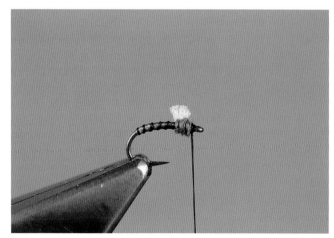

17. Color the thread with dark brown permanent marker. Take several wraps behind the hook eye to create a small head.

18. Whip-finish the head and trim the tying thread flush to the hook.

19. Completed Foam Wing Emerger.

Upto's Midge Emerger

This pattern was shown to us over 25 years ago by Dr. Jeff Uptograf, who is not only an emergency-room physician, but he is also a fanatical fly fisherman and creative fly tier. We've had tremendous luck fishing this pattern in and under the surface, in both lakes and streams.

Biots from the leading edge of a goose or duck quill are a useful body material and also have some application for wings on the midge adult (see Tak's Biot Midge Adult, page 220). The biot creates a smooth body, or one that has a slightly raised rib. Strip, but do not cut, the quill from the stem of the feather. At the base of the fiber, note that there is a slight indentation (notch) that will help you determine how to create a smooth or ribbed body. To create a smooth body, tie the biot by the tip with the notch facing toward the rear of the hook. Face the notch to the front of the hook to create a ribbed effect. Attach the hackle pliers to the tip of the biot and make sure that the hackle pliers are in-line with the biot. If you place the tip of the biot at an angle to the hackle pliers, you run the risk of cutting the biot while you wrap it.

Materials

Hook:	#18 Tiemco 2488
Thread:	Black 8/0 Uni
Tail:	Amber Antron
Abdomen:	White goose biot
Wing Bud:	White poly yarn
Thorax:	Gray Super Fine

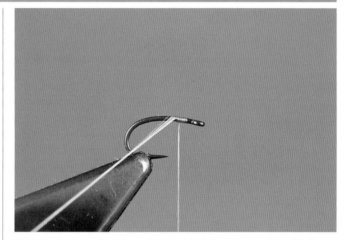

1. Attach the tying thread one-third the distance of the hook shank back from the hook eye, and make several wraps to the midpoint of the hook.

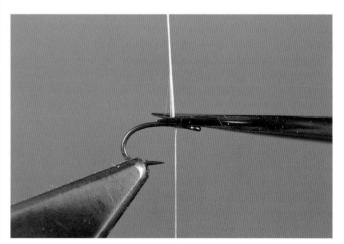

2. Trim the tag end of the tying thread.

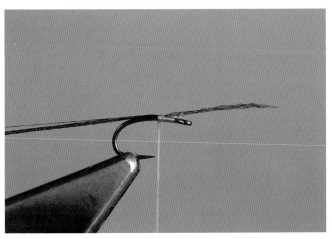

3. Attach eight to ten fibers of amber Antron yarn. (We like to make our trailing shucks sparse.)

4. Wrap the tying thread in touching wraps toward the hook bend opposite the barb.

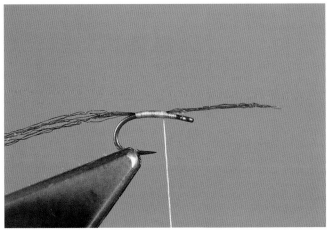

5. Wrap the thread forward in touching wraps to one-third the distance behind the hook eye.

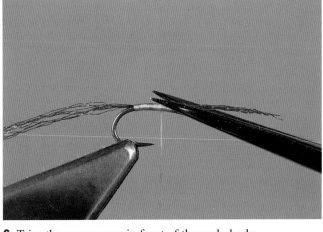

6. Trim the excess yarn in front of the underbody.

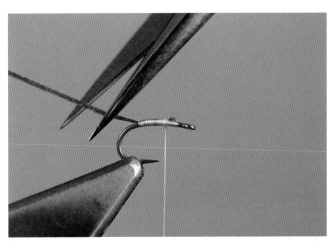

7. Trim the rear portion of the yarn so that it is about the length of the body. This simulates the trailing shuck.

8. Wrap the thread forward to a point two eye widths behind the hook eye. Attach the poly yarn with several wraps of tying thread.

9. Wrap the tying thread over the poly yarn to the hook bend where the trailing shuck starts.

12. Wrap the tying thread forward to where you first tied in the poly yarn.

10. Wrap the tying thread forward two or three wraps.

13. Wrap the biot forward toward the hook eye.

11. Tie in the goose biot.

14. Continue to wrap the biot forward to one eye width behind the hook eye.

15. Tie off the biot with several wraps of thread.

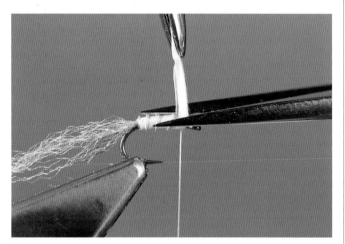

16. Trim the excess biot.

17. Wrap the tying thread over the remaining biot stubs.

18. Pull the poly yarn over the biot body and thorax and tie in, forming a loop wing. Tie off the poly yarn by taking two wraps of thread over the yarn. Secure and trim the excess yarn.

19. Trim the excess poly yarn.

20. Dub on a small amount of gray Super Fine.

21. Dub a tapered head with the last wrap behind the hook eye.

23. Trim the tying thread flush to the hook. Completed Upto's Midge Emerger.

22. Whip-finish the head.

Emerger Patterns

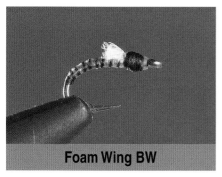

Foam Wing BW

Originator: Rick Takahashi
Tier: Rick Takahashi

Hook:	#18-26 Tiemco 2488
Thread:	White 17/0 Uni
Body:	Tying thread
Rib:	Tying thread
Wing:	White foam
Head:	Tying thread

Note: Foam for the wing is from electronics packaging. For the rib and head, color the tying thread with black Sharpie marker. Coat entire fly with Griff's Thin Head Cement. Other hook(s): Dai-Riki 125.

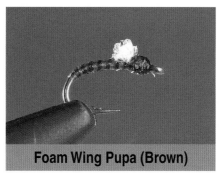

Foam Wing Pupa (Brown)

Originator: Rick Takahashi
Tier: Rick Takahashi

Hook:	#18-26 Tiemco 2488
Thread:	White 17/0 Uni
Body:	Tying thread
Rib:	Tying thread
Wing:	White poly yarn
Head:	Tying thread

Note: Color the thread for the body with olive Charptak marker, and the thread for the rib and the head with black Sharpie marker. Other hook(s): Dai-Riki 125.

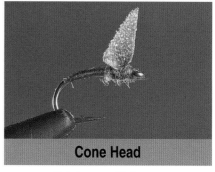

Cone Head

Originator: Unknown
Tier: Rick Takahashi

Hook:	#18-26 Tiemco 2488
Thread:	White 17/0 Uni
Body:	Tying thread
Wing:	Gray Larva Lace foam
Thorax:	Gray Super Fine

Note: Color the tying thread used for the body with light gray Chartpak marker. Other hook(s): Tiemco 2487 or Dai-Riki 125.

Foam Wing Zebra

Originator: Unknown
Tier: Rick Takahashi

Hook: #18-26 Tiemco 2488
Thread: White 8/0 Uni
Rib: Tying thread
Wing: White Larva Lace foam
Head: Tying thread
Note: For the rib and head, color the tying thread with black Sharpie marker. Other hook(s): Tiemco 2487 or Dai-Riki 125.

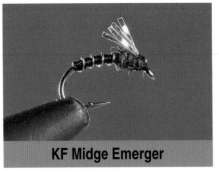

KF Midge Emerger

Originator: Paul Freeman
Tier: Paul Freeman

Hook: #20-26 Tiemco 2487
Thread: Black 8/0 Uni
Body: Tying thread
Rib: Copper Lagartun wire (extra fine)
Wing: Pearl Krystal Flash
Head: Black 8/0 Uni
Thorax: Mahogany Super Fine
Note: Other hook(s): Tiemco 2457 or Dai-Riki 135.

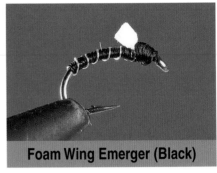

Foam Wing Emerger (Black)

Originator: Unknown
Tier: Paul Freeman

Hook: #20-24 Tiemco 2487
Thread: Black 8/0 Uni
Body: Tying thread
Rib: Silver Lagartun wire (extra fine)
Wing: White closed-cell foam
Head: Tying thread
Note: Other hook(s): Tiemco 2457 or Dai-Riki 135.

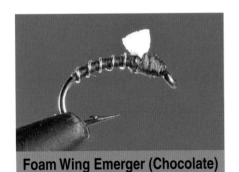

Foam Wing Emerger (Chocolate)

Originator: Unknown
Tier: Paul Freeman

Hook: #20-24 Tiemco 2487
Thread: Brown 8/0 Uni
Body: Tying thread
Rib: Silver Lagartun wire (extra fine)
Wing: Closed-cell white foam
Head: Tying thread
Note: Other hook(s): Tiemco 2457 or Dai-Riki 135.

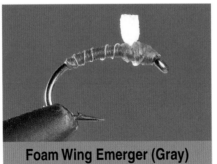

Foam Wing Emerger (Gray)

Originator: Unknown
Tier: Paul Freeman

Hook: #20-24 Tiemco 2487
Thread: Gray 8/0 Uni
Body: Tying thread
Rib: Silver Lagartun wire (extra fine)
Wing: Closed-cell white foam
Head: Tying thread
Note: Other hook(s): Tiemco 2457 or Dai-Riki 135.

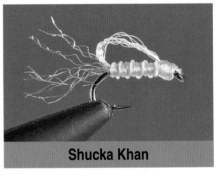

Shucka Khan

Originator: Paul Freeman
Tier: Paul Freeman

Hook: #20-24 Tiemco 100
Thread: Cream 8/0 Uni
Body: Tying thread
Tail: Copper brown Antron
Wing: White Antron

Puff Emerger

Originator: Paul Freeman
Tier: Paul Freeman

Hook:	#20-24 Tiemco 100
Thread:	Camel 8/0 Uni
Body:	Tying thread
Rib:	Silver Lagartun wire (extra fine)
Wing:	White closed-cell foam
Hackle:	Brown

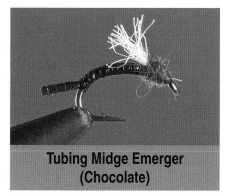

Tubing Midge Emerger (Chocolate)

Originator: Unknown
Tier: Solitude Fly Company

Hook:	#18-24 Daiichi 1120
Thread:	Dark brown 8/0 Uni
Tail:	Brown Midge Tubing, flattened
Body:	Brown Micro Tubing
Wing:	White Hi-Vis
Thorax:	Chocolate brown rabbit dubbing

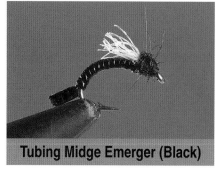

Tubing Midge Emerger (Black)

Originator: Unknown
Tier: Solitude Fly Company

Hook:	#18-24 Daiichi 1120
Thread:	Black 8/0 Uni
Tail:	Black Midge Tubing, flattened
Body:	Black Micro Tubing
Wing:	White Hi-Vis
Thorax:	Black rabbit dubbing

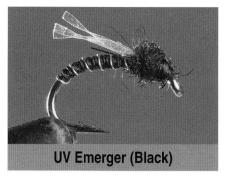

UV Emerger (Black)

Originator: Unknown
Tier: Solitude Fly Company

Hook:	#18-26 Daiichi 1130
Thread:	Black 8/0 Uni
Body:	Tying thread
Rib:	Gold Ultra Wire (extra small)
Wing:	Pearl UV Krystal Flash
Head:	Black rabbit dubbing

Sidewinder Emerger

Originator: Bear Goode
Tier: Solitude Fly Company

Hook:	#20-26 Daiichi 1130
Thread:	Yellow 6/0 Uni
Body:	Yellow 6/0 Uni
Rib:	Black 6/0 Uni
Wing:	Light dun poly yarn
Head:	Black 8/0 Uni

Poly Wing Emerger (Chocolate)

Originator: Greg Faught
Tier: Solitude Fly Company

Hook:	#18-22 Daiichi 1120
Thread:	Brown 8/0 Uni
Body:	Brown 8/0 Uni
Rib:	Copper Ultra Wire (extra small)
Wing:	White Hi-Vis
Thorax:	Tying thread

Poly Wing Emerger (Black)

Originator: Greg Faught
Tier: Solitude Fly Company

Hook:	#18-22 Daiichi 1120
Thread:	Black 8/0 Uni
Rib:	Silver Ultra Wire (extra small)
Body:	Tying thread
Wing:	White Hi-Vis
Thorax:	Tying thread

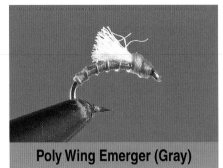

Poly Wing Emerger (Gray)

Originator: Greg Faught
Tier: Solitude Fly Company

Hook:	#18-22 Daiichi 1120
Thread:	Rusty dun 8/0 Uni
Rib:	Silver Ultra Wire (extra small)
Body:	Tying thread
Wing:	White Hi-Vis
Thorax:	Tying thread

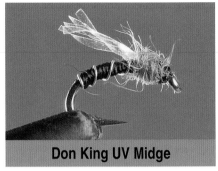

Don King UV Midge

Originator: Unknown
Tier: Solitude Fly Company

Hook:	#18-22 Daiichi 1120
Thread:	Black 8/0 Uni
Rib:	Silver Ultra Wire (extra small)
Body:	Tying thread
Wing:	Pearl UV Krystal Flash
Thorax:	Gray rabbit dubbing

Black Beauty Emerger

Originator: Unknown
Tier: Solitude Fly Company

Hook:	#18-22 Daiichi 1120
Thread:	Black 8/0 Uni
Tail:	White Hi-Vis
Rib:	Silver Ultra Wire (extra small)
Body:	Tying thread
Wing:	White Hi-Vis
Thorax:	Gray rabbit dubbing

Bead Wing Midge (Brown)

Originator: Unknown
Tier: Solitude Fly Company

Hook:	#18-24 Daiichi 1120
Thread:	Brown 8/0 Uni
Body:	Tying thread
Rib:	Copper Ultra Wire (extra small)
Wing:	Pearl glass bead
Thorax:	Brown rabbit

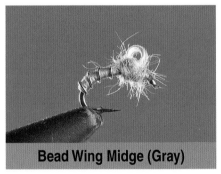

Bead Wing Midge (Gray)

Originator: Unknown
Tier: Solitude Fly Company

Hook:	#18-24 Daiichi 1120
Thread:	Gray 8/0 Uni
Body:	Tying thread
Rib:	Copper Ultra Wire (extra small)
Wing:	Pearl glass bead
Thorax:	Gray muskrat

Bead Wing Midge (Black)

Originator: Unknown
Tier: Solitude Fly Company

Hook:	#18-24 Daiichi 1120
Thread:	Black 8/0 Uni
Body:	Tying thread
Rib:	Copper Ultra Wire (extra small)
Wing:	Pearl glass bead
Thorax:	Black rabbit dubbing

KF Flasher (Olive)

Originator: Unknown
Tier: Solitude Fly Company

Hook:	#18-24 Daiichi 1120
Thread:	Olive 8/0 Uni
Body:	Tying thread
Rib:	Copper Ultra Wire (extra small)
Wing:	Pearl Krystal Flash
Thorax:	Light olive hare's ear dubbing

KF Flasher (Chocolate)

Originator: Unknown
Tier: Solitude Fly Company

Hook:	#18-24 Daiichi 1120
Thread:	Brown 8/0 Uni
Body:	Tying thread
Rib:	Copper Ultra Wire (extra small)
Wing:	Pearl Krystal Flash
Thorax:	Chocolate brown rabbit dubbing

KF Flasher (Black)

Originator: Unknown
Tier: Solitude Fly Company

Hook:	#18-24 Daiichi 1120
Thread:	Black 8/0 Uni
Rib:	Copper Ultra Wire (extra small)
Body:	Tying thread
Wing:	Pearl Krystal Flash
Thorax:	Black rabbit dubbing

Foam Back Emerger (Chocolate)

Originator: Greg Faught
Tier: Solitude Fly Company

Hook:	#18-24 Daiichi 1120
Thread:	Black 8/0 Uni
Tail:	Brown Antron
Body:	Chocolate hare's ear dubbing
Rib:	Copper Ultra Wire (extra small)
Wing:	White closed-cell foam
Thorax:	Chocolate hare's ear dubbing

Hurricane Midge Emerger (Black)

Originator: Gary Hayes
Tier: Solitude Fly Company

Hook:	#18-24 Daiichi 1270
Bead:	Clear glass
Thread:	Black 6/0 Danville
Body:	Black Ultra Wire (extra small)
Wing:	White CDC
Thorax:	Black rabbit dubbing

Hurricane Midge Emerger (Red)

Originator: Gary Hayes
Tier: Solitude Fly Company

Hook:	#18-24 Daiichi 1270
Bead:	Clear glass
Thread:	Black 6/0 Danville
Body:	Red Ultra Wire (extra small)
Wing:	White CDC
Thorax:	Black rabbit dubbing

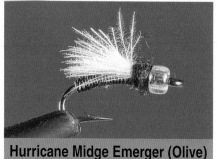

Hurricane Midge Emerger (Olive)

Originator: Gary Hayes
Tier: Solitude Fly Company

Hook:	#18-24 Daiichi 1270
Bead:	Clear glass
Thread:	Black 6/0 Danville
Body:	Green Ultra Wire (extra small)
Wing:	White CDC
Thorax:	Black rabbit dubbing

BH UV Z-Midge (Pearl)

Originator: Unknown
Tier: Solitude Fly Company

Hook:	#16-20 Daiichi 1120
Bead:	Black Cyclops
Thread:	White 6/0 Danville
Rib:	Black Ultra Wire (extra small)
Body:	Pearl Flashabou
Wing:	Pearl UV Krystal Flash
Thorax:	Black ostrich herl

BH UV Z-Midge (Olive)

Originator: Unknown
Tier: Solitude Fly Company

Hook:	#16-20 Daiichi 1120
Bead:	Gold Cyclops
Thread:	Olive 6/0 Danville
Body:	Olive Flashabou
Rib:	Gold Ultra Wire (extra small)
Wing:	Pearl UV Krystal Flash
Thorax:	Black ostrich herl

BH UV Z-Midge (Black)

Originator: Unknown
Tier: Solitude Fly Company

Hook:	#16-20 Daiichi 1120
Bead:	Black Cyclops
Thread:	Black 6/0 Danville
Body:	Black Flashabou
Rib:	Gold Ultra Wire (extra small)
Wing:	Pearl UV Krystal Flash
Thorax:	Black ostrich herl

BH K Flasher (Chocolate)

Originator: Greg Faught
Tier: Solitude Fly Company

Hook:	#18-22 Daiichi 1120
Bead:	Gold Cyclops
Thread:	Dark brown 8/0 Uni
Body:	Tying thread
Rib:	Copper Ultra Wire (extra small)
Wing:	Pearl UV Krystal Flash
Thorax:	Brown rabbit dubbing

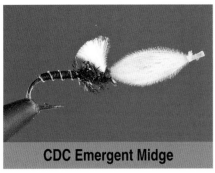

CDC Emergent Midge

Originator: James Wallach
Tier: James Wallach

Hook:	#20-24 Tiemco 100
Thread:	Black 8/0 Uni
Body:	Tying thread
Rib:	Silver Danville wire (fine)
Legs:	Peacock herl
Wing:	White CDC
Thorax:	Peacock herl

Darlon Hatching Midge

Originator: James Wallach
Tier: James Wallach

Hook:	#20-24 Tiemco 2488
Bead:	Hematite glass
Thread:	Gray 8/0 Uni
Body:	Tying thread over Darlon
Shuck/Wings:	Dark dun Darlon
Rib:	Silver Danville wire (fine)
Thorax:	Cream Super Fine

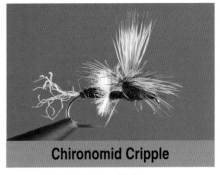

Chironomid Cripple

Originator: Unknown
Tier: Solitude Fly Company

Hook:	#14 Daiichi 1100
Thread:	Black 6/0 Danville
Tail:	White Hi-Vis
Body:	Black Super Fine
Rib:	Silver Ultra Wire (extra small)
Hackle:	Grizzly
Thorax:	White ostrich herl
Post:	Elk mane
Back:	Elk hair

Hatching Midge (Black)

Originator: Unknown
Tier: Solitude Fly Company

Hook:	#14-22 Daiichi 1130
Thread:	Black 6/0 Danville
Tail:	Clear Midge Tubing, flattened
Body:	Clear Midge Tubing
Rib:	White UTC Monofilament Thread
Wing:	Z-Wing
Gills:	White poly yarn
Hackle:	Dun

Hatching Midge (Olive)

Originator: Unknown
Tier: Solitude Fly Company

Hook:	#14-22 Daiichi 1130
Thread:	Gray 6/0 Danville
Tail:	Clear Midge Tubing, flattened
Body:	Clear Midge Tubing
Rib:	Black UTC mono thread
Wing:	Clear Medallion Sheeting
Gills:	White poly yarn
Hackle:	Dun

Dandelion (Red)

Originator: Unknown
Tier: Solitude Fly Company

Hook:	#18-22 Daiichi 1130
Thread:	Camel 8/0 Uni
Body:	Red Micro Tubing
Thorax:	Peacock herl
Post:	White Hi-Vis
Hackle:	Brown

Dandelion (Brown)

Originator: Unknown
Tier: Solitude Fly Company

Hook:	#18-22 Daiichi 1130
Thread:	Camel 8/0 Uni
Body:	Brown Micro Tubing
Thorax:	Peacock herl
Post:	White Hi-Vis
Hackle:	Brown

Dandelion (Olive)

Originator: Unknown
Tier: Solitude Fly Company

Hook:	#18-22 Daiichi 1130
Thread:	Olive 8/0 Uni
Body:	Tying thread
Rib:	Copper Lagartun wire (extra fine)
Thorax:	Peacock herl
Post:	White Hi-Vis
Hackle:	Medium dun

Three Dollar Dip (Brown)

Originator: Blue Ribbon Flies
Tier: Umpqua Feather Merchants

Hook:	#14-18 Tiemco 2457
Bead:	Gold metal
Thread:	Brown 8/0 Uni
Body:	Tying thread
Rib:	Gold Ultra Wire (extra small)
Wing:	Bleached deer hair

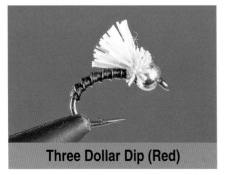

Three Dollar Dip (Red)

Originator: Blue Ribbon Flies
Tier: Umpqua Feather Merchants

Hook:	#14-18 Tiemco 2457
Bead:	Gold metal
Thread:	Red 8/0 Uni
Body:	Tying thread
Rib:	Red Ultra Wire (extra small)
Wing:	Bleached deer hair

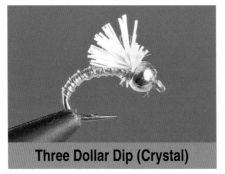

Three Dollar Dip (Crystal)

Originator: Blue Ribbon Flies
Tier: Umpqua Feather Merchants

Hook:	#14-18 Tiemco 2457
Bead:	Gold metal
Thread:	Pearl Krystal Flash
Body:	Tying thread
Rib:	Gold Ultra Wire (extra small)
Wing:	Bleached deer hair

Three Dollar Dip (Olive)

Originator: Blue Ribbon Flies
Tier: Umpqua Feather Merchants

Hook:	#14-18 Tiemco 2457
Bead:	Gold metal
Thread:	Olive 8/0 Uni
Body:	Tying thread
Rib:	Gold Ultra Wire (extra small)
Wing:	Bleached deer hair

Mathews's Serendipity

Originator: Craig Mathews
Tier: Umpqua Feather Merchants

Hook:	#14-20 Tiemco 2487
Thread:	Red 8/0 Uni
Body:	Red Z-lon, twisted
Wing case:	Trimmed deer hair

Midgling (Olive)

Originator: Mike Mercer
Tier: Umpqua Feather Merchants

Hook:	#16-20 Tiemco 2457 or 2487
Bead:	Green glass
Thread:	Olive 8/0 Uni
Tail:	Pearl Angel Hair
Underbody:	Pearl Krystal Flash
Body:	Olive Midge Tubing
Wing case:	Pearl Krystal Flash
Collar:	Olive ostrich herl

Midgling (Root Beer)

Originator: Mike Mercer
Tier: Umpqua Feather Merchants

Hook:	#16-20 Tiemco 2457 or 2487
Bead:	Root beer glass
Thread:	Brown 8/0 Uni
Tail:	Pearl Angel Hair
Underbody:	Pearl Krystal Flash
Body:	Brown Midge Tubing
Wing case:	Pearl Krystal Flash
Collar:	Olive brown ostrich herl

Trailing Shuck Midge (Olive)

Originator: Unknown
Tier: Umpqua Feather Merchants

Hook:	#20-22 Tiemco 101
Thread:	Black 8/0 Uni
Tail:	Brown Z-lon
Body:	Tying thread
Back:	White Z-lon
Legs:	Black hackle
Thorax:	Peacock herl

Sprout Midge

Originator: Morgan/Larsen
Tier: Umpqua Feather Merchants

Hook:	#18-24 Tiemco 2487
Thread:	Gray 14/0 Gordon Griffiths
Shuck:	Orange Krystal Flash
Body:	Tying thread
Post:	White foam cylinder
Thorax:	Tying thread
Hackle:	Grizzly
Wing:	Natural CDC

Morgan's Midge

Originator: Morgan/Larsen
Tier: Umpqua Feather Merchants

Hook:	#18-24 Tiemco 2487
Thread:	Black 8/0 Uni
Tail:	Amber Krystal Flash
Body:	Brown tying thread
Rib:	Tying thread, twisted
Wing:	Tan CDC
Hackle:	Dark dun rooster
Head:	Tying thread

Snowshoe Emerger

Originator: Jim Cannon
Tier: Umpqua Feather Merchants

Hook: #18-20 Tiemco 2488
Thread: Black 8/0 Uni
Wing: Snowshoe rabbit foot
Body: Brown Midge Tubing
Thorax: Brown Ice Dub
Note: The hair for the wing should come from snowshoe rabbit hind foot, from the front half of the foot. 33% bleached white, 33% dyed black, and 33% pearl Ice Dub blended together.

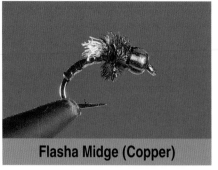

Flasha Midge (Copper)

Originator: Mark Boname
Tier: Stone Creek

Hook: #18-22 Dai-Riki 135
Bead: Root beer glass
Thread: Black 8/0 Uni
Body: Copper Flashabou
Wing: White Z-lon
Thorax: Peacock herl

Flasha Midge (Red)

Originator: Mark Boname
Tier: Stone Creek

Hook: #18-22 Dai-Riki 135
Bead: Clear glass
Thread: Red 8/0 Uni
Body: Red Flashabou
Wing: White Z-lon
Thorax: Peacock herl

Flasha Midge (Black)

Originator: Mark Boname
Tier: Stone Creek

Hook: #18-22 Dai-Riki 135
Bead: Black glass
Thread: Black 8/0 Uni
Body: Black Flashabou
Wing: White Z-lon
Thorax: Peacock herl

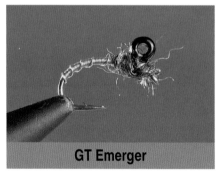

GT Emerger

Originator: Gordon Tharrett
Tier: Umpqua Feather Merchants

Hook: #16-20 Tiemco 2457
Bead: Black glass
Thread: Gray 8/0 Uni
Body: Tying thread
Rib: Silver Ultra Wire (extra small)
Thorax: Gray Spirit River Emergence dubbing

Para Hi-Vis (Gray)

Originator: Greg Faught
Tier: Solitude Fly Company

Hook: #16-18 Daiichi 1130
Thread: Gray 8/0 Uni
Body: Gray Super Fine
Post: Fl. orange Z-lon
Hackle: Grizzly

Para Hi-Vis (Olive)

Originator: Greg Faught
Tier: Solitude Fly Company

Hook:	#16-18 Daiichi 1130
Thread:	Gray 8/0 Uni
Body:	Olive brown Super Fine
Post:	Fl. orange Z-lon
Hackle:	Dun

Para Hi-Vis (Chocolate)

Originator: Greg Faught
Tier: Solitude Fly Company

Hook:	#16-18 Daiichi 1130
Thread:	Rust 8/0 Uni
Body:	Rust Super Fine
Post:	Fl. orange Z-lon
Hackle:	Grizzly

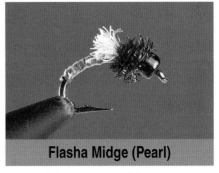

Flasha Midge (Pearl)

Originator: Mark Boname
Tier: Stone Creek

Hook:	#18-22 Dai-Riki 135
Bead:	Black glass
Thread:	Black 8/0 Uni
Body:	Pearl Flashabou
Wing:	White Z-lon
Thorax:	Peacock herl

Soft Hackle

Originator: John Nichols
Tier: John Nichols

Hook:	#16-20 Tiemco 2457
Thread:	Red 8/0 Uni
Body:	Peacock dubbing
Hackle:	Starling

Cream Flash

Originator: Rick Takahashi
Tier: Rick Takahashi

Hook:	#20-26 Tiemco 2488
Body:	Cream 70-denier UTC
Rib:	Tying thread colored dark brown
Flash:	Pearl Krystal Flash
Wing:	Closed cell packing foam
Head:	Black 8/0 Uni

Trailing Shuck Emerger

Originator: Rick Takahashi
Tier: Rick Takahashi

Hook:	#22-26 Tiemco 2488
Thread:	White 17/0 Uni colored with black Sharpie
Tail:	Orange Krystal Flash with ends melted with lighter
Body:	Olive polyester paintbrush fiber
Wing:	Fl. white Hi-Vis coated with fl. pink paint
Hackle:	Grizzly

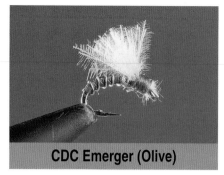

CDC Emerger (Olive)

Originator: Russell Ellis
Tier: Russell Ellis

Hook:	#20-22 Tiemco 2487
Thread:	Olive 8/0 Uni
Body:	Tying thread
Rib:	Gold Lagartun wire (extra fine)
Wing:	Yellow Trouthunter Premium CDC

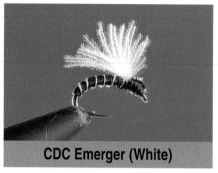

CDC Emerger (White)

Originator: Russell Ellis
Tier: Russell Ellis

Hook:	#20-22 Tiemco 2487
Thread:	Black 8/0 Uni
Body:	Tying thread
Rib:	Gold Lagartun wire (extra fine)
Wing:	Natural white Trouthunter Premium CDC

Ostrich Herl Midge (Olive)

Originator: Russell Ellis
Tier: Russell Ellis

Hook:	#20-22 Tiemco 2487
Thread:	Olive 8/0 Uni
Body:	Tying thread
Rib:	Copper Lagartun wire (extra fine)
Wing:	Black ostrich herl plumes

Ostrich Herl Midge (Tan)

Originator: Russell Ellis
Tier: Russell Ellis

Hook:	#20-22 Tiemco 2487
Thread:	Rusty dun 8/0 Uni
Body:	Tying thread
Rib:	Gold Lagartun wire (extra fine)
Wing:	Black ostrich herl plumes

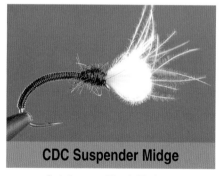

CDC Suspender Midge

Originator: Henk Verhaar
Tier: Henk Verhaar

Hook:	#16-22 Tiemco 2487
Thread:	Red 8/0 Uni
Underbody:	Tying thread
Body:	Nylon monofilament
Thorax:	Red Spectrablend dubbing
Wing:	CDC

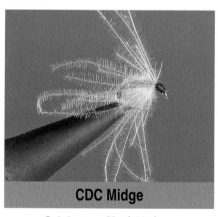

CDC Midge

Originator: Henk Verhaar
Tier: Henk Verhaar

Hook:	#16 Tiemco 2487
Thread:	Black 8/0 Uni
Body:	Tan CDC
Collar:	Cream CDC
Head:	Tying thread

Note: This pattern was inspired by Hans Weilenmann's CDC & Elk.

Paraloop Midge Emerger

Originator: Martin Westbeek
Tier: Martin Westbeek

Hook: #20 Partridge Klinkhammer
Thread: Charcoal 16/0 Tiemco
Body: Peccary hair
Thorax: Peacock herl
Paraloop post: White poly yarn
Hackle: Whiting speckled badger saddle
Note: The badger hackles have a blurred outline, which I think looks more alive and moving than other hackle. Substitute with a grizzly hackle if you wish.

Snowshoe Bubble Emerger

Originator: Martin Westbeek
Tier: Martin Westbeek

Hook: #17 Tiemco 102Y
Thread: Charcoal 16/0 Tiemco
Tail: Dark dun snowshoe hare
Body: Dark dun snowshoe hare underfur
Wing: Dark dun snowshoe hare
Note: The Bubble Emerger was originally a CDC fly.

Snowshoe Palomino Midge

Originator: Brett Smith
Tier: Martin Westbeek

Hook: #16-18 Tiemco 2488
Thread: Charcoal 16/0 Tiemco
Body: Tan Ultra Chenille
Thorax: Natural squirrel SLF
Wing: Natural cream snowshoe hare

Flash Midge

Originator: Scott Stisser
Tier: Scott Stisser

Hook: #18-20 Tiemco 2487 or 2488
Thread: Black 6/0 Danville
Body: Pearl Krystal Flash
Thorax: Olive dubbing
Hackle: Black ostrich herl

Suspender Midge

Originator: John Mundinger
Tier: John Mundinger

Hook: #20 Mustad 94840
Thread: Black 8/0 Uni
Shuck: White Antron
Body: Tying thread
Rib: Peacock Krystal Flash
Wing post: White closed-cell foam
Hackle: Grizzly
Thorax: Peacock herl

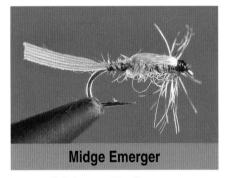

Midge Emerger

Originator: Ken Iwamasa
Tier: Ken Iwamasa

Hook: #18-20 Mustad 94833
Thread: Brown 14/0 Gordon Griffiths
Shuck: Gray duck quill
Thorax: Tan dubbing
Legs: Grizzly hackle
Back: White poly yarn

Coming Out Midge Emerger

Originator: Jeff Henkemeyer
Tier: Jeff Henkemeyer

Hook:	#18-22 Tiemco 2487
Thread:	Black 8/0 Uni
Tail:	Grizzly hen hackle tip
Body:	Black thread
Wing:	White Z-lon
Hackle:	Grizzly

Coming Out Midge Emerger (Holographic Silver)

Originator: Jeff Henkemeyer
Tier: Jeff Henkemeyer

Hook:	#18-22 Tiemco 2487
Thread:	Black 8/0 Uni
Tail:	Grizzly hackle tips
Body:	Holographic Tinsel (small)
Wing:	White Z-lon
Hackle:	Grizzly strung saddle

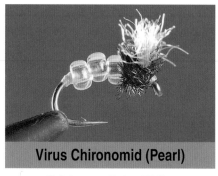

Virus Chironomid (Pearl)

Originator: Rainy Riding
Tier: Rainy's Fly Company

Hook:	#18-22 Tiemco 2487
Body:	Pearl clear beads
Thread:	White 8/0 Uni
Thorax:	Peacock herl
Wing:	White poly yarn

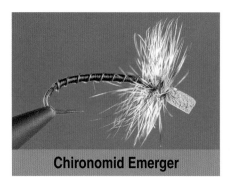

Chironomid Emerger

Originator: John Shewey
Tier: Rainy's Fly Company

Hook:	#12-16 Tiemco 200R
Thread:	Red 6/0 Uni
Body:	Tying thread
Rib:	Copper Ultra Wire (small)
Hackle:	Grizzly
Thorax:	Peacock herl
Gills:	Gray Evazote Foam (⅛ mm)

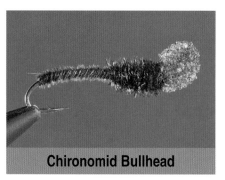

Chironomid Bullhead

Originator: John Shewey
Tier: Rainy's Fly Company

Hook:	#12-16 Tiemco 200R
Thread:	Black 8/0 Uni
Body:	Natural pheasant tail
Rib:	Gold Lagartun wire (fine)
Thorax:	Peacock herl
Gills:	Gray foam

Crystal Serendipity (Green)

Originator: Rainy Riding
Tier: Rainy's Fly Company

Hook:	#16-18 Tiemco 2487
Thread:	White 6/0 Uni
Body:	Olive Krystal Flash, twisted
Thorax:	Natural deer hair

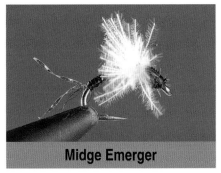

Midge Emerger

Originator: Todd Smith
Tier: Rainy's Fly Company

Hook: #18-22 Tiemco 2487
Thread: Black 8/0 Uni
Tail: Root beer Krystal Flash
Body: Black Krystal Flash
Wing: White Trouthunter CDC
Wing case: Black Stretch Flex
Thorax: Black Nature's Spirit dubbing

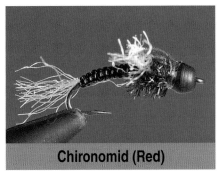

Chironomid (Red)

Originator: Rainy Riding
Tier: Rainy's Fly Company

Hook: #10-18 Tiemco 2302
Bead: Black metal
Thread: Clear 8/0 Uni
Shuck: White Antron
Rib: Red D Rib
Wing case: Black duck quill
Thorax: Peacock herl
Gills: White Antron

Death Midge Emerger

Originator: Jason Haslam
Tier: Rainy's Fly Company

Hook: #18-22 Tiemco 2487
Thread: Black 8/0 Uni
Body: Black and white Coats & Clark rayon thread, twisted
Wing: Light dun CDC
Hackle: Grizzly

Crystal Serendipity (Red)

Originator: Rainy Riding
Tier: Rainy's Fly Company

Hook: #16-18 Tiemco 2487
Bead: Gold metal
Thread: White 6/0 Uni
Body: Red Krystal Flash, twisted
Thorax: Natural deer hair

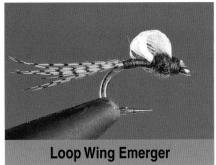

Loop Wing Emerger

Originator: John Gordon
Tier: John Gordon

Hook: #20 Tiemco 2488
Thread: Brown 8/0 Uni
Tail: Wood duck
Body: Tying thread
Thorax: Mahogany Super Fine
Wing: White Antron

Antron Wing Emerger

Originator: John Gordon
Tier: John Gordon

Hook: #24 Tiemco 2488
Thread: Black 8/0 Uni
Body: Tying thread
Rib: Copper Ultra Wire (extra small)
Thorax: Black Super Fine
Wing: White Antron

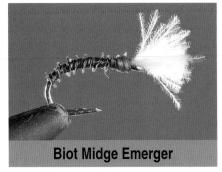

Biot Midge Emerger

Originator: John Gordon
Tier: John Gordon

Hook:	#20-24 Tiemco 2488
Thread:	Olive 8/0 Uni
Body:	Rusty brown goose biot
Thorax:	Tying thread
Wing:	White CDC puff

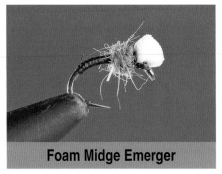

Foam Midge Emerger

Originator: John Gordon
Tier: John Gordon

Hook:	#24-26 Tiemco 2487
Thread:	Black 8/0 Uni
Body:	Tying thread
Thorax:	Gray Super Fine
Wing:	White closed-cell foam

Bubble Midge

Originator: Unknown
Tier: Dennis Shaw

Hook:	#12-18 Kamasan B100
Thread:	Black 70-denier UTC
Body:	Tying thread
Rib:	Mylar Tinsel
Thorax:	Black SLF Midge Pupa
Wing:	Two CDC feathers
Wing buds:	Grizzly hackle, pearl flash

Shrouded Buzzer

Originator: Dennis Shaw
Tier: Dennis Shaw

Hook:	#14-20 K14ST
Thread:	Black 10/0 Bennechi
Body:	Black 8/0 Uni
Rib:	Pearl Mylar tinsel (fine)
Thorax:	70% clear Antron, 30% black seal fur

Note: Brush the thorax with Velcro so that it shrouds the body. Apply floatant to the top of the shroud only and fish as you would a suspended Buzzer.

C and C Midge

Originator: Stuart Croft and Dave Calvert
Tier: Dennis Shaw

Hook:	#16-22 K14ST
Thread:	Olive 10/0 Bennechi
Tail:	White poly yarn
Body:	Olive beaver
Thorax:	Grizzly hackle
Wing:	White poly yarn

Midge 1

Originator: Chip Drozenski
Tier: Chip Drozenski

Hook:	#20-24 Tiemco 2487
Thread:	Black 8/0 Uni
Shuck:	Grizzly hackle point and CDC
Body:	Peacock herl
Wing:	Natural and dun CDC

TF No Name

Originator: Chip Drozenski
Tier: Chip Drozenski

Hook: #16-24 Tiemco 2487
Thread: Black 8/0 Uni
Shuck: CDC
Body: Peacock herl
Thorax: Peacock herl
Wing: Natural CDC

Black Emerger

Originator: Alex Ferguson
Tier: Alex Ferguson

Hook: #10-14 Partridge YMM2A
Thread: Black 8/0 Uni
Body: Tying thread
Rib 1:   Red Ultra Wire
                  (extra small)
Rib 2:   Fine copper wire
Wing buds: Goose biots dyed pale hot
                  orange
Hackle: Greenwells hen
Note: Coat the body and rib with Super
Glue and Sally Hansen Hard As Nails.

Brown Emerger

Originator: Alex Ferguson
Tier: Alex Ferguson

Hook: #10-14 Partridge YMM2A
Thread: Medium brown 8/0 Uni
Body: Tying thread
Rib 1:   UTC Mirage Tinsel (small)
Rib 2:   Fine copper wire
Wing buds: Goose biots dyed pale hot
                  orange
Hackle: Greenwells hen
Note: Coat the body and rib with Super
Glue and Sally Hansen Hard As Nails.

Green Emerger

Originator: Alex Ferguson
Tier: Alex Ferguson

Hook: #10-14 Partridge YMM2A
Thread: Medium olive 8/0 Uni
Body: Tying thread
Rib 1:   Pearl Uni Mylar (fine)
Rib 2:   Fine copper wire
Wing buds: Goose biots dyed pale hot
                  orange
Hackle: Greenwells hen dyed dark
Note: Coat the body and rib with Super
Glue and Sally Hansen Hard As Nails.

Fiery Brown Sugar Cube Buzzer

Originator: John Mapson
Tier: Alex Ferguson

Hook: #10-14 Partridge YMM2A
Thread: Brown 10/0 Power Silk
Post: Booby Cord
Body: Fiery brown seal fur
Rib: Gold Uni French tinsel
Thorax: Hot scarlet seal fur

Brown Stewart Type Emerger

Originator: Alex Ferguson
Tier: Alex Ferguson

Hook: #10-14 Partridge YMM2A
Thread: Brown 10/0 Power Silk
Body: Stripped peacock quill
Rib: Gold Uni French oval tinsel
Thorax: Hot orange seal fur,
              brushed with Velcro
Hackle: Greenwells cock or hen
Note: This pattern was inspired by W. C.
Stewart's famous spiders.

Black Widow Emerger

Originator: Chad Gauerke
Tier: Chad Gauerke

Hook:	#20 Dai-Riki 135
Bead:	Clear Quick Silver
Thread:	Black 8/0 Uni
Body:	Tying thread
Rib:	Silver Lagartun wire (fine)
Wing:	Jungle cock
Thorax:	Black Super Fine

Super Purple Hazard

Originator: Chad Gauerke
Tier: Chad Gauerke

Hook:	#20 Dai-Riki 270
Bead:	Purple aqua Czech
Thread:	Purple 8/0 Uni
Body:	Tying thread
Rib:	Silver Lagartun wire (fine)
Wing:	Purple Krystal Flash
Wing Case:	UTC Mirage Tinsel
Gills:	Natural CDC

Mighty Q Midge

Originator: Chad Gauerke
Tier: Chad Gauerke

Hook:	#20 Dai-Riki 135
Bead:	Wine glass
Thread:	Black 8/0 Uni
Body:	Gold Lagartun wire (fine)
Thorax:	Bronze peacock Arizona dubbing
Wing:	Olive CDC

Zebra Puff

Originator: Chad Gauerke
Tier: Chad Gauerke

Hook:	#20 Dai-Riki 135
Bead:	Silver mercury glass
Thread:	Black 10/0 Gudebrod
Body:	Tying thread
Rib:	Silver Lagartun wire (fine)
Thorax:	Bronze peacock Arizona dubbing
Gills:	Medium dun CDC

Purple Weapon

Originator: Chad Gauerke
Tier: Chad Gauerke

Hook:	#20 Dai-Riki 270
Thread:	Purple 8/0 Uni
Body:	Tying thread
Rib:	Blue Lagartun wire (fine)
Wing:	Jungle cock, split
Head:	Tying thread

Hatching Midge

Originator: Chad Gauerke
Tier: Chad Gauerke

Hook:	#12 YK6 ST
Thread:	Black 8/0 Uni
Bead:	Silver crystal Czech
Wing buds:	UTC Mirage Tinsel
Body:	Tying thread
Rib:	Silver Lagartun wire (fine)
Thorax:	Peacock Simiseal dubbing
Wing:	Natural CDC
Head:	Tying thread

Olive Parachute Hopper Midge

Originator: Unknown
Tier: Alex Ferguson

Hook:	#10-14 Hyabusa 752
Thread:	Olive 10/0 Power Silk
Body:	An equal mix of medium olive and brown olive seal fur brushed with Velcro
Rib:	Gold oval tinsel (fine)
Post:	Booby Cord
Legs:	Pheasant tail fibers dyed olive, knotted
Hackle:	Medium red game cock dyed olive

Claret Parachute Hopper Midge

Originator: Alex Ferguson
Tier: Alex Ferguson

Hook:	#10-14 Hyabusa 752
Thread:	Red 10/0 Power Silk
Body:	An equal mix of dark claret, medium claret, and crimson seal fur brushed with Velcro
Rib:	Gold oval tinsel (fine)
Post:	Booby Cord
Legs:	Six cock pheasant tail fibers dyed olive, knotted
Hackle:	Medium red game cock dyed olive

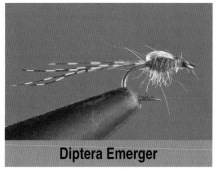

Diptera Emerger

Originator: Mike Kimball
Tier: Russell Stanton

Hook:	#26 Partridge K1A
Thread:	Tan 10/0 Gudebrod
Tail:	Teal flank barbs
Thorax:	Gray beaver
Wing case:	Poly yarn

Zebra Midge (Variation #1)

Originator: Russell Stanton
Tier: Russell Stanton

Hook:	#22 Tiemco 101
Thread:	White 10/0 Gudebrod
Body:	Dental floss
Rib:	Black Coats & Clark
Wing buds:	White Z-lon
Thorax:	Black beaver

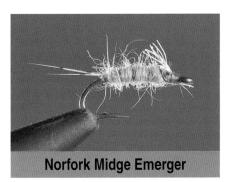

Norfork Midge Emerger

Originator: Russell Stanton
Tier: Russell Stanton

Hook:	#22 Tiemco 101
Thread:	Gray 10/0 Gudebrod
Tail:	Dun hackle
Body:	Gray (60%), olive (20%), and brown (20%) dubbing
Rib:	Copper Lagartun wire (fine)
Wing buds:	White Z-lon

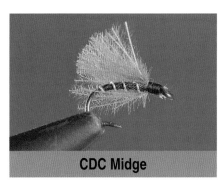

CDC Midge

Originator: Russell Stanton
Tier: Russell Stanton

Hook:	#24 Partridge K1A
Thread:	Black 12/0 Bennechi
Body:	Tying thread
Wing:	Natural CDC, trimmed
Rib:	Silver Lagartun wire (extra fine)

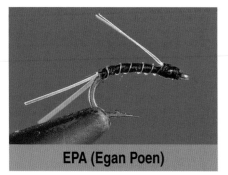

EPA (Egan Poen)

Originator: Kelli Sandoval
Tier: Kelli Sandoval

Hook:	#22-26 Tiemco 2488
Thread:	Black 70-denier UTC
Shuck/Wing:	Pearl Krystal Flash
Body:	Tying thread
Rib:	Copper Lagartun wire (extra fine)
Head:	Tying thread

Glitter Wing Emerger (Golden)

Originator: Rick Takahashi
Tier: Rick Takahashi

Hook:	#18-24 Tiemco 2487
Thread:	White 8/0 Uni
Body:	Golden olive Glitter Thread
Wing:	Pearl Glitter Thread
Collar:	Black Super Fine

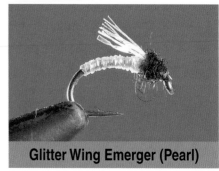

Glitter Wing Emerger (Pearl)

Originator: Rick Takahashi
Tier: Rick Takahashi

Hook:	#18-24 Tiemco 2487
Thread:	White 8/0 Uni
Body:	Pearl Glitter Thread
Wing:	Pearl Glitter Thread
Collar:	Black Super Fine

Glitter Wing Emerger (Black)

Originator: Rick Takahashi
Tier: Rick Takahashi

Hook:	#18-24 Tiemco 2487
Thread:	White 8/0 Uni
Body:	Black Glitter Thread
Wing:	Pearl Glitter Thread
Collar:	Black Super Fine

Glitter Wing Emerger (Tan)

Originator: Rick Takahashi
Tier: Rick Takahashi

Hook:	#18-24 Tiemco 2487
Thread:	White 8/0 Uni
Body:	Pearl Glitter Thread
Wing:	Pearl Glitter Thread
Collar:	Black Super Fine

Note: Color the Glitter Thread for the body with tan Chartpak marker.

Glitter Wing Emerger (Rust)

Originator: Rick Takahashi
Tier: Rick Takahashi

Hook:	#18-24 Tiemco 2487
Thread:	White 8/0 Uni
Body:	Rust Glitter Thread
Wing:	Pearl Glitter Thread
Collar:	Black Super Fine

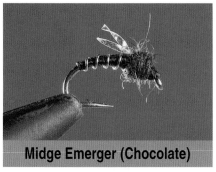

Midge Emerger (Chocolate)

Originator: Unknown
Tier: Rick Takahashi

Hook:	#18-24 Tiemco 2487
Thread:	Brown 8/0 Uni
Body:	Tying thread
Rib:	Copper Lagartun wire (fine)
Wing:	Pearl Krystal Flash
Collar:	Brown Super Fine

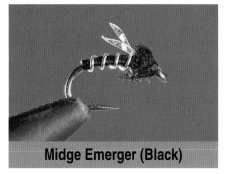

Midge Emerger (Black)

Originator: Unknown
Tier: Rick Takahashi

Hook:	#18-24 Tiemco 2487
Thread:	Black 8/0 Uni
Body:	Tying thread
Rib:	Silver Lagartun wire (fine)
Wing:	Pearl Krystal Flash
Collar:	Black Super Fine

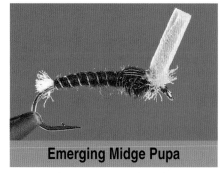

Emerging Midge Pupa

Originator: Paul Lasha
Tier: Rick Takahashi

Hook:	#12-16 Tiemco 2302
Thread:	Black 8/0 Uni
Body:	Black wool yarn
Tail:	White poly yarn
Rib:	Silver Lagartun wire (fine)
Collar:	Peacock herl
Wing case:	Olive pheasant tail
Gills:	White poly yarn
Emerging pupa:	Tan foam

Hanging Midge (Black)

Originator: Rick Takahashi
Tier: Rick Takahashi

Hook:	#12-16 Tiemco 206BL
Thread:	Black 8/0 Uni
Body:	Tying thread
Tail:	White poly yarn
Rib:	Silver Lagartun wire (fine)
Thorax:	Peacock herl
Wing buds:	Orange goose biots
Wing case:	CDC colored dark brown
Gills:	Tan CDC

Hanging Midge (Olive)

Originator: Rick Takahashi
Tier: Rick Takahashi

Hook:	#12-16 Tiemco 206BL
Thread:	Olive 8/0 Uni
Body:	Tying thread
Tail:	White poly yarn
Rib:	Orange thread
Thorax:	Peacock herl
Wing buds:	Orange goose biots
Wing case:	CDC colored tan
Gills:	Tan CDC

Hanging Midge (Gray)

Originator: Rick Takahashi
Tier: Rick Takahashi

Hook:	#12-16 Tiemco 206BL
Thread:	White 8/0 Uni
Body:	Tying thread
Tail:	White poly yarn
Rib:	Pearl Krystal Flash
Thorax:	Peacock herl
Wing buds:	Orange goose biots
Wing case:	CDC colored tan
Gills:	Tan CDC

Note: For the body, color the tying thread with gray Chartpak marker.

Hanging Midge (Olive)

Originator: Rick Takahashi
Tier: Rick Takahashi

Hook:	#12-16 Tiemco 206BL
Thread:	White 8/0 Uni
Tail:	White poly yarn
Body:	Tying thread
Rib:	Pearl Krystal Flash
Thorax:	Peacock herl
Wing buds:	Orange goose biots
Wing case:	CDC colored tan
Gills:	Two tan CDC feathers

Note: For the body, color the tying thread with olive Chartpak marker.

Micro Flashback (Black)

Originator: Bill Black
Tier: Spirit River

Hook:	#12-18 Spear-It D312
Thread:	Tan 8/0 Uni
Body:	Black Flex-Floss
Rib:	Tying thread
Flash:	Pearl Mirror Flash
Wing:	Tan CDC puff
Thorax:	Black Fine and Dry
Wing case:	Pearl Mirror Flash

Note: Other hook(s): Daiichi 1260.

Micro Flashback (Red)

Originator: Bill Black
Tier: Spirit River

Hook:	#18-22 Spear-It CS200
Thread:	Red 8/0 Uni
Body:	Red Flex-Floss
Rib:	Black 8/0 Uni
Flash:	Pearl Mirror Flash
Wing:	White CDC puff
Thorax:	Brown Fine and Dry
Wing case:	Pearl Mirror Flash

Note: Other hook(s): Daiichi 1270.

Micro Flashback (Brown)

Originator: Bill Black
Tier: Spirit River

Hook:	#18-22 Spear-It CS200
Thread:	Black 8/0 Uni
Body:	Brown Flex-Floss
Rib:	Tying thread
Flash:	Pearl Mirror Flash
Wing:	Tan CDC puff
Thorax:	Olive Fine and Dry
Wing case:	Pearl Mirror Flash

Note: Other hook(s): Daiichi 1270.

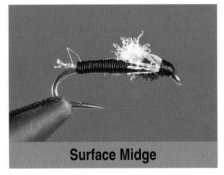

Surface Midge

Originator: Rico Moore
Tier: Rico Moore

Hook:	#18-20 Tiemco 3761
Thread:	Black 10/0 Gudebrod
Tail:	Pearl Krystal Flash
Body:	Black Ultra Wire (small)
Wing buds:	UV pearl Ice Dub
Thorax:	UV black Ice Dub
Legs:	White Fluoro Fibre

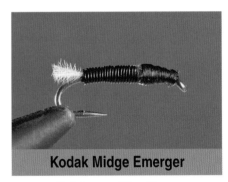

Kodak Midge Emerger

Originator: Rico Moore
Tier: Rico Moore

Hook:	#18-20 Tiemco 3761
Thread:	Black 10/0 Gudebrod
Tail:	Coq de Leon
Body:	Black Ultra Wire (small)
Thorax:	Tying thread

Breaking the Surface Midge

Originator: Rico Moore
Tier: Rico Moore

Hook:	#18-24 Tiemco 2487
Thread:	Black 10/0 Gudebrod
Tail:	White CDC
Body:	Tying thread
Rib:	Black Ultra Wire (small)
Wing case:	Black foam
Wing:	White CDC

Midge #3

Originator: Chip Drozenski
Tier: Chip Drozenski

Hook:	#18-24 Tiemco 2487
Thread:	Black 8/0 Uni
Shuck:	Pearl Krystal Flash
Body:	Tying thread
Rib:	Silver Lagartun wire (extra fine)
Wing:	White Antron
Thorax:	Gray Super Fine
Hackle:	Grizzly tied Hackle Stacker style

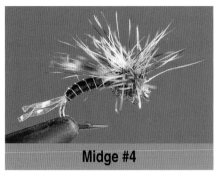

Midge #4

Originator: Chip Drozenski
Tier: Chip Drozenski

Hook:	#18-24 Tiemco 2487
Thread:	Black 8/0 Uni
Shuck:	Pearl Krystal Flash
Body:	Tying thread
Rib:	Silver Lagartun wire (extra fine)
Wing:	Grizzly hackle tips
Thorax:	Gray Super Fine
Hackle:	Grizzly tied Hackle Stacker style

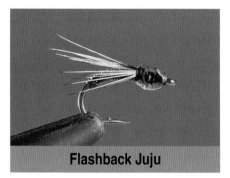

Flashback Juju

Originator: Charlie Craven (variation)
Tier: Chad Gauerke

Hook:	#20 Dai-Riki 125
Thread:	White 10/0 Uni
Body:	Brown Super Hair
Rib:	Red Super Hair
Wing:	Jungle fowl
Wing case:	UTC Mirage Tinsel
Head:	Black 8/0 Uni

Brown Orange Paraloop Emerger

Originator: Sue Armstrong
Tier: Sue Armstrong

Hook:	#12-20 Tiemco 2487
Thread:	Dark brown 70-denier UTC
Body:	Tying thread
Rib:	Burnt orange 70-denier UTC
Thorax:	Dark brown Super Fine
Hackle:	Grizzly

Mountain Midge

Originator: Jeremy Davies
Tier: Jeremy Davies

Hook:	#12-20 Tiemco 2487
Thread:	Olive 8/0 Uni
Tail:	Brown Antron
Body:	Natural peacock Arizona dubbing
Rib:	Gold Lagartun wire (extra fine)
Wing:	White Antron
Hackle:	Grizzly

Griffith's Gnat Emerger

Originator: Craig Mathews
Tier: Craig Mathews

Hook:	#18-24 Tiemco 2488
Thread:	Olive 70-denier UTC
Shuck:	Olive Z-lon
Body:	Tying thread
Thorax:	Peacock herl
Hackle:	Grizzly

Improved Zelon Midge

Originator: Craig Mathews
Tier: Craig Mathews

Hook:	#18-24 Tiemco 2488
Thread:	Olive 70-denier UTC
Shuck:	White Z-lon
Body:	Tying thread
Thorax:	Black Super Fine
Wing:	White Z-lon

Three Dollar Dipity

Originator: Craig Mathews
Tier: Craig Mathews

Hook:	#18-24 Tiemco 2488
Thread:	Red 8/0 Uni
Body:	Tying thread
Rib:	Copper Lagartun wire (fine)
Wing:	White deer hair, clipped
Head:	Tying thread

Snowshoe Emerger

Originator: Jim Cannon
Tier: Jim Cannon

Hook:	#18-22 Tiemco 2488
Thread:	Black 8/0 Uni
Wing:	Snowshoe rabbit foot hair
Body:	Black UTC Vinyl D Rib

Note: Wing is a blend of 33% bleached white hair, 33% dyed black hair, and 33% pearl Ice Dub.

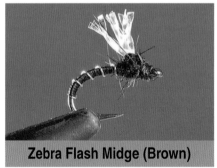

Zebra Flash Midge (Brown)

Originator: Unknown
Tier: Pacific Fly Group

Hook:	#20-24 Tiemco 2488
Thread:	Brown 8/0 Uni
Body:	Tying thread
Rib:	Silver Ultra Wire (extra small)
Thorax:	Black dubbing
Wing:	Pearl Krystal Flash

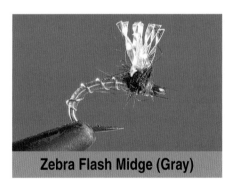

Zebra Flash Midge (Gray)

Originator: Unknown
Tier: Pacific Fly Group

Hook:	#20-24 Tiemco 2488
Thread:	Light gray 8/0 Uni
Body:	Tying thread
Rib:	Silver Ultra Wire (extra small)
Thorax:	Black dubbing
Wing:	Pearl Krystal Flash

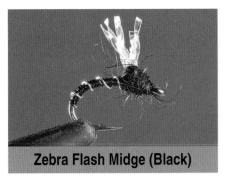

Zebra Flash Midge (Black)

Originator: Unknown
Tier: Pacific Fly Group

Hook:	#20-24 Tiemco 2488
Thread:	Black 8/0 Uni
Body:	Tying thread
Rib:	Silver Ultra Wire (extra small)
Thorax:	Black dubbing
Wing:	Pearl Krystal Flash

Flash Midge (Gray)

Originator: Johnny Gomez
Tier: Pacific Fly Group

Hook:	#20-24 Daiichi 1130
Thread:	Light gray 8/0 Uni
Tail:	Brown hackle
Body:	Tying thread
Thorax:	Light gray dubbing
Wing:	Pearl Krystal Flash

Flash Midge (Black)

Originator: Johnny Gomez
Tier: Pacific Fly Group

Hook:	#20-24 Daiichi 1130
Thread:	Black 8/0 Uni
Tail:	Black hackle
Body:	Tying thread
Thorax:	Black dubbing
Wing:	Pearl Krystal Flash

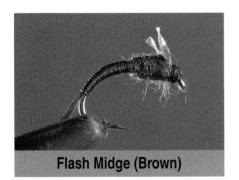

Flash Midge (Brown)

Originator: Johnny Gomez
Tier: Pacific Fly Group

Hook:	#20-24 Daiichi 1130
Thread:	Dark brown 8/0 Uni
Tail:	Brown hackle
Body:	Tying thread
Thorax:	Brown Super Fine
Wing:	Pearl Krystal Flash

Chironomid Emerger (Olive)

Originator: Dennis Komatsu
Tier: Pacific Fly Group

Hook:	#16-20 Daiichi 1560
Thread:	Black 6/0 Uni
Tail/Gills:	White poly yarn
Body:	Stripped olive hackle stem
Wing:	Grizzly hen cape
Thorax:	Peacock herl

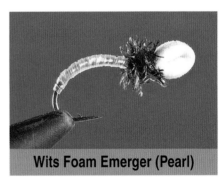

Wits Foam Emerger (Pearl)

Originator: Willie Kamura
Tier: Pacific Fly Group

Hook:	#16-20 Daiichi 1130
Thread:	White 6/0 Uni
Body:	Pearl Krystal Flash
Post:	White 2mm foam
Thorax:	Peacock herl

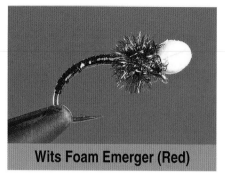

Wits Foam Emerger (Red)

Originator: Willie Kamura
Tier: Pacific Fly Group

Hook:	#16-20 Daiichi 1130
Thread:	Light gray 6/0 Uni
Body:	Red Krystal Flash
Post:	White 2mm foam
Thorax:	Peacock herl

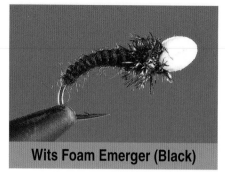

Wits Foam Emerger (Black)

Originator:Willie Kamura
Tier: Pacific Fly Group

Hook:	#16-20 Daiichi 1130
Thread:	Black 6/0 Uni
Body:	Black Super Fine
Post:	White 2mm foam
Thorax:	Peacock herl

Wits Foam Emerger (Green)

Originator: Willie Kamura
Tier: Pacific Fly Group

Hook:	#16-20 Daiichi 1130
Thread:	White 6/0 Uni
Body:	Olive Krystal Flash
Post:	White 2mm foam
Thorax:	Peacock herl

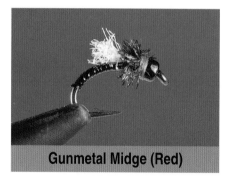

Gunmetal Midge (Red)

Originator: Tom Whitly
Tier: Pacific Fly Group

Hook:	#16-20 Daiichi 1130
Bead:	Gunmetal Killer Caddis
Thread:	Gray 8/0 Uni
Body:	Red Flashabou
Wing:	White Antron
Thorax:	Peacock herl

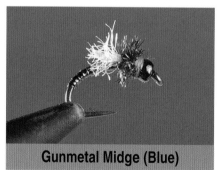

Gunmetal Midge (Blue)

Originator: Tom Whitly
Tier: Pacific Fly Group

Hook:	#16-20 Daiichi 1130
Bead:	Gunmetal Killer Caddis
Thread:	Gray 8/0 Uni
Body:	Blue Flashabou
Wing:	White Antron
Thorax:	Peacock herl

Gunmetal Midge (Green)

Originator: Tom Whitly
Tier: Pacific Fly Group

Hook:	#16-20 Daiichi 1130
Bead:	Gunmetal Killer Caddis
Thread:	Gray 8/0 Uni
Body:	Pearl Flashabou
Wing:	White Antron
Thorax:	Peacock herl

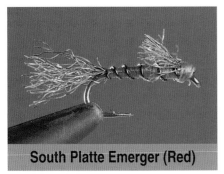

South Platte Emerger (Red)

Originator: Unknown
Tier: Pacific Fly Group

Hook: #16-22 Daiichi 1100
Thread: Light gray 8/0 Uni
Body: Tying thread
Rib: Red Ultra Wire
(extra small)
Tail/Wing: Pink Antron

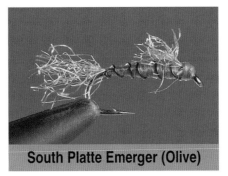

South Platte Emerger (Olive)

Originator: Unknown
Tier: Pacific Fly Group

Hook: #16-22 Daiichi 1100
Thread: Light gray 8/0 Uni
Body: Tying thread
Rib: Olive Ultra Wire
(extra small)
Tail/Wing: Light olive Antron

Top Secret Midge

Originator: Pat Dorsey
Tier: Pat Dorsey

Hook: #20-26 Tiemco 2488
Thread: Brown 8/0 Uni
Body: Tying thread
Rib: White 6/0 Uni
Wing: White Fluoro Fibre
Thorax: Rust Super Fine
Note: Other hook(s): Dai-Riki 125.

Dryemerger (Amber)

Originator: James Ferrin
Tier: Pacific Fly Group

Hook: #16-22 Daiichi 1120
Thread: Tan 6/0 Uni
Post: White Antron
Hackle: Brown
Body: Amber UTC Vinyl D Rib
Wing buds: White Antron
Thorax: Peacock herl

Dryemerger (Brassie)

Originator: James Ferrin
Tier: Pacific Fly Group

Hook: #16-22 Daiichi 1120
Thread: Tan 6/0 Uni
Post: White Antron
Hackle: Grizzly
Body: Red Ultra Wire
(extra small)
Wing buds: White Antron
Thorax: Peacock herl

Dryemerger (Black Silhouette)

Originator: James Ferrin
Tier: Pacific Fly Group

Hook: #16-22 Daiichi 1120
Thread: Black 6/0 Uni
Post: Black Antron
Hackle: Black
Body: Black UTC Vinyl D Rib
Thorax: Black ostrich herl

Dryemerger (Black)

Originator: James Ferrin
Tier: Pacific Fly Group

Hook:	#16-22 Daiichi 1120
Thread:	Black 6/0 Uni
Post:	White Antron
Hackle:	Black
Body:	Tying thread
Rib:	Copper Ultra Wire (small)
Wing buds:	White Antron
Thorax:	Peacock herl

Dryemerger (Olive)

Originator: James Ferrin
Tier: Pacific Fly Group

Hook:	#16-22 Daiichi 1120
Thread:	Olive 6/0 Uni
Post:	White Antron
Hackle:	Light dun
Body:	Tying thread
Rib:	Copper Ultra Wire (small)
Wing buds:	White Antron
Thorax:	Peacock herl

Dryemerger (Gray)

Originator: James Ferrin
Tier: Pacific Fly Group

Hook:	#16-22 Daiichi 1120
Thread:	Light gray 6/0 Uni
Post:	White Antron
Hackle:	Light dun
Body:	Tying thread
Rib:	Copper Ultra Wire (small)
Wing buds:	White Antron
Thorax:	Peacock herl

Dryemerger (Red)

Originator: James Ferrin
Tier: Pacific Fly Group

Hook:	#16-22 Daiichi 1120
Thread:	Tan 6/0 Uni
Post:	White Antron
Hackle:	Brown
Body:	Red Micro Tubing
Wing buds:	White Antron
Thorax:	Peacock herl

Brassie Dryemerger (Copper)

Originator: James Ferrin
Tier: Pacific Fly Group

Hook:	#16-22 Daiichi 1120
Thread:	Tan 6/0 Uni
Post:	White Antron
Hackle:	Brown and grizzly
Body:	Copper Ultra Wire (extra small)
Wing buds:	White Antron
Thorax:	Peacock herl

Lady McConnell

Originator: Unknown
Tier: Brian Chan

Hook:	#10-16 Mustad R30
Thread:	Black 8/0 Uni
Tail:	White Z-lon and grizzly hackle tip
Body:	Black dubbing
Back:	Deer hair
Hackle:	Grizzly

EA's Micro Midge

Originator: Eric Pettine
Tier: Eric Pettine

Hook:	#22-26 Tiemco 101
Thread:	Medium gray 10/0 Gudebrod
Tail:	Medium gray Antron
Body:	Medium gray blue dun hackle
Overbody:	Black closed-cell foam
Hackle:	Dun

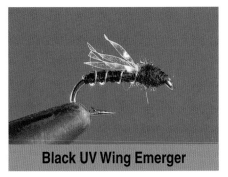

Black UV Wing Emerger

Originator: ATF Fly Shop
Tier: Tim Mack

Hook:	#22-26 Tiemco 100
Thread:	Black 10/0 Bennechi
Body:	Tying thread
Rib:	Copper Lagartun wire (fine)
Wing:	Pearl UV Krystal Flash
Thorax:	Black Super Fine

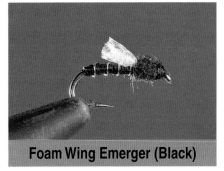

Foam Wing Emerger (Black)

Originator: ATF Fly Shop
Tier: Tim Mack

Hook:	#22-26 Tiemco 100
Thread:	Black 10/0 Bennechi
Body:	Tying thread
Rib:	Copper Lagartun wire (fine)
Wing:	White thin packaging foam
Thorax:	Black Super Fine

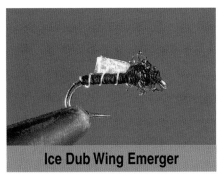

Ice Dub Wing Emerger

Originator: ATF Fly Shop
Tier: Tim Mack

Hook:	#22-26 Tiemco 100
Thread:	Black 10/0 Bennechi
Body:	Tying thread
Rib:	Silver Lagartun wire (fine)
Wing:	White thin packaging foam
Thorax:	Black Ice Dub

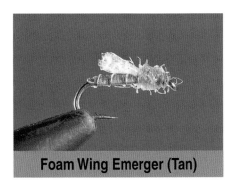

Foam Wing Emerger (Tan)

Originator: ATF Fly Shop
Tier: Tim Mack

Hook:	#22-26 Tiemco 100
Thread:	Tan 10/0 Bennechi
Body:	Tying thread
Rib:	Gold Lagartun wire (fine)
Wing:	White packaging foam
Thorax:	Tan Ice Dub

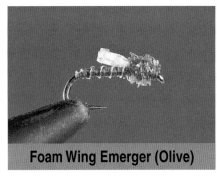

Foam Wing Emerger (Olive)

Originator: ATF Fly Shop
Tier: Tim Mack

Hook:	#22-26 Tiemco 100
Thread:	Olive 10/0 Bennechi
Body:	Tying thread
Rib:	Gold Lagartun wire (fine)
Wing:	White packaging foam
Thorax:	Olive Ice Dub

Midgie Modger (Black)

Originator: Unknown
Tier: Montana Fly Company

Hook:	#10-14 MFC 7048
Bead:	Black glass
Thread:	Black 6/0 Uni
Wing:	White Gator Hair
Tail:	Black Flashabou Accent
Body:	Black Ultra Wire
Thorax:	Natural peacock herl

Midgie Modger (Red)

Originator: Unknown
Tier: Montana Fly Company

Hook:	#14-20 MFC 7045
Thread:	Black 6/0 Uni
Bead:	Red glass
Tail:	Black Flashabou Accent
Body:	Red Ultra Wire
Wing:	White Gator Hair
Thorax:	Natural peacock herl

Otter's Micro Midge Emerger (Black)

Originator: Walt Mueller
Tier: Montana Fly Company

Hook:	#20-22 MFC 7000
Thread:	Black 8/0 Uni
Body:	Black UTC Vinyl D Rib
Wing:	Bright white Antron Body Wool
Head:	Black Frog's Hair

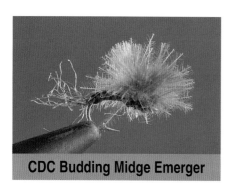

CDC Budding Midge Emerger

Originator: Unknown
Tier: Montana Fly Company

Hook:	#16-22 MFC 7048
Thread:	Black 8/0 Uni
Tail:	Rusty brown Z-lon
Body:	Black Super Floss and brown Tentacles
Thorax:	Peacock Wing N' Flash
Post:	White 4mm foam tube
Hackle:	Natural dun CDC

Black Midge Cripple

Originator: Unknown
Tier: Montana Fly Company

Hook:	#10-14 MFC 7048
Thread:	Black 8/0 Uni
Tail:	Pearl Krystal Flash
Body:	Black Flashabou Accent
Thorax:	Black Frog's Hair
Wing:	White CDC
Hackle:	Grizzly

CDC Winged Midge

Originator: Unknown
Tier: Montana Fly Company

Hook:	#10-14 MFC 7009 or Daiichi 1120
Thread:	Black 8/0 Uni
Tail:	Pearl Krystal Flash
Body:	Black Flashabou Accent
Wing:	White CDC
Wing case:	Black Spider Legs
Thorax:	Black Frog's Hair

Gray Midge Soft Hackle

Originator: Yancey Cox
Tier: Yancey Cox

Hook:	#19-21 Tiemco 103BL
Thread:	Brown 14/0 Gordon Griffiths
Body:	Tying thread
Rib:	Twisted tying thread
Hackle:	Starling

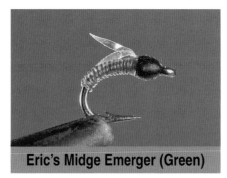

Eric's Midge Emerger (Green)

Originator: Jason Goodale
Tier: Jason Goodale

Hook:	#18-24 Tiemco 2488
Thread:	Green 10/0 Bennechi
Underbody:	Tying thread
Body:	.005 clear mono
Wing:	Pearl Krystal Flash
Head:	Black 10/0 covered with Loon UV Knot Sense

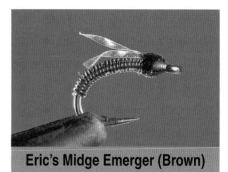

Eric's Midge Emerger (Brown)

Originator: Jason Goodale
Tier: Jason Goodale

Hook:	#18-24 Tiemco 2488
Thread:	Brown 10/0 Bennechi
Underbody:	Tying thread
Body:	.005 clear mono
Wing:	Pearl Krystal Flash
Head:	Black 10/0 covered with Loon UV Knot Sense

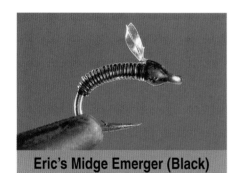

Eric's Midge Emerger (Black)

Originator: Jason Goodale
Tier: Jason Goodale

Hook:	#18-24 Tiemco 2488
Thread:	Black 10/0 Bennechi
Underbody:	Tying thread
Body:	.005 clear mono
Wing:	Pearl Krystal Flash
Head:	Black 10/0 covered with Loon UV Knot Sense

Eric's Midge Emerger (Olive)

Originator: Jason Goodale
Tier: Jason Goodale

Hook:	#18-24 Tiemco 2488
Thread:	Olive 10/0 Bennechi
Underbody:	Tying thread
Body:	.005 clear mono
Wing:	Pearl Krystal Flash
Head:	Black 10/0 covered with Loon UV Knot Sense

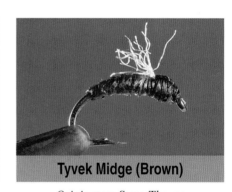

Tyvek Midge (Brown)

Originator: Steve Thrapp
Tier: Steve Thrapp

Hook:	#18-24 Tiemco 2487
Thread:	Black 8/0 Uni
Body:	Tyvek colored with brown Chartpak marker
Wing:	White Antron
Thorax:	Tying thread

L2HF Emerger

Originator: Al Ritt
Tier: Al Ritt

Hook: #16-22 Tiemco 2487
Thread: Black 14/0 Gordon Griffiths
Gills/Wing: Clear organza
Bead: Gunmetal glass
Underbody: Red 70-denier UTC
Body: Clear Micro Tubing
Rib: Silver Ultra Wire (extra small)
Thorax: Black peacock Ice Dub
Hackle: Starling

Vincent Vertical Midge (VVM)

Originator: Vincent Su
Tier: Vincent Su

Hook: #18-22 Tiemco 100
Thread: Tan 8/0 Uni
Body: Light olive UTC Vinyl D Rib
Post: White poly yarn
Thorax: Peacock Ice Dub
Hackle: Grizzly

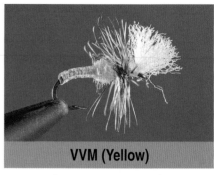

VVM (Yellow)

Originator: Vincent Su
Tier: Vincent Su

Hook: #18-22 Tiemco 100
Thread: White 8/0 Uni
Body: Yellow UTC Vinyl D Rib
Post: White poly yarn
Thorax: Yellow Ice Dub
Hackle: Grizzly

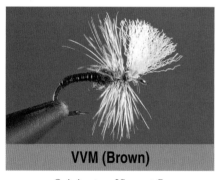

VVM (Brown)

Originator: Vincent Su
Tier: Vincent Su

Hook: #18-22 Tiemco 100
Thread: Tan 8/0 Uni
Body: Root beer UTC Vinyl D Rib
Post: White poly yarn
Thorax: Peacock Ice Dub
Hackle: Grizzly

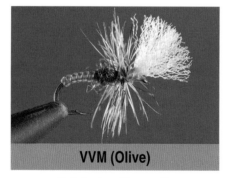

VVM (Olive)

Originator: Vincent Su
Tier: Vincent Su

Hook: #18-22 Tiemco 100
Thread: Olive 8/0 Uni
Body: Olive UTC Vinyl D Rib
Post: White poly yarn
Thorax: Peacock Ice Dub
Hackle: Grizzly

VVM (Black)

Originator: Vincent Su
Tier: Vincent Su

Hook: #18-22 Tiemco 100
Thread: Black 8/0 Uni
Body: Black UTC Vinyl D Rib
Post: White poly yarn
Thorax: Peacock Ice Dub
Hackle: Grizzly

Micro Chartreuse

Originator: Ron Donahue
Tier: Ron Donahue

Hook: #26 Tiemco 101
Thread: Chartreuse 8/0 Uni
Body: Tying thread
Wing: Chartreuse Antron
Head: Tying thread

Olive Star

Originator: Stan Benton
Tier: Stan Benton

Hook: #16-18 Tiemco 2487
Thread: Olive 14/0 Gordon Griffiths
Body: Olive Midge Bodi
Tag: Fl. lime green 6/0 Danville
Wing: Hen hackle
Hackle: Starling

Macaw Midge

Originator: Stan Benton
Tier: Stan Benton

Hook: #18-24 Tiemco 2487
Thread: Black 8/0 Uni
Body: Blue and gold macaw herl
from the tail feather
Wing: White Darlon
Collar: Trico Stalcup's Dry Fly
Dub

Shuckin' Midge

Originator: Stan Benton
Tier: Stan Benton

Hook: #22 Tiemco 2487
Thread: Tan 14/0 Gordon Griffiths
Bead: Silver metal
Shuck: White Darlon and pearl
Krystal Flash
Body: Tying thread
Collar: Cream beaver dubbing

Starling and Black

Originator: Stan Benton
Tier: Stan Benton

Hook: #18-22 Tiemco 2487
Thread: Black 8/0 Uni
Bead: Copper metal
Body: Black Ultra Wire (small)
Hackle: Starling

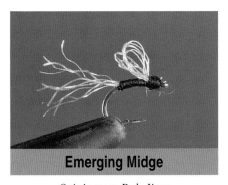

Emerging Midge

Originator: Rob Jiron
Tier: Rob Jiron

Hook: #18-22 Tiemco 2488
Thread: Black 8/0 Uni
Body: Tying thread
Shuck/Wing: White Antron

UV Pearl Soft Hackle Midge

Originator: Juan Ramirez
Tier: Juan Ramirez

Hook:	#20-24 Tiemco 2488
Thread:	White 14/0 Gordon Griffiths
Body:	Pearl UV Krystal Flash
Wing:	Dun hen hackle over white sparkle organza
Thorax:	UV gray Ice Dub

Note: Coat body with Loon Hard Head.

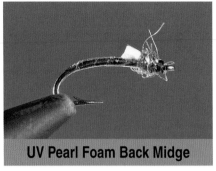

UV Pearl Foam Back Midge

Originator: Juan Ramirez
Tier: Juan Ramirez

Hook:	#20-24 Dai-Riki 270
Thread:	Black 14/0 Gordon Griffiths
Body:	Pearl UV Krystal Flash
Thorax:	White foam covered by UV gray Ice Dub

Note: Coat body with Loon Hard Head.

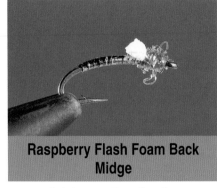

Raspberry Flash Foam Back Midge

Originator: Juan Ramirez
Tier: Juan Ramirez

Hook:	#20-24 Dai-Riki 270
Thread:	Gray 14/0 Gordon Griffiths
Body:	Pearl Krystal Flash dyed red
Thorax:	White foam covered by UV gray Ice Dub

Note: Coat body with Loon Hard Head.

Black Cherry Soft Hackle Midge

Originator: Juan Ramirez
Tier: Juan Ramirez

Hook:	#20-24 Tiemco 2488
Thread:	Black 14/0 Gordon Griffiths
Body:	Pearl Krystal Flash dyed red
Thorax:	Black hen hackle

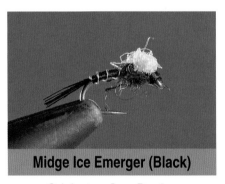

Midge Ice Emerger (Black)

Originator: Juan Ramirez
Tier: Juan Ramirez

Hook:	#20-24 Tiemco 2487
Thread:	Black 14/0 Gordon Griffiths
Tail:	Black hackle
Body:	Tying thread
Rib:	Copper Ultra Wire (fine)
Thorax:	Black Super Fine
Legs:	Black Fluoro Fibre
Wing:	UV pearl Ice Dub

Note: Tie in the dubbing for the wing as you would for a floating nymph.

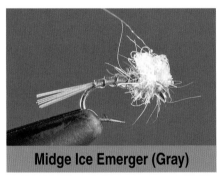

Midge Ice Emerger (Gray)

Originator: Juan Ramirez
Tier: Juan Ramirez

Hook:	#20-24 Tiemco 2457
Thread:	Gray 14/0 Gordon Griffiths
Tail:	Dun hackle
Body:	Tying thread
Rib:	Copper Ultra Wire (extra small)
Legs:	Gray Antron
Wing:	UV Callibaetis Ice Dub
Thorax:	Gray rabbit dubbing

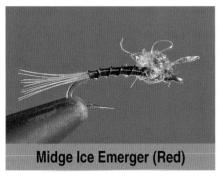

Midge Ice Emerger (Red)

Originator: Juan Ramirez
Tier: Juan Ramirez

Hook: #20-24 Tiemco 200R
Thread: Red 14/0 Gordon Griffiths
Tail: Dun hackle
Rib: Red Ultra Wire
(extra small)
Body: Tying thread
Legs: Dun hackle
Wing: UV gray Ice Dub

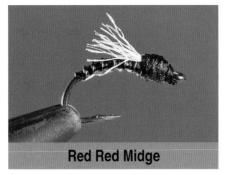

Red Red Midge

Originator: Steve Thrapp
Tier: Steve Thrapp

Hook: #18-22 Mustad C49S
Thread: Red 70-denier UTC
Rib: Red Ultra Wire
(extra small)
Body: Tying thread
Wing: White Antron
Thorax: Black tying thread

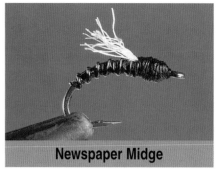

Newspaper Midge

Originator: Steve Thrapp
Tier: Steve Thrapp

Hook: #18-22 Mustad C49S
Thread: Black 8/0 Uni
Body: Tying thread
Rib: Red Ultra Wire
(extra small)
Wing: White Antron
Thorax: Tying thread

Ice Bead Midge

Originator: Steve Thrapp
Tier: Steve Thrapp

Hook: #18-22 Mustad C49S
Bead: Gunmetal Killer Caddis
Thread: Black 8/0 Uni
Body: Tying thread
Rib: Silver Ultra Wire
(extra small)
Wing: White Antron
Thorax: Peacock Ice Dub

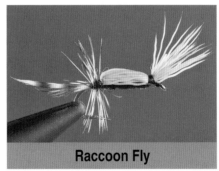

Raccoon Fly

Originator: Unknown
Tier: Steve Thrapp

Hook: #14-18 Tiemco 100
Thread: Black 70-denier UTC
Tail: Grizzly hackle tip
Hackle: Grizzly
Underbody: Black Uni Floss
Body: Tying thread
Back/Wing: Elk hair
Thorax: Tying thread

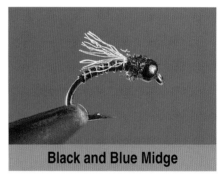

Black and Blue Midge

Originator: Steve Thrapp
Tier: Steve Thrapp

Hook: #18-20 Dai-Riki 135
Bead: Gunmetal Killer Caddis
Thread: Black 70-denier UTC
Body: Tying thread
Rib: Blue Ultra Wire
(extra small)
Thorax: Black Ice Dub
Wing: White Fluoro Fibre

Little Brown Midge

Originator: Steve Thrapp
Tier: Steve Thrapp

Hook: #18-22 Mustad C49S
Thread: Rust brown 70-denier UTC
Body: Tying thread
Rib: Copper brown Ultra Wire (extra small)
Wing: White Antron
Head: Black thread

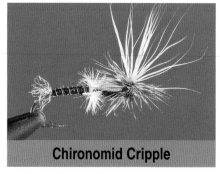

Chironomid Cripple

Originator: Peter Koga
Tier: Peter Koga

Hook: #14 Tiemco 2312
Thread: Black 8/0 Uni
Tail: White poly yarn
Body: Black Super Fine
Rib: Silver Lagartun wire (fine)
Gills: Ostrich
Wing: Elk hair
Hackle: Grizzly

Ostrich Buzzer

Originator: Peter Durisik
Tier: Peter Durisik

Hook: #10-14 Dohiku G 644BL
Thread: Brown Fly DK-80
Abdomen: Ostrich
Rib: Red Flexi Floss with gold Lagartun wire (fine)
Collar: Fl. orange marabou
Throat: Pearl Krystal Flash
Thorax: American squirrel or brown hare's ear dubbing

Suspender Black Buzzer

Originator: Peter Durisik
Tier: Peter Durisik

Hook: #10-12 Dohiku G 644BL
Thread: Black Fly DK-80
Abdomen: Tying thread
Tag: Fl. orange 70-denier UTC
Rib: Silver Flashabou
Thorax: Red 70-denier UTC
Wing: Natural CDC
Note: Coat entire fly except wing with Sally Hansen Hard As Nails.

CDC Black Buzzer

Originator: Peter Durisik
Tier: Peter Durisik

Hook: #10-16 Dohiku G 644BL
Thread: Black Fly DK-80
Tail: Orange Krystal Flash
Abdomen: Tying thread
Rib: Black Hends Body Quill
Collar: Fl. orange Hends thread
Thorax: American squirrel or black hare's ear dubbing
Wing: White CDC

CDC PT Buzzer

Originator: Peter Durisik
Tier: Peter Durisik

Hook: #10-16 Dohiku G 644BL
Thread: Brown Fly DK-80
Tail: Orange Krystal Flash
Abdomen: Pheasant tail
Rib: Gold Ultra Wire (extra small)
Throat: Fl. orange Hends thread
Thorax: American squirrel or brown hare's ear dubbing
Wing: Natural CDC

Double Rib Midge Cripple

Originator: Jude Duran
Tier: Jude Duran

Hook: #10-18 Daiichi 1100
Thread: Black 12/0 Bennechi
Body: White 12/0 Bennechi
Rib: Black tying thread
Wing case: Trimmed deer hair
Thorax: Black tying thread
Hackle: Grizzly

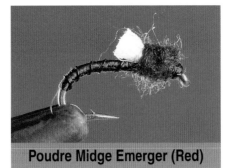

Poudre Midge Emerger (Red)

Originator: Mark McMillan
Tier: Mark McMillan

Hook: #18-26 Tiemco 2487
Thread: Red 70-denier UTC
Rib: Black Lagartun wire (fine)
Abdomen: Tying thread
Wing: White 1mm Rainy's crosslink foam cylinder
Thorax: Red Super Fine

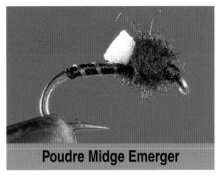

Poudre Midge Emerger

Originator: Mark McMillan
Tier: Mark McMillan

Hook: #18-26 Tiemco 2487
Thread: Black 70-denier UTC
Rib: Olive 8/0 Uni
Abdomen: Black thread
Wing: White 1mm Rainy's crosslink foam cylinder
Thorax: Black Super Fine

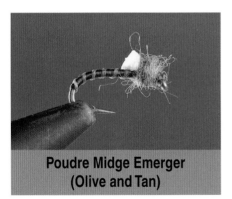

Poudre Midge Emerger (Olive and Tan)

Originator: Mark McMillan
Tier: Mark McMillan

Hook: #18-26 Tiemco 2487
Thread: Gray 70-denier UTC
Rib: Tan 8/0 Uni
Abdomen: Dark gray 70-denier UTC
Wing: White 1mm Rainy's crosslink foam cylinder
Thorax: Tan Super Fine

Grizzly Zebra Emerger

Originator: Jeremy Berela
Tier: Jeremy Berela

Hook: #18-26 Daiichi 1130
Thread: Black 12/0 Bennechi
Shuck: Grizzly hackle
Rib: Silver Lagartun wire (extra fine)
Body: Black thread
Wing: Pearl Krystal Flash
Thorax: Black Super Fine

Stuck in the Shuck Midge

Originator: Jeremy Berela
Tier: Jeremy Berela

Hook: #18-24 Daiichi 1130
Thread: Black 12/0 Bennechi
Trailing shuck: Organza
Body: Black and clear Super Hair
Wing: Light dun CDC
Legs: Grizzly hackle

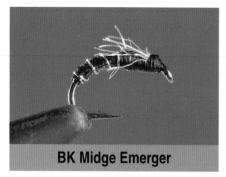

BK Midge Emerger

Originator: Jeremy Berela
Tier: Jeremy Berela

Hook: #18-22 Daiichi 1130
Thread: Black 12/0 Bennechi
Body: Pearl and black Krystal Flash
Rib: Silver Lagartun wire (extra fine)
Thorax: Black thread
Wing case: White Z-lon
Legs: Z-lon

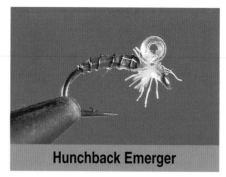

Hunchback Emerger

Originator: Jeff Ehlert
Tier: Jeff Ehlert

Hook: #18-22 Tiemco 2487
Thread: Gray 8/0 Uni
Body: Tying thread
Rib: Blue Lagartun wire (fine)
Thorax: Tying thread
Bead: Clear mercury
Wing: White organza
Note: Bead is tied on top of thorax with Kevlar thread.

Parri Midge

Originator: Dave Parri
Tier: Dave Parri

Hook: #18-20 Tiemco 200R
Thread: Black 8/0 Uni
Shuck: White Antron
Body: Tying thread
Thorax: Black and gray rabbit dubbing
Wing case/Wing: White Antron

DM's Olive Midge Emerger

Originator: Dennis Martin
Tier: Dennis Martin

Hook: #18-24 Tiemco 2488
Thread: Black 14/0 Gordon Griffiths
Body: Light olive Midge Tubing
Wing: White Antron
Thorax: Black Super Fine

Foam Head Zebra Midge

Originator: Unknown
Tier: Jerry Saiz

Hook: #18-24 Tiemco 2487
Thread: Black 8/0 Uni
Body: Tying thread
Rib: Silver Lagartun wire (fine)
Thorax: Gray Super Fine
Wing case: White closed-cell foam
Head: Black 8/0 Uni

Zebra Midge Emerger

Originator: Unknown
Tier: Jerry Saiz

Hook: #18-24 Tiemco 200R
Thread: Black 8/0 Uni
Tail: Light dun hackle
Body: Tying thread
Rib: Silver Lagartun wire (fine)
Thorax: Gray Super Fine
Wing: Dun Fluoro Fibre
Head: Black 8/0 Uni

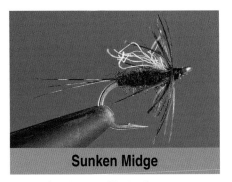

Sunken Midge

Originator: Kevin Compton
Tier: Kevin Compton

Hook:	#20 Gaelic Supreme Wide Gap Midge
Thread:	Black 10/0 Gudebrod
Shuck:	Whiting Coq de Leon
Body:	Black Fly-Rite dubbing
Hackle:	Starling shoulder feather
Wing:	White Antron

Mighty Midge

Originator: Hans Van Klinken
Tier: Kevin Compton

Hook:	#20 Partridge K14ST
Thread:	Black 10/0 Gudebrod
Body:	Natural gray goose biot
Wing case:	Natural CDC
Thorax:	Peacock herl
Post:	CDC

Hub's Twisted Sister Midge (Cream)

Originator: Jerry Hubka
Tier: Jerry Hubka

Hook:	#18-22 Daiichi 1140
Thread:	Tan 8/0 Uni
Tail:	Pearl Krystal Flash
Body:	Tan floss, twisted
Thorax:	Brown Super Fine
Gills:	White poly yarn
Wing case:	Pearl Krystal Flash

Hub's Twisted Sister Midge (Olive)

Originator: Jerry Hubka
Tier: Jerry Hubka

Hook:	#18-22 Daiichi 1140
Thread:	Olive 8/0 Uni
Tail:	Pearl Krystal Flash
Body:	Dark olive floss, twisted
Thorax:	Fine dark dubbing
Gills:	White poly yarn
Wing case:	Pearl Krystal Flash

Lil' Red Riser Emerger

Originator: Jerry Hubka
Tier: Jerry Hubka

Hook:	#16-20 Tiemco 200R
Bead:	Red glass
Tail:	White poly yarn
Thread:	Red 8/0 Uni
Body:	Red rainbow Tiewell Sparkleflash
Thorax:	Peacock herl
Gills:	White poly yarn
Note:	Coat body with Griff's Thin Head Cement.

Upper Colorado Midge (Black)

Originator: Dave Parri
Tier: Dave Parri

Hook:	#20 Tiemco 200R
Thread:	Black 8/0 Uni
Body:	Tying thread
Wing:	Gray mallard wing
Legs:	Black Unique Hair
Thorax:	Gray Super Fine

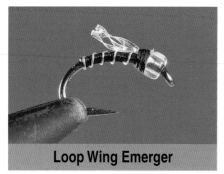

Loop Wing Emerger

Originator: Jeff Ehlert
Tier: Jeff Ehlert

Hook:	#18-24 Tiemco 2487
Bead:	Clear glass
Thread:	Black 8/0 Uni
Body:	Tying thread
Rib:	Silver Lagartun wire (fine)
Wing:	Pearl Krystal Flash

Pop Up Midge

Originator: Unknown
Tier: Bubba Smith

Hook:	#18-24 Tiemco 206BL
Thread:	Black 8/0 Uni
Body:	Tying thread
Rib:	Silver Lagartun wire (fine)
Wing:	White Fluoro Fibre
Hackle:	Grizzly

Reversed Paraloop Midge

Originator: Unknown
Tier: Bubba Smith

Hook:	#18-24 Tiemco 206BL
Thread:	Black 8/0 Uni
Body:	Tying thread
Rib:	Silver Lagartun wire (fine)
Hackle:	Grizzly tied Paraloop style

Sorry Charlie Midge

Originator: Unknown
Tier: Bubba Smith

Hook:	#18-24 Tiemco 200R
Thread:	Black 8/0 Uni
Body:	Black and olive Fish Hair
Thorax:	Muskrat
Wing:	White Fluoro Fibre

Holo Black Beauty

Originator: Unknown
Tier: Bubba Smith

Hook:	#18-24 Tiemco 200R
Bead:	Clear glass with black center
Thread:	Black 8/0 Uni
Body:	Black Holographic Flashabou
Wing:	White Fluoro Fibre
Thorax:	Muskrat dubbing

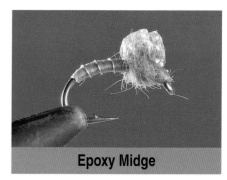

Epoxy Midge

Originator: Unknown
Tier: Bubba Smith

Hook:	#18-24 Tiemco 2487
Thread:	Cream 8/0 Uni
Body:	Tying thread
Rib:	Silver Lagartun wire (fine)
Wing:	Silver Midge Braid covered with epoxy
Thorax:	Muskrat dubbing

Suspender Pupa Emerger

Originator: Rick Takahashi
Tier: Rick Takahashi

Hook: #10-16 Tiemco 108SP-BL
Thread: White 70-denier UTC
Thorax/Head: Tying thread
Abdomen: Latex strip
Wing: Pearl Krystal Flash
Post: White poly yarn
Hackle: Grizzly
Note: Color the thread for the thorax and head and the latex for the abdomen with sand Chartpak marker.

Suspended Thread Emerger

Originator: Rick Takahashi
Tier: Rick Takahashi

Hook: #14-16 Tiemco 108SP-BL
Thread: Black 8/0 Uni
Thorax/Head: Tying thread
Abdomen: Tan Coats & Clark
Post: White poly yarn
Hackle: Grizzly

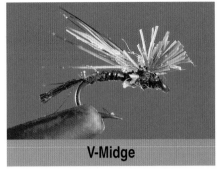

V-Midge

Originator: Yukiteru Yamagishi
Tier: Yukiteru Yamagishi

Hook: #20-26 Tiemco 100; #28
                   Partridge K1A
Thread: Black 8/0 Uni
Tail: Tying thread
Body: Black thread
Thorax: Tying thread
Wing: Deer hair

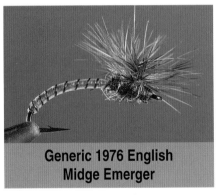

Generic 1976 English Midge Emerger

Originator: Unknown
Tier: Roy Christie

Hook: #12-20 Partridge 15BN
Thread: Brown Pearsall's silk
Body: Mother of pearl Mylar
Rib: Tying thread
Thorax: Black seal fur
Hackle: Grizzly dyed brown

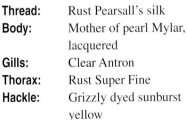

Reversed Parachute Midge Emerger

Originator: Roy Christie
Tier: Roy Christie

Hook: #12-16 Drennan Sedge
Thread: Rust Pearsall's silk
Body: Mother of pearl Mylar,
                   lacquered
Gills: Clear Antron
Thorax: Rust Super Fine
Hackle: Grizzly dyed sunburst
                   yellow

Generic 1976 English Midge Emerger

Originator: Unknown
Tier: Roy Christie

Hook: #16 Partridge Flashpoint F
                   Wire
Thread: Brown Pearsall's silk
Body: Tying thread
Rib: Copper Lagartun wire
                   (fine)
Thorax: Hare's ear dyed orange
Hackle: Grizzly dyed sunburst
                   yellow

Avon Special Emerger

Originator: Roy Christie
Tier: Roy Christie

Hook:	#12-18 Varivas 2200
Thread:	Hot orange 8/0 Uni
Tail:	Clear Antron
Body:	Mother of pearl Mylar
Wing:	Wood duck
Hackle:	Grizzly dyed sunburst yellow
Wing case:	Red swan biots
Thorax:	Black hare's ear

U Shaped Buzzer

Originator: Roy Christie
Tier: Roy Christie

Hook:	#12-16 Partridge Flashpoint F Wire
Thread:	Hot Orange 8/0 Uni
Body:	Mother of pearl Mylar, lacquered
Posts:	White CDC mixed with yellow
Thorax:	Brown hare's ear

Wingcased Avon Special Emerger

Originator: Roy Christie
Tier: Roy Christie

Hook:	#10-16 Daiichi 1270
Thread:	Yellow Pearsall's silk
Body:	Mother of pearl Mylar
Rib:	Nylon monofilament
Wing case:	Wood duck colored with orange marker
Hackle:	Grizzly dyed golden olive
Thorax:	Orange rabbit fur

Note: Lacquer the entire body and wing case.

Avon Special U Buzzer

Originator: Roy Christie
Tier: Roy Christie

Hook:	#12-18 Varivas 2200
Thread:	Hot orange 8/0 Uni
Tail:	White CDC
Body:	Mother of pearl Mylar
Wing:	Wood duck
Hackle:	Grizzly dyed gold olive
Thorax:	Tying thread

U Shaped Buzzer

Originator: Unknown
Tier: Roy Christie

Hook:	#10-20 Partridge Nymph or K14ST
Thread:	Yellow Pearsall's silk
Posts:	Natural CDC
Body:	Mother of pearl Mylar, lacquered

Winter Wonder Midge

Originator: John Larson
Tier: John Larson

Hook:	#24-26 Gamakatsu S13S-M
Thread:	Gray 8/0 Uni
Body:	PMD colored horse tail
Wing:	White CDC and white Fluoro Fibre
Head:	Thread colored with tan Prismacolor marker

Saint Juan's Ghost

Originator: John Larson
Tier: John Larson

Hook: #22 Tiemco 200R
Bead: Clear mercury
Thread: White Spiderweb
Body: Mirage Tinsel
Rib: Monofilament
Thorax: White Super Fine
Wing: White CDC
Note: Coat the rib and body with Wet and Wild Rock Solid Nail Polish.

T Hole Cherry Bomb

Originator: John Larson
Tier: John Larson

Hook: #18-24 Tiemco 2488
Bead: Pink mercury
Thread: Fl. pink 8/0 Uni
Body: Tying thread
Rib: Red Lagartun wire (fine)
Wing: Pearl Krystal Flash
Thorax: Shrimp Ice Dub

Juan Shot

Originator: John Larson
Tier: John Larson

Hook: #28-30 Tiemco 518
Thread: White Spiderweb
Tail: Lemon wood duck
Body: Fl. chartreuse Flash Cord
Wing: White CDC
Head: Light chartreuse Ice Dub
Note: Coat body with Wet and Wild Rock Solid Nail Polish.

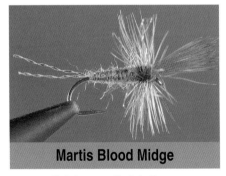

Martis Blood Midge

Originator: Ralph Cutter
Tier: Ralph Cutter

Hook: #12-18 Tiemco 100
Thread: Orange 6/0 Uni
Tails: Pearl Krystal Flash
Abdomen: Orange Antron dubbing
Wing: Orange deer hair
Hackle: Furnace saddle

Cross Dresser

Originator: Jason Borger
Tier: Jason Borger

Hook: #14-28 TAR 101
Thread: Gray 8/0 Uni
Shuck: Dark sand Targus SST
Abdomen: Light olive and light gray Targus Super Dry, blended
Hackle: Light dun
Wing: Gray Antron
Note: This pattern adds a shuck, V wing, and a body color that allows the fly to work well during many midge and mayfly hatches (that's the cross-dresser part) to the venerable and highly effective Griffith's Gnat.

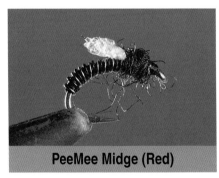

PeeMee Midge (Red)

Originator: Steve Schweitzer
Tier: Steve Schweitzer

Hook: #18-20 Tiemco 2457
Thread: Black 12/0 Bennechi
Body: Tying thread
Rib: Red and black Lagartun wire (fine)
Wing: Closed-cell sheet packing foam
Head: Red and black Super Fine

PeeMee Midge (Peacock)

Originator: Steve Schweitzer
Tier: Steve Schweitzer

Hook: #18-20 Tiemco 2457
Thread: Black 12/0 Bennechi
Body: Tying thread
Rib: Gold Lagartun wire (fine)
Wing: Closed-cell sheet packing foam
Head: Peacock dubbing

PeeMee Midge

Originator: Steve Schweitzer
Tier: Steve Schweitzer

Hook: #18-20 Tiemco 2457
Thread: Black 12/0 Bennechi
Body: Tying thread
Rib: Olive thread
Wing: Closed-cell sheet packing foam
Head: Black and red Super Fine

Midge Floating Pupa

Originator: Noritaka Osada
Tier: Noritaka Osada

Hook: #19-23 Tiemco 212Y
Thread: Tan 16/0 Tiemco
Abdomen: Olive 16/0 Tiemco
Rib: Black Danville 3/0 Monocord
Thorax: Synthetic peacock
Wing: Cream CDC

Midge Stillborn

Originator: Noritaka Osada
Tier: Noritaka Osada

Hook: #19-23 Tiemco 112Y
Thread: Tan 16/0 Tiemco
Abdomen: Tying thread
Rib: Black Danville 3/0 Monocord
Thorax: Synthetic peacock
Wing: Cream CDC, Z-lon, Melty Fiber

Midge Stillborn

Originator: Noritaka Osada
Tier: Noritaka Osada

Hook: #19-23 Tiemco 212Y
Thread: Olive 16/0 Tiemco
Shuck: Z-lon and Melty Fiber
Abdomen: Tying thread
Rib: Black Danville 3/0 Monocord
Thorax: Synthetic peacock
Wing: Cream CDC

Christmas Midge

Originator: Jeremy Davies
Tier: Jeremy Davies

Hook: #10-20 Tiemco 2487
Tail: Green Antron
Thread: Olive 8/0 Uni
Body: Green Holographic Tinsel
Rib: Red Uni Wire (small)
Thorax: Natural peacock Arizona dubbing

Heavy Metal Midge

Originator: Jeremy Davies
Tier: Jeremy Davies

Hook:	#10-20 Tiemco 2487
Bead:	Black metal
Thread:	Olive 8/0 Uni
Tail:	Green Antron
Body:	Black Holographic Tinsel
Rib:	Green Uni Wire (small)
Thorax:	Olive brown Ice Dub

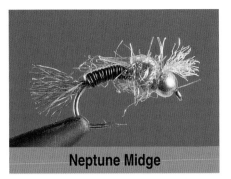

Neptune Midge

Originator: Jeremy Davies
Tier: Jeremy Davies

Hook:	#10-18 Tiemco 2487
Bead:	Gold metal
Thread:	Olive 8/0 Uni
Tail:	Green Antron
Body:	Blue and green Lagartun wire (fine)
Wing case:	White Antron
Back:	Pearl Flashabou

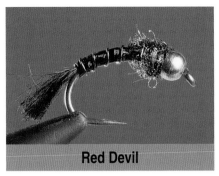

Red Devil

Originator: Jeremy Davies
Tier: Jeremy Davies

Hook:	#10-20 Tiemco 2487BL
Bead:	Gold metal
Thread:	Red 8/0 Uni
Tail:	Red floss
Body:	Red UTC Holographic Tinsel
Rib:	Red Uni Wire (small)
Thorax:	Red Ice Dub

Ultra Flash Midge (Red)

Originator: Jeremy Davies
Tier: Jeremy Davies

Hook:	#10-20 Tiemco 2487
Bead:	Gold metal
Thread:	Red 8/0 Uni
Tail:	Red Antron
Body:	Red Holographic Tinsel
Rib:	Copper Uni Wire (small)
Wing case:	White Antron
Thorax:	Natural peacock Arizona dubbing

Ultra Flash Midge (Green)

Originator: Jeremy Davies
Tier: Jeremy Davies

Hook:	#10-20 Tiemco 2487
Bead:	Gold metal
Thread:	Olive 8/0 Uni
Tail:	Green Antron
Body:	Green Holographic Tinsel
Rib:	Gold Uni Wire (small)
Wing case:	White Antron
Thorax:	Natural peacock Arizona dubbing

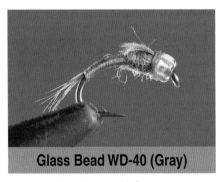

Glass Bead WD-40 (Gray)

Originator: Unknown
Tier: Pacific Fly Group

Hook:	#20-24 Daiichi 1130
Bead:	Diamond Killer Caddis
Thread:	Light gray 8/0 Uni
Tail/Wing case:	Mallard dyed wood duck
Body:	Tying thread
Thorax:	Light gray Super Fine

Glass Bead WD-40 (Black)

Originator: Unknown
Tier: Pacific Fly Group

Hook:	#20-24 Daiichi 1130
Bead:	Diamond Killer Caddis
Thread:	Black 8/0 Uni
Tail/Wing case:	Mallard dyed wood duck
Body:	Tying thread
Thorax:	Black Super Fine

Glass Bead WD-40 (Brown)

Originator: Unknown
Tier: Pacific Fly Group

Hook:	#20-24 Daiichi 1130
Bead:	Diamond Killer Caddis
Thread:	Dark brown 8/0 Uni
Tail/Wing case:	Mallard dyed wood duck
Body:	Tying thread
Thorax:	Rust Super Fine

WD-40

Originator: Mark Engler
Tier: Duranglers Fly Shop

Hook:	#18-24 Tiemco 2487
Thread:	Brown 8/0 Uni
Tail:	Mallard dyed wood duck
Body:	Tying thread
Head:	Brown Super Fine
Wing case:	Mallard dyed wood duck

Flashback WD

Originator: Mark Engler
Tier: Duranglers Fly Shop

Hook:	#18-22 Tiemco 2487
Thread:	Gray 8/0 Uni
Tail:	Mallard
Body:	Tying thread
Thorax:	Gray Super Fine
Wing case:	Pearl Mylar

Chocolate Flashback WD

Originator: Mark Engler
Tier: Duranglers Fly Shop

Hook:	#18-22 Tiemco 2487
Thread:	Brown 8/0 Uni
Tail:	Mallard dyed wood duck
Body:	Tying thread
Thorax:	Brown Super Fine
Wing case:	Pearl Mylar

WD Flashy (Black)

Originator: Unknown
Tier: Montana Fly Company

Hook:	#16-22 MFC 7045
Thread:	Black 8/0 Uni
Tail:	Mallard dyed wood duck
Body:	Tying thread
Thorax:	Gunmetal Wing N' Flash
Wing case:	Mallard dyed wood duck

WD Flashy (Dark Olive)

Originator: Unknown
Tier: Montana Fly Company

Hook: #16-22 MFC 7045
Thread: Olive dun 8/0 Uni
Tail: Mallard dyed wood duck
Body: Tying thread
Thorax: Gunmetal Wing N' Flash
Wing case: Mallard dyed wood duck

WD Flashy (Light Olive)

Originator: Unknown
Tier: Montana Fly Company

Hook: #16-22 MFC 7045
Thread: Olive dun 8/0 Uni
Tail: Mallard dyed wood duck
Body: Tying thread
Thorax: Gunmetal Wing N' Flash
Wing case: Mallard dyed wood duck

WD Flashy (Red)

Originator: Unknown
Tier: Montana Fly Company

Hook: #16-22 MFC 7045
Thread: Red 8/0 Uni
Tail: Mallard dyed wood duck
Body: Tying thread
Thorax: Gunmetal Wing N' Flash
Wing case: Mallard dyed wood duck

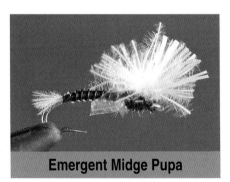

Emergent Midge Pupa

Originator: Ed Engle
Tier: Ed Engle

Hook: #18-22 Tiemco 200R
Thread: Black 10/0 Gudebrod
Tail: White CDC
Body: Tying thread
Rib: Copper brown Ultra Wire (small)
Wing: Tan Medallion Sheeting
Post: Deer hair
Hackle: White CDC

Emergent Midge Adult

Originator: Ed Engle
Tier: Ed Engle

Hook: #18-24 Tiemco 100
Thread: Black 8/0 Uni
Body: Tying thread
Wing: Bleached deer or elk hair
Thorax: Black beaver dubbing
Post: Wing butt
Hackle: Grizzly

CDC "Yusurika" Stillborn

Originator: Hisashi Suzuki
Tier: Hisashi Suzuki

Hook: #28-30 Tiemco 518
Thread: Tan Tiemco 16/0
Shuck: 6X monofilament
Thorax: Tying thread
Wing: Cream CDC

Tying the Adult

THE MIDGE PUPA hangs under the surface of the water (meniscus), and as the adult emerges and penetrates the film, it pulls itself out of its pupal shuck. When riding on the surface film, the adult insect resembles a mosquito. The insect is ready to take flight shortly after emergence. When midges are hatching, trout can go on a feeding rampage, taking adults as they emerge or while allowing their wings to dry on the water's surface, sometimes becoming selective to this stage.

The adult stage can be divided into single adults, or clusters of adult midges clumped together either due to wind drift or for mating purposes. Fishing individual adult patterns can be a challenge, requiring a precise presentation and drift. The midge cluster represents the midge in a mating mass, or midges that have otherwise bunched together to form a mass of bodies and wings. The advantage of fishing midge cluster patterns is that you can use a slightly larger fly. The classic midge cluster is the Griffith's Gnat, and it is still one of the best cluster patterns you can tie.

Adult midges can look like mosquitoes at first glance, but they do not bite.

Tak's Biot Wing Adult

R ick developed this fly to mimic the adult midges he encountered on the San Juan River. One of the difficulties of fishing a midge adult is being able to see the pattern in the surface film. The white biot wing and grizzly hackle in this pattern make it easier to spot the fly. Like the naturals, the wings are shorter than their bodies.

Materials

Hook:	#20 Tiemco 2488
Abdomen:	Black 8/0 Uni or white 17/0 colored with marker
Rib:	Silver Lagartun wire (extra fine)
Wing:	White goose biot
Hackle:	Grizzly

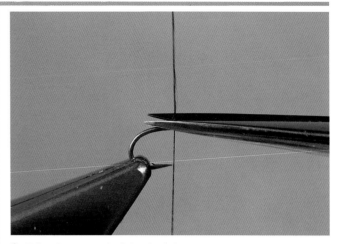

2. Trim the tag end of the thread.

1. Attach the tying thread at the two-thirds point on the hook shank and make several wraps.

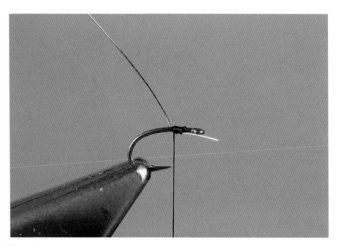

3. Tie in the wire, leaving a small tag end.

For hackle, use the smallest feathers you can find on the neck, or try midge saddle hackles, which provide feathers with long stems and short hackles, allowing you to tie midges as small as sizes 20 to 26.

4. Pull the wire back until it slides under the tying thread. Wrap the tying thread over the wire to the hook bend.

5. Wrap the tying thread forward in touching wraps to a point one eye width behind the hook eye.

6. Start wrapping the wire toward the hook eye in evenly spaced wraps to create the rib.

7. Wrap the wire to a point one eye width back from the hook eye, and tie off the wire with several wraps of thread.

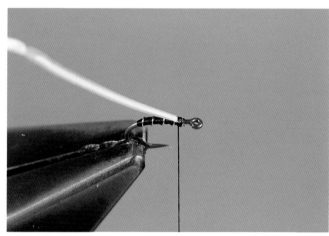

8. Trim the excess wire. Tie in a white biot by the tip, so that the biot curves away from the hook.

9. Wrap over the biot several times to secure it.

10. Trim the fibers from the end of the hackle stem, trim the stem short, and tie it in at the base of the biot wing.

11. Wrap the thread to just behind the hook eye.

12. Wrap the saddle hackle two or three times toward the hook eye until it is one eye width behind the hook eye.

13. Tie off the saddle hackle with two wraps of the tying thread.

14. Trim the saddle hackle flush to the hook.

15. Create a tapered head from the hackle to the hook eye. Whip-finish and trim the excess thread.

16. Trim the biot about one-quarter to one-half the length of the body.

17. Trim the bottom of the hackle flush with the underside of the hook shank. The completed Biot Wing Adult.

CDC Wing Adult

Cul de canard, also known as CDC, are the feathers located near the preening glands of waterfowl such as ducks and geese. The microbarbs in the individual fibers trap air, which floats the feather naturally. Adding paste or liquid floatant to these feathers only ruins the natural floatation properties of the feather. Small emergers and adults can both be tied using these feathers. In addition to floating well, CDC feathers make a wonderful wing profile. For treating flies with CDC, see "Keeping High and Dry" on page 269.

Materials
Hook:	#20 Tiemco 2488
Thread:	Black 8/0 Uni
Abdomen:	Black 8/0 Uni
Wing:	Cul de canard, white or dun

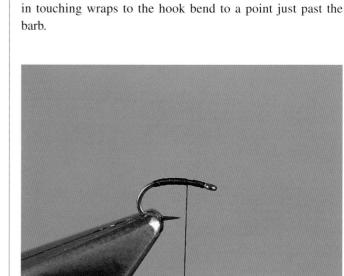

2. Trim the tag end of the tying thread. Wrap the tying thread in touching wraps to the hook bend to a point just past the barb.

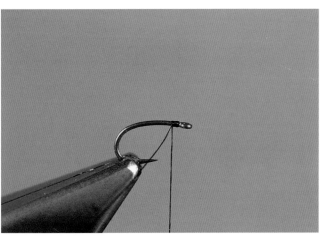

1. Attach the tying thread behind the hook eye, taking several wraps to secure the tying thread.

3. Continue wrapping the tying thread forward to a point one eye width behind the hook eye.

4. Wrap the tying thread to form a small ball.

5. Tie in a white CDC feather so that the tips face toward the rear of the hook.

6. Pull the butt end of the CDC feather forward toward the hook eye until the tips are as long as you want them.

7. Take several more wraps of tying thread over the CDC stem to secure the feather.

8. Trim the excess CDC feather flush with the hook.

9. Wrap the thread over the exposed butt ends of the CDC feather, creating a tapered head. Whip-finish and trim the tying thread flush with the hook.

10. Completed CDC Wing Adult.

Mule Midge

This adult midge pattern is the brainchild of Dr. Kevin Rogers of Steamboat Springs, Colorado. While pursuing his PhD at Colorado State University, Kevin developed this pattern to mimic the numerous midge adults found on the Poudre River. He and his wife, Emily, would test hookless version of this pattern on the Poudre, and the trout loved it. The Mule got its name because Kevin said it outfished and was more reliable than the popular Palomino Midge.

Materials

Hook:	#18-24 Tiemco 2488
Thread:	White 17/0 Uni
Body:	EZ Magic Dub, colors to match naturals
Wing:	White or dun CDC
Legs:	Black CDC

1. Attach the tying thread at the two-thirds point on the hook shank and trim the tag end of the thread.

2. Tie in a one-inch-long piece of Magic Dub.

3. Trim the Magic Dub just beyond the hook bend.

4. Wrap the tying thread toward the hook eye.

5. Tie in a CDC feather by its butt section with two wraps of tying thread. The tip of the CDC should extend past the hook eye. Pull the butt end of the CDC feather back toward the hook bend until you start compressing the CDC fibers together. Take several more wraps of tying thread to secure it.

6. Trim the butt end of the CDC feather at the midpoint of the hook. Wrap the tying thread toward the hook eye until it is one eye width behind the eye.

7. With two wraps of the tying thread, tie in a bundle of gray CDC fibers that have been pulled from the stem of a CDC feather selected from the middle of the bundle.

8. Turn the bundle of CDC fibers sideways so that they are perpendicular to the hook shank, much like a spent wing. These will be trimmed to form the legs.

9. Fold the CDC feather over the bundled CDC fibers, and take several wraps over the CDC to attach it behind the legs.

10. Trim each side of the bundled CDC fibers short to form the legs on each side of the body.

13. Whip-finish behind the legs.

11. The trimmed legs should look like this.

14. The finished Mule Midge. It's a little more complicated than some of the other patterns we show in this book, but the results are worth it.

12. Trim the CDC feather the same length as the Magic Dub body. If desired, cut the wing a bit shorter than the body.

Griffith's Gnat

The Griffith Gnat, developed by George Griffith, is one of the classic midge cluster patterns, and it is as effective today as it was when it was invented. Anglers have used this pattern for years to imitate a midge emerging into an adult, but in our opinion this pattern also mimics a cluster of midges very well. Tak's High Post Midge is a version of this basic design.

Materials

Hook:	#20 Tiemco 100
Thorax/head:	Black 70-denier UTC or 8/0 Uni
Body:	Peacock herl
Hackle:	Metz Micro Barb grizzly saddle

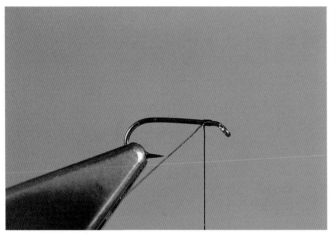

1. Attach the thread one eye width back from the hook eye and take several wraps toward the hook bend. Trim the tag end.

2. Tie in the wire, leaving a tag end.

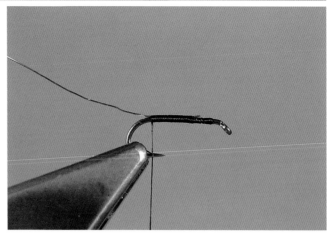

3. Pull the wire until it slides under the thread base. Wrap the tying thread back to the hook bend to a point opposite the barb.

4. Wrap the tying thread forward to a point three eye widths behind the hook eye.

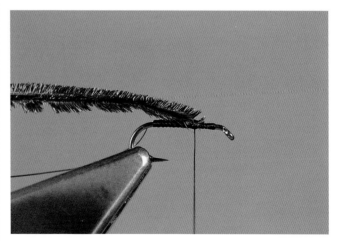

5. Trim the tips of two peacock herls and tie them in by the tips.

6. Wrap the tying thread over the peacock herl to the hook bend.

9. Tie in the grizzly saddle hackle by the butt end with two wraps of thread.

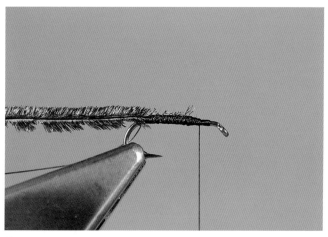

7. Wrap the tying thread to a point two eye widths behind the hook eye.

10. Wrap the peacock toward the hook bend in evenly spaced wraps.

8. Wrap the peacock herl forward in touching wraps to a point one eye width behind the hook eye, and tie off the peacock herl with two wraps of tying thread. Trim the excess peacock herl.

11. Wrap the peacock back to the hook bend to a point opposite the barb.

12. Wrap the wire in front of and over the hackle stem to secure the hackle at the hook bend. You can now let go of the hackle.

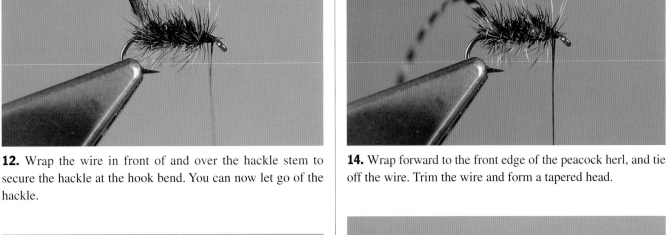

14. Wrap forward to the front edge of the peacock herl, and tie off the wire. Trim the wire and form a tapered head.

13. Wrap the wire in evenly spaced wraps forward toward the hook eye.

15. Whip-finish the head. Trim the wire flush to the hook. Trim the hackle at the hook bend.

High Post Midge Cluster

This pattern is similar to the Griffith's Gnat, but it is tied in black with an extra-long post for visibility. Rick designed this pattern because he wanted a pattern that would sit flush in the surface film. The black post contrasts nicely with the lighter surface of the water, especially in glare. The pattern has a thread body instead of the Griffith's Gnat's peacock herl, and the trimmed hackle on the bottom allows the fly to sit lower in the water. To help see the fly even more, you can get above and to the side of the fish, cast well upstream of the feeding fish, and pull the fly into the fish's feeding lane. The high post and the small wake on the water will help you find the fly. When the fly is in the fish's feeding lane, drop the rod tip and let it float drag free to the trout.

Materials

Hook:	#20 Tiemco 100
Thorax/head:	Black 70-denier UTC or 8/0 Uni
Body:	Tying thread
High post:	Black Antron
Hackle:	Black Metz Micro Barb Saddle
Rib:	Tying thread

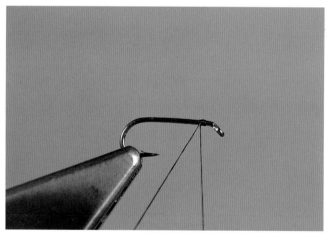

1. Attach the thread one eye width back from the eye.

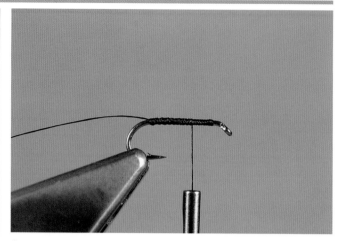

2. Wrap the tying thread over the tag end of the thread toward the hook bend. Continue to wrap the tying thread with touching wraps toward the hook bend to a point opposite the hook barb. Wrap the tying thread forward in touching wraps to the two-thirds point on the hook shank. The tag end will be used as a rib later, so do not trim it.

3. Attach the yarn with two wraps of tying thread.

4. Grasp the front end of the yarn, and take a single wrap in front of it to force it upright.

5. Trim the rear half of the fibers flush to the hook.

6. Attach hackle with shiny side facing toward the hook eye.

7. Wrap the hackle to the hook bend in evenly spaced wraps.

8. Grasp the tag end of the tying thread and take a wrap in front of and over the stem of the saddle hackle to secure it to the hook.

9. Continue to wrap the thread in evenly spaced wraps to the front of the hackle. Tie off the thread with several wraps of thread.

10. Trim the excess thread flush to the hook.

11. Trim the feather.

14. Trim the bottom of the hackle.

12. Whip-finish the head. Trim the tying thread flush to the hook.

15. The completed High Post Midge Cluster.

13. Trim the wing post 1½ to 2 times the length of fly's body.

Black Midge Cluster

This pattern was one of the first cluster patterns that Rick tied and fished. It is an easy pattern to tie and is good practice for tying parachutes. This pattern represents a tight jumble of adult midges that have been trapped in the surface film of the water. It looks similar to a yarn strike indicator, and is easy to spot on the water. Rick uses this pattern as an alternative to the Griffith's Gnat and Tak's High Post Midge Cluster, especially on rivers where the fish are not highly selective.

Materials

Hook:	#20 Tiemco 100
Thorax/head:	Black 8/0 Uni
Post:	Black poly yarn
Hackle:	Black Metz Micro Barb Saddle

1. Attach the thread in the middle of the hook shank. Trim the excess tying thread flush to the hook.

2. Attach the yarn with several wraps of thread.

3. Wrap the tying thread around the yarn to form a post. Wrap the thread up the post to provide a stiff base on which to wrap the parachute hackle.

4. Attach the hackle on the front end of the post on the side nearest you.

5. Wrap the hackle around the post starting from the base, up the post, and then back down to the base of the post.

6. Wrap the hackle over the near side of the hook and tie off.

8. Trim the post about the length of the hook shank, and the fly is finished.

7. Trim the hackle, whip-finish, and trim the excess thread.

Adult Patterns

Adult Patterns

High Post Midge (Black)

Originator: Rick Takahashi
Tier: Rick Takahashi

Hook: #22-28 Tiemco 2488
Thread: White 17/0 Uni
Tail: Black Krystal Flash
Body: Tying thread
Rib: Tying thread
Wing: Black Antron
Hackle: Black

Note: Color the tying thread with black Pantone marker for the body.

High Post Midge (Brown/Gray)

Originator: Rick Takahashi
Tier: Rick Takahashi

Hook: #22-28 Tiemco 2488
Thread: White 17/0 Uni
Tail: Black Krystal Flash
Body: Tying thread
Rib: Tying thread
Wing: Black Antron
Hackle: Grizzly

Note: Color thread with warm gray Chartpak marker for the body; brown for the rib.

High Post Midge (Black/White)

Originator: Rick Takahashi
Tier: Rick Takahashi

Hook: #22-28 Tiemco 2488
Thread: White 17/0 Uni
Tail: Black Krystal Flash
Body: Tying thread
Rib: Tying thread
Wing: Black Antron
Hackle: Grizzly

Note: Color thread with warm black Sharpie marker for the body.

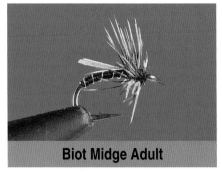

Biot Midge Adult

Originator: Rick Takahashi
Tier: Rick Takahashi

Hook:	#20-26 Tiemco 2488
Thread:	Black 8/0 Uni
Body:	Tying thread
Rib:	Silver Ultra Wire (extra small)
Wing:	White biot
Hackle:	Grizzly

Extended Body Adult

Originator: Rick Takahashi
Tier: Rick Takahashi

Hook:	#20-24 Tiemco 2488
Thread:	Black 8/0 Uni
Body:	Black EZ Magic Dub
Wing:	White biot tied tip first
Hackle:	Black

Parachute Midge (Black)

Originator: Unknown
Tier: Solitude Fly Company

Hook:	#18-24 Daiichi 1100
Thread:	Black 6/0 Danville
Tail:	Black hackle
Body:	Black Super Fine
Wing:	White Hi-Vis
Hackle:	Black

Parachute Midge (Brown)

Originator: Unknown
Tier: Solitude Fly Company

Hook:	#18-24 Daiichi 1100
Thread:	Brown 6/0 Danville
Tail:	Brown hackle
Body:	Brown Super Fine
Wing:	White Hi-Vis
Hackle:	Brown

Parachute Midge (White)

Originator: Unknown
Tier: Solitude Fly Company

Hook:	#18-24 Daiichi 1100
Thread:	Cream 6/0 Danville
Tail:	Cream hackle
Body:	Light cahill Super Fine
Wing:	White Hi-Vis
Hackle:	Cream

Parachute Midge (Olive)

Originator: Unknown
Tier: Solitude Fly Company

Hook:	#18-24 Daiichi 1100
Thread:	Olive 6/0 Danville
Tail:	Dun hackle
Body:	BWO Super Fine
Wing:	White Hi-Vis
Hackle:	Dun

Parachute Midge (Dun/Grizzly)

Originator: Unknown
Tier: Solitude Fly Company

Hook: #18-24 Daiichi 1100
Thread: Dun 6/0 Danville
Tail: Dun hackle
Body: Gray Super Fine
Wing: White Hi-Vis
Hackle: Grizzly

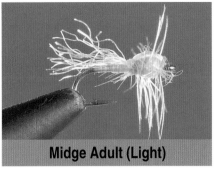

Midge Adult (Light)

Originator: Unknown
Tier: Umpqua Feather Merchants

Hook: #22-24 Tiemco 101
Thread: Cream 6/0 Uni
Body: Tying thread
Wing: White Z-lon
Thorax: Ginger dubbing
Hackle: Ginger

Midge Adult (Dark)

Originator: Unknown
Tier: Umpqua Feather Merchants

Hook: #22-24 Tiemco 101
Thread: Black 6/0 Uni
Body: Tying thread
Wing: White Z-lon
Thorax: Peacock herl
Hackle: Dark dun

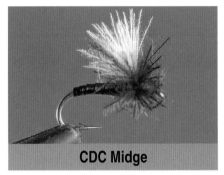

CDC Midge

Originator: Unknown
Tier: Umpqua Feather Merchants

Hook: #20-22 Tiemco 100
Thread: Black 6/0 Uni
Body: Stripped black ostrich herl
Wing: Black Z-lon and White CDC
Thorax: Black Super Fine
Legs: Black CDC

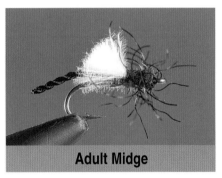

Adult Midge

Originator: Brad Befus
Tier: Umpqua Feather Merchants

Hook: #20-22 Tiemco 101
Thread: Black 6/0 Uni
Body: Twisted black Z-lon
Wing: White CDC
Thorax: Black 8/0 Uni
Legs: Black Z-lon

Black Smut

Originator: John Nichols
Tier: John Nichols

Hook: #16-20 Tiemco 921
Thread: Black 8/0 Uni
Body: Stripped peacock herl
Wing: White organza
Thorax: Black Super Fine
Hackle: Black

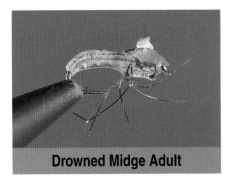

Drowned Midge Adult

Originator: Brian Yamauchi
Tier: Brian Yamauchi

Hook: #18-24 Tiemco 100
Thread: White 17/0
Body: Latex coated with Loon
             UV Knot Sense
Wing: Clear Medallion Sheeting
Legs: Orvis Trilobel pure Antron

Atière

Originator: Martin Westbeek
Tier: Martin Westbeek

Hook: #16 Daiichi 1180
Thread: Charcoal 16/0 Tiemco
Body: Two gray goose fibers
Wing: Two silver badger feather
             tips
Hackle: Black Whiting saddle

Olive Midge Adult

Originator: Scott Stisser
Tier: Scott Stisser

Hook: #18-26 Tiemco 2487 or
             2488
Thread: Black 12/0 Gordon
             Griffiths
Wing: White poly yarn and Celo
             Z-Wing
Body: Stripped olive hackle stem
Thorax: Dark olive dubbing
Hackle: Olive ostrich herl

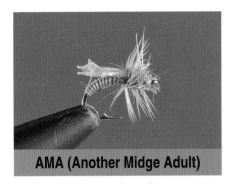

AMA (Another Midge Adult)

Originator: Scott Stisser
Tier: Scott Stisser

Hook: #18-26 Tiemco 2487 or
             2488
Thread: Gray or black 6/0 Danville
Wing: Celo Z-Wing
Body: Stripped grizzly hackle
             stem
Thorax: Gray dubbing
Hackle: Dun saddle

Hi Vis Foam Wing Adult

Originator: Scott Stisser
Tier: Scott Stisser

Hook: #18-20 Tiemco 2487 or
             2488
Thread: Gray or black 6/0 Danville
Wing: Dun hen hackle tips
Body: Stripped grizzly hackle
             stem
Thorax: Gray dubbing
Hackle: Dun Whiting saddle
Post: Chartreuse foam

Parachute Peacock

Originator: John Mundinger
Tier: John Mundinger

Hook: #20 Mustad 94833
Thread: Dark dun 12/0 Bennechi
Tail: Medium dun hackle
Body: Peacock herl
Post: White Widow's Web
Hackle: Medium dun

Midge Flea

Originator: Jeff Henkemeyer
Tier: Jeff Henkemeyer

Hook: #26 Tiemco 100
Thread: Black 8/0 Uni
Body: Black CDC dubbing
Wing: Natural CDC
Head: Black CDC dubbing

Adult Midge

Originator: Jason Haslam
Tier: Rainy's Fly Company

Hook: #18-22 Tiemco 200R
Thread: Black 14/0 Gordon
Griffiths
Body: Black Antron
Wing: Medium dun CDC
Thorax: Tying thread
Hackle: Grizzly

CDC Hackle Stacker

Originator: Todd Smith
Tier: Rainy's Fly Company

Hook: #18-22 Tiemco 100
Thread: Black 8/0 Uni
Tail: Light dun Microfibetts
Body: Black goose biot
Wing: CDC
Note: The wing is a mixture of 70% light dun, 30% natural dark dun, and dun CDC in a dubbing loop. Attach Hackle Stacker style and trim square in front.

Black Midge

Originator: Goran Grba
Tier: Milan Kupresanin

Hook: #24 Tiemco 508
Thread: Black 10/0 Uni
Body: Black biot
Wing: Natural CDC
Hackle: Hare's ear

Black Smut

Originator: Russell Stanton
Tier: Russell Stanton

Hook: #20 Tiemco 101
Thread: Black 10/0 Gudebrod
Body: Black beaver
Wing: Dark dun hackle
Hackle: Grizzly

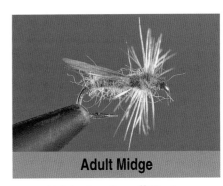

Adult Midge

Originator: Russell Stanton
Tier: Russell Stanton

Hook: #22 Tiemco 100
Thread: Gray 10/0 Gudebrod
Body: Gray beaver or muskrat
Wing: Hackle tips
Thorax: Gray beaver or muskrat
Hackle: Dun

Adult Midge

Originator: Russell Stanton
Tier: Russell Stanton

Hook:	#22 Daiichi 1140
Thread:	Black 10/0 Gudebrod
Body:	Tying thread
Rib:	Copper Lagartun wire (fine)
Wing:	White goose biot, trimmed
Hackle:	Grizzly

Hi-Vis Midge (Olive)

Originator: Spirit River
Tier: Spirit River

Hook:	#18-20 Spear-It CS048
Thread:	Olive 6/0 Uni
Body:	Tying thread
Rib:	Copper Lagartun wire (fine)
Wing:	Fl. pink Hi-Vis
Thorax:	Medium olive Fine and Dry
Hackle:	Grizzly

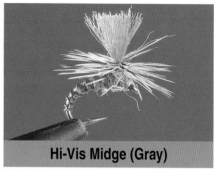

Hi-Vis Midge (Gray)

Originator: Spirit River
Tier: Spirit River

Hook:	#18-20 Spear-It CS048
Thread:	Gray 6/0 Uni
Body:	Tying thread
Rib:	Copper Lagartun wire (fine)
Wing:	Fl. pink Hi-Vis
Thorax:	Adams gray Fine and Dry
Hackle:	Grizzly

Hi-Vis Midge (Cream)

Originator: Spirit River
Tier: Spirit River

Hook:	#18-20 Spear-It CS048
Thread:	Cream 6/0 Uni
Body:	Tying thread
Rib:	Copper Lagartun wire (fine)
Wing:	Fl. pink Hi-Vis
Thorax:	Light cahill Fine and Dry
Hackle:	Grizzly

Hi-Vis Midge (Black)

Originator: Spirit River
Tier: Spirit River

Hook:	#18-20 Spear-It CS048
Thread:	Black 6/0 Uni
Body:	Tying thread
Rib:	Copper Lagartun wire (fine)
Wing:	Fl. pink Hi-Vis
Thorax:	Black Fine and Dry
Hackle:	Grizzly

Halo Midge Paraloop Style

Originator: Sue Armstrong
Tier: Sue Armstrong

Hook:	#16-20 Tiemco 2487
Thread:	Black 70-denier UTC
Shuck/Post:	White SAAP Float-Vis
Body:	Black UTC Holographic Tinsel (medium)
Thorax:	Black Super Fine
Hackle:	Grizzly

Eric's Midge

Originator: Eric Pettine
Tier: Eric Pettine

Hook:	#16-22 Tiemco 101
Thread:	Medium gray 10/0 Gudebrod
Tail:	Medium gray Antron
Body:	Medium blue dun hackle
Overbody:	Black closed-cell foam
Indicator:	Burnt orange Antron
Head:	Tying thread

Hi-Viz Adult

Originator: ATF Fly Shop
Tier: Tim Mack

Hook:	#22-24 Tiemco 100
Thread:	Black 10/0 Bennechi
Body:	Black Super Fine
Wing:	Orange foam
Hackle:	Black
Tail:	Black Microfibetts

Parachute Black Midge Adult

Originator: ATF Fly Shop
Tied by: Tim Mack

Hook:	#22-24 Tiemco 100
Thread:	Black 10/0 Bennechi
Tail:	Black Microfibetts
Body:	Black Super Fine
Wing:	White Antron
Hackle:	Black

Gray Sam Midge

Originator: Unknown
Tier: Duranglers Fly Shop

Hook:	#18-24 Tiemco 501
Thread:	Black 14/0 Gordon Griffiths
Body:	Tan Tier's Lace
Wing:	White CDC
Thorax:	Black Super Fine
Hackle:	Grizzly

Gray Biot Midge Adult

Originator: Unknown
Tier: Duranglers Fly Shop

Hook:	#18-24 Tiemco 2488
Thread:	Brown 14/0 Gordon Griffiths
Body:	Tying thread
Wing:	Light gray biot over CDC
Hackle:	Grizzly

Biot Adult Midge (Black)

Originator: Unknown
Tier: Montana Fly Company

Hook:	#20 MFC 701
Thread:	Black 8/0 Uni
Tail:	Black hackle
Body:	Black turkey biot
Hackle:	Black

CDC Hackle Stacker Midge

Originator: Unknown
Tier: Montana Fly Company

Hook:	#10-14 MFC 7001
Thread:	Black 8/0 Uni
Body:	Black Flashabou Accent
Thorax:	Black Super Fine
Wing:	White CDC

Spotter Midge

Originator: Mary Dette
Tier: Bob Magill

Hook:	#20-22 Mustad Viking 94833
Thread:	Black 8/0 Uni
Tail:	Black hackle
Body:	Tying thread
Wing:	White duck quill
Hackle:	Black

L2HF Dry Fly

Originator: Al Ritt
Tier: Al Ritt

Hook:	#16-22 Tiemco 100 or 101
Thread:	Olive 14/0 Gordon Griffiths
Body:	Olive quill
Thorax:	Whiting olive dyed grizzly
Back:	Gator Hair
Indicator:	Fl. pink Antron

Spent Wing Midge

Originator: Rob Jiron
Tier: Rob Jiron

Hook:	#18-22 Tiemco 100
Thread:	Black 8/0 Uni
Body:	Tying thread
Wing:	White Darlon

Para Midge-Gician

Originator: Kevan Evans
Tier: Kevan Evans

Hook:	#18-24 Tiemco 2487
Thread:	Purple 8/0 Uni
Body:	Tying thread
Rib:	Fire orange 8/0 Uni
Post:	Yellow Antron
Hackle:	Grizzly hackle
Wing:	White Swiss Straw

X-tended Rag'n Midge-Gician

Originator: Kevan Evans
Tier: Kevan Evans

Hook:	#18-24 Tiemco 2487
Thread:	Fire orange 8/0
Body:	Red Krystal Flash
Wing:	White Swiss Straw
Post:	Yellow Antron
Hackle:	Grizzly hackle

Note: Coat the body with Loon UV Knot Sense.

"O" Shoot Midge (Red)

Originator: Scott Stisser
Tier: Scott Stisser

Hook: #18-24 Tiemco 2487
Thread: Red 6/0 Uni
Body: Tying thread
Rib: Silver Lagartun wire (fine)
Wing: Mylar tinsel
Thorax: Black dubbing
Post: White poly yarn
Hackle: Brown ostrich

"O" Shoot Midge (Pearl)

Originator: Scott Stisser
Tier: Scott Stisser

Hook: #18-24 Tiemco 2487
Thread: Olive 6/0 Uni
Body: Pearl Krystal Flash
Wing: Mylar tinsel
Thorax: Black dubbing
Post: White poly yarn
Hackle: Black ostrich

Adult Midge (Black)

Originator: Scott Stisser
Tier: Scott Stisser

Hook: #18-24 Tiemco 2487
Thread: Black 6/0 Uni
Body: Stripped grizzly hackle stem
Wing: Mylar tinsel
Thorax: Black dubbing
Wing case: White foam strip
Hackle: Dark dun

CDC Parachute Midge (Black)

Originator: Shane Stalcup
Tier: Dennis Martin

Hook: #18-24 Tiemco 2488
Thread: Black 14/0 Gordon Griffiths
Body: Goose biot dyed black
Wing: White poly yarn
Hackle: Black CDC
Thorax: Light olive Superdry

CDC Parachute Midge (Olive)

Originator: Shane Stalcup
Tier: Dennis Martin

Hook: #18-24 Tiemco 2487
Thread: Olive 14/0 Gordon Griffiths
Body: Goose biot dyed olive
Wing: White poly yarn
Hackle: Natural CDC
Thorax: Gray Superdry

CDC Parachute Midge (Tan)

Originator: Shane Stalcup
Tier: Dennis Martin

Hook: #18-24 Tiemco 2487
Thread: Olive 14/0 Gordon Griffiths
Body: Goose biot dyed tan
Wing: White poly yarn
Hackle: Tan CDC
Thorax: Light gray Superdry

Dangler

Originator: Ed Koch
Tier: Kevin Compton

Hook:	#20 Grip 11011BL
Thread:	Yellow 10/0 Gudebrod
Tail:	Whiting Coq de Leon
Body:	Pale yellow Kreinik
Hackle:	Whiting Farms grizzly saddle

No Name Midge

Originator: Ed Shenk
Tier: Kevin Compton

Hook:	#20 Grip 14723BL
Thread:	Blue dun 10/0 Gudebrod
Body:	Muskrat belly fur
Hackle:	Whiting Farms grizzly saddle

Brown Midge

Originator: Ed Koch
Tier: Kevin Compton

Hook:	#20 Grip 11011BL
Thread:	Brown 10/0 Gudebrod
Tail:	Whiting brown hackle
Body:	Tying thread
Hackle:	Whiting Farms brown grizzly saddle

Peg's Midge Variant

Originator: Peg Myers
Tier: Kevin Compton

Hook:	#20 Tiemco 100 SP-BL
Thread:	Black 10/0 Gudebrod
Tail:	Whiting grizzly hackle tip
Body:	Pale peacock herl
Hackle:	Whiting Farms grizzly variant

Dangler

Originator: Kevin Compton
Tier: Kevin Compton

Hook:	#20 Grip 11013BL
Thread:	Black 10/0 Gudebrod
Body:	Tan CDC
Legs:	Tan CDC
Wing:	Whiting Coq de Leon hen neck feather tip

Lipstick Midge

Originator: Dennis Smith
Tier: Dennis Smith

Hook:	#20 Tiemco 2488
Thread:	Olive 8/0 Uni
Body:	Red orange Micro Tubing, crimped
Wing:	Wood duck
Thorax:	Hare's ear dubbing

CDC Adult Midge

Originator: Unknown
Tier: Bubba Smith

Hook: #18-20 Tiemco 531
Thread: Black 8/0 Uni
Tail: Black hackle
Body: Tying thread
Hackle: Black Henry's Fork Hackle

Paraloop Adult Midge

Originator: Unknown
Tier: Bubba Smith

Hook: #18-24 Tiemco 900BL
Thread: Black 8/0 Uni
Tail: Black hackle
Body: Tying thread
Wing: White Fluoro Fibre
Hackle: Grizzly tied Paraloop style

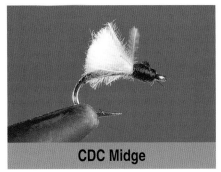

CDC Midge

Originator: Unknown
Tier: Bubba Smith

Hook: #18-24 Tiemco 2488
Thread: Black 8/0 Uni
Body: Tying thread
Wing: White CDC
Head: Tying thread

Hopper's Dry Midge

Originator: Unknown
Tier: Bruce Hopper

Hook: #22 Tiemco 101
Thread: Black 8/0 Uni
Tail: Black Microfibetts
Body: Tying thread
Hackle: Whiting Farms grizzly saddle

Dry Midge Egg Layer

Originator: Roy Christie
Tier: Roy Christie

Hook: #12-16 Drennan Sedge
Thread: Brown Pearsall's silk
Hackle: Grizzly
Wing: Tiemco Aero Dry Wing and Krystal Flash
Thorax: Gray Super Fine and pheasant tail

Copper Wire Hare's Ear

Originator: Roy Christie
Tier: Roy Christie

Hook: #16 Gaelic Supreme Syl Nemes Soft Hackle
Thread: Copper wire
Body: Natural hare's mask dubbing

Upside Down Dry Midge

Originator: Roy Christie
Tier: Roy Christie

Hook:	#10-16 Daiichi 1270
Thread:	Antique gold Pearsall's silk
Body:	Peacock herl, stripped
Wing:	Tiemco Aero Dry Wing and Krystal Flash
Thorax:	Rabbit dubbing
Thorax cover:	Pheasant tail
Hackle:	Grizzly

Hellsgate Butt Biter

Originator: John Larson
Tier: John Larson

Hook:	#32 Tiemco 518
Thread:	Black 14/0 Gordon Griffiths
Body:	Black horse tail
Wing:	Clear Swiss Straw under dun CDC

Note: Coat body with Wet and Wild Rock Solid Nail Polish.

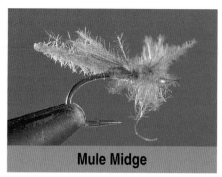

Mule Midge

Originator: Kevin Rogers
Tier: Rick Takahashi

Hook:	#18-24 Tiemco 2488
Thread:	White 17/0 Uni
Body:	Tan Micro Dub
Legs:	Light dun CDC
Wing:	Natural CDC

Antron Mule

Originator: Kevin Rogers
Tier: Rick Takahashi

Hook:	#18-24 Tiemco 2488
Thread:	White 17/0 Uni
Body:	Tan Micro Dub
Legs:	Dun CDC
Wing:	White Antron

Hi-Vis Midge

Originator: Steve Schweitzer
Tier: Steve Schweitzer

Hook:	#20-22 Tiemco 101
Thread:	Black 12/0 Bennechi
Body:	Stripped peacock herl coated with head cement
Post:	Fl. orange Chick-A-Bou
Hackle:	Whiting Farms Midge Saddle

Midge Parachute

Originator: Noritaka Osada
Tier: Noritaka Osada

Hook:	#19-23 Tiemco 212Y
Thread:	Black 16/0 Tiemco
Post:	Pink Tiemco Aero Dry Wing
Rib:	Black mono thread
Body:	Tan 16/0 Tiemco thread
Thorax:	Synthetic peacock
Hackle:	Dun

Midge Cripple

Originator: Noritaka Osada
Tier: Noritaka Osada

Hook: #19-23 Tiemco 112Y
Thread: Tan 16/0 Tiemco
Shuck: Z-lon and Melty Fiber
Abdomen: Tying thread
Rib: Green Danville 3/0 Monocord
Thorax: Black 16/0 Tiemso thread
Wing: Cream CDC
Hackle: Dun

Midge Spent

Originator: Noritaka Osada
Tier: Noritaka Osada

Hook: #19-23 Tiemco 112Y
Thread: Olive 16/0 Tiemco
Abdomen: Tying thread
Rib: Black Danville 3/0 Monocord
Thorax: Black Super Fine
Wing: Cream CDC

Midge Adult

Originator: Noritaka Osada
Tier: Noritaka Osada

Hook: #19-23 Tiemco 112Y
Thread: Black 16/0 Tiemco
Abdomen: Olive 16/0 Tiemco
Rib: Black Danville 3/0 Monocord
Thorax: Black 16/0 Tiemco
Wing: Cream CDC
Hackle: Dun

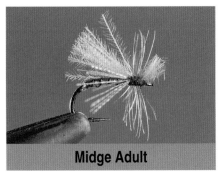

Midge Adult

Originator: Noritaka Osada
Tier: Noritaka Osada

Hook: #19-23 Tiemco 112Y
Thread: Black 16/0 Tiemco
Abdomen: Olive 16/0
Rib: Black Danville 3/0 Monocord
Thorax: Black 16/0
Wing: Cream CDC and Tiemco Molfo Fiber
Hackle: Dun

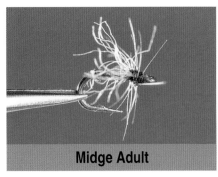

Midge Adult

Originator: Noritaka Osada
Tier: Noritaka Osada

Hook: #32 Tiemco 518
Thread: Black 16/0 Tiemco
Abdomen: Tan 16/0 Tiemco
Thorax: Black 16/0 Tiemco
Wing: Ram's wool
Hackle: Light blue dun

Cluster Patterns

Hi-Vis Griffith's Gnat

Originator: Unknown
Tier: Umpqua Feather Merchants

Hook:	#18-22 Tiemco 100
Thread:	Black 6/0 Uni
Body:	Peacock herl
Rib:	Gold Ultra Wire (extra small)
Post:	Fl. pink Float Hi-Vis
Hackle:	Grizzly

Griffith's Gnat

Originator: Unknown
Tier: Umpqua Feather Merchants

Hook:	#18-22 Tiemco 101
Thread:	Black 6/0 Uni
Body:	Peacock herl
Hackle:	Grizzly

Paraloop Midge Cluster

Originator: Martin Westbeek
Tier: Martin Westbeek

Hook:	#17 Tiemco 102Y
Thread:	Charcoal 16/0 Tiemco
Body:	Peacock herl
Post:	White poly yarn, doubled
Hackle:	Whiting speckled badger saddle

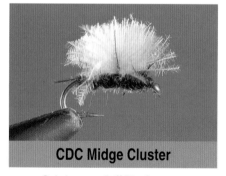

CDC Midge Cluster

Originator: Jeff Henkemeyer
Tier: Jeff Henkemeyer

Hook:	#22 Tiemco 100
Thread:	Black 14/0 Gordon Griffiths
Body:	Black CDC dubbing
Wing:	Natural CDC

Sparkle Tail Midge

Originator: Rainy Riding
Tier: Rainy's Fly Company

Hook:	#18-20 Tiemco 100
Thread:	Black 8/0 Uni
Tail:	White Antron
Body:	Gunmetal glass beads
Hackle:	Grizzly

Split Tail Midge

Originator: Rainy Riding
Tier: Rainy's Fly Company

Hook:	#14-20 Tiemco 100
Thread:	Black 8/0 Uni
Tail:	Pearl Krystal Flash
Body:	Gunmetal glass beads
Hackle:	Olive dyed grizzly

Double Hackle Stacker

Originator: Jason Haslam
Tier: Rainy's Fly Company

Hook: #16-18 Tiemco 100
Thread: Black 8/0 Uni
Body: Tying thread
Hackle: Two grizzly tied Hackle
Stacker style

Sparkle Tail Midge (Pearl)

Originator: Rainy Riding
Tier: Rainy's Fly Company

Hook: #18-20 Tiemco 100
Thread: Black 8/0 Uni
Tail: White Antron
Body: Pearl glass beads
Hackle: Grizzly

Split Tail Midge (Black)

Originator: Rainy Riding
Tier: Rainy's Fly Company

Hook: #14-20 Tiemco 100
Thread: Black 8/0 Uni
Body: Gunmetal glass beads
Tail: Pearl Krystal Flash
Hackle: Black

Midge Cluster Paraloop

Originator: Sue Armstrong
Tier: Sue Armstrong

Hook: #12-18 Daiichi 1330
Thread: Black 70-denier UTC
Body: Peacock herl
Hackle: Dark barred ginger

Arizona Dot

Originator: Jeremy Davies
Tier: Jeremy Davies

Hook: #10-20 Tiemco 100
Thread: Olive 8/0 Uni
Body: Natural peacock Arizona
dubbing
Hackle: Grizzly

Double Cluster

Originator: Rick Takahashi
Tier: Rick Takahashi

Hook: #16-22 Tiemco 100
Thread: Black 8/0 Uni
Body: Peacock Ice Dub
Wing: Black Z-lon

Double Threat Cluster

Originator: Rick Takahashi
Tier: Rick Takahashi

Hook: #16-22 Tiemco 100
Thread: Black 70-denier UTC
Body: Tying thread
Wing: Black Antron
Hackle: Grizzly trimmed flat on the bottom

Snowshoe Cluster Midge

Originator: Jim Cannon
Tier: Jim Cannon

Hook: #18-22 Tiemco 2487
Thread: Black 8/0 Uni
Wing: Snowshoe rabbit foot hair
Hackle: Grizzly
Note: For the wing, blend 33% bleached white rabbit, 33% dyed black rabbit, and 33% pearl Ice Dub.

High-Vis Parachute Midge

Originator: Unknown
Tier: Montana Fly Company

Hook: #10-14 MFC 7000
Thread: Black 6/0 Uni
Post: Fl. orange Antron Body Wool
Body: Peacock herl
Hackle: Grizzly

Double Parachute Midge

Originator: Unknown
Tier: Montana Fly Company

Hook: #10-14 MFC 7000
Thread: Black 8/0 Uni
Body: Peacock herl
Posts: Black Widow's Web
Hackle: Grizzly

Gould's Chernobyl Gnat

Originator: Unknown
Tier: Montana Fly Company

Hook: #10-14 MFC 7000
Thread: Black 8/0 Uni
Body: Black foam
Legs: Black Centipede Legs
Hackle: Grizzly

Carlson's LOZO Midge

Originator: Unknown
Tier: Montana Fly Company

Hook: #10-14 MFC 7000
Thread: Black 6/0 Uni
Body: Peacock herl
Wing: White calf tail
Hackle: Grizzly

DM's White Midge Cluster

Originator: Dennis Martin
Tier: Dennis Martin

Hook: #18-24 Tiemco 100
Thread: White 14/0 Gordon Griffiths
Body: White Midge Tubing
Hackle: White

Gray Herl Midge

Originator: Ed Koch
Tier: Kevin Compton

Hook: #20 Partridge K1A
Thread: Gray 10/0 Gudebrod
Body: Gray ostrich herl
Tail: Grizzly

Extended Disco Orgy

Originator: Kevan Evans
Tier: Kevan Evans

Hook: #20 Tiemco 101
Thread: Fl. pink 8/0 Uni
Body: Pink Diamond Midge Braid
Wing: Clear white Swiss Straw
Thorax: Tying thread
Hackle: Grizzly

Hackle Stacker Midge Cluster

Originator: Unknown
Tier: Bubba Smith

Hook: #18-24 Tiemco 100
Thread: Black 8/0 Uni
Body: Tying thread
Hackle: Grizzly tied Paraloop style

Double Parachute Midge Cluster

Originator: Unknown
Tier: Bubba Smith

Hook: #18-22 Tiemco 100
Thread: Black 8/0 Uni
Body: Tying thread
Hackle: Grizzly tied Paraloop style

Flat Mating Midge

Originator: Roy Christie
Tier: Roy Christie

Hook: #10 Daiichi 1270
Thread (rear): Claret Pearsall's silk
Hackle (rear): Grizzly dyed brown
Thorax (rear): Brown Super Fine
Thread: Primrose Pearsall's silk
Hackle: Grizzly dyed olive yellow
Thorax: Olive Super Fine
Bodies: Tying thread

Cluster Midge

Originator: Masa Katsumata
Tier: Masa Katsumata

Hook:	#16 Tiemco 206BL
Thread:	Black 8/0 Uni
Abdomen:	Tying thread
Wing:	Clear Medallion Sheeting
Hackle:	Black Whiting Midge Saddle

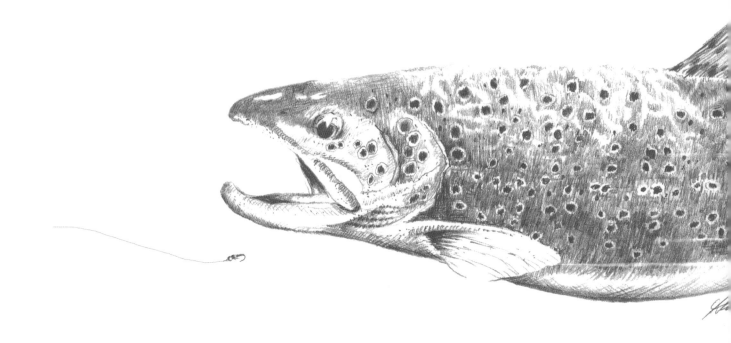

PART

Fishing the Midge:
Tips from the Masters

FISHING WITH SMALL flies can present a daunting challenge to many fly anglers, who may be intimidated by the lighter tippets, smaller flies, and precise drifts required when fishing these patterns. But, as with everything else, the more you do it, the better you become. This section of the book delves into the variety of techniques, rigs, and nuances associated with fly fishing with midges, from the perspective of a number of fly fishers who fish a lot midges. You'll find some similarities in each individual's approach and the subtleties that can sometimes mean the difference between catching and not catching fish. The puzzle of successful midge fly fishing isn't solved by using just one technique or approach. To that end, we've asked avid midge anglers around the world to discuss the equipment they prefer to fish with, how they prepare to fish, tippets and the flies or rigs they prefer, and strategies that they use in a variety of situations ranging from stillwaters to tailwaters.

A beauty from B.C. Dr. Brian Chan, stillwater master from British Columbia, releases one of the many Kamloops rainbows that have mistaken his chironomid patterns as the "real deal."

Curing the Fly Fisher's Curse

Dr. Eric Pettine

Jujubee Midge

MANY ANGLERS FEEL they are not up to catching trout when the fish are feeding on insects the size of dandruff. Even though trout will often feed heavily on these tiny insects, the hatch is considered "too technical" for the average angler. Not only do many anglers assume they cannot fish midges hatches effectively, but many guides assume their clients would not be able to catch trout during a microhatch.

As a matter of fact, it isn't difficult. To catch trout on dry flies, whether using large or small patterns, it's only necessary to cast 20 feet of line with delicacy and accuracy. Rig a dry-fly rod with about 12 feet of leader. Add a little tuft of poly yarn to the tippet to imitate the fly. Then spend five or ten minutes each day casting to a target. Within a week or two, you'll be able to cast well enough to fish any hatch effectively.

Not all fly rods will cast only 20 or 30 feet well. A stiff rod is great for flinging flies, lead, indicators—and occasionally, the guide—out of the drift boat. That rod will not cast a short line accurately or with delicacy. Most graphite rods will cast a

Author Jerry Hubka looks over his selection of midges to find that special pattern that will bring a trout to the net.

long line much better than they will cast a short line, but effective fly fishers generally are only casting 20 or 30 feet when fishing for trout.

Next you need to tie (or buy) some midge imitations. I like having size 18 to 26. I favor patterns that can be tied in any size without varying the materials. For visibility, I add a small burnt orange or chartreuse post to patterns tied in sizes 18 and 20. A white post is a poor choice since there is already so much white flotsam on the surface of most streams. Size 24 or 26 dry flies are hard to see, so I fish them as a dropper off a larger pattern. For example, I will fish a size 18 midge pattern with a post as the top fly, and the smaller pattern tied off the hook bend on about 18 inches of 7X tippet.

It is essential that you get your fly to the fish. Trout feed with an economy of movement. A stonefly is worth a trip across the river, since it provides plenty of energy. A midge by itself does not provide much in the way of nutrient, and the fish cannot afford to move far to feed on such meager fare. Instead, they let the river bring the food to them. The advantage for the angler is that trout feeding on surface insects have to stay close

to the surface and their cone of vision out of the water is narrow. However, your cast must be accurate to get the fly into the trout's feeding lane. Using caution, you can get close to the trout, making a short and accurate cast possible.

The next problem is that midges hatch so profusely—during a heavy hatch these tiny insects could be measured only by the metric ton—it is often hard to compete with the naturals during the height of the hatch. A better time to fish is before the hatch gets too heavy but after the trout have started feeding on them. An even better opportunity is just as the hatch starts to wane but while the fish are still looking for the insects. During this period, the trout get greedy, and it is possible to take advantage of that. Hunt for bigger fish during the height of the hatch so that when your window of opportunity comes, you won't need to waste precious time on small fish.

Don't expect to run up the score on the trout when fishing a microhatch. The ultimate challenge is to find a bigger trout sipping midges off the surface and, with a little luck, fool it. You cannot expect to land many of these fish using tiny hooks and ultrafine tippets, but the reward equals the effort.

The Midge Game

Craig Mathews

$3.00 Dipity

LIKE MOST ANGLERS, I fought fishing tiny midge patterns on fragile tippets and long leaders to wary trout for many seasons. Now, I successfully fish midge hatches every month of the year. Where I used to balk at tying on a size 20 to 26 fly to a 12-inch leader and adding a long length of tippet, usually of about 2 to 4 feet, I now look forward to "the game." And to successfully play that game, one has to be at the top of theirs. Below are a few points to consider.

Because there is nothing unique about a trout's riseform as it takes midges, the actual presence of midges on the water is the strongest clue that the fish are eating them. I get as close as I can to trout rising to midges. Experience will show you how close you can approach without spooking fish, and each fish may be different. By wading on my knees or sliding along the shoreline on my butt, I can often get within 10 feet, which is

necessary to keep track of my fly and keep it from dragging. If necessary, I lift the leader off the water so it won't become trapped in mixed currents and drag the fly, which can be a problem when casting a long line. To help me see my fly, or where it lands, I drive my forward cast so that the fly lands well above the working trout, landing with a splat. With a little practice, this "splat cast" will help you pick up your tiny pattern as it floats toward the target.

At the top of my list of important gear for midge fishing are Hat Eyes, clip-on magnifiers that attach to the bill of my hat and allow me to tie tiny flies on 6X or 7X tippets. They also help me find the right midge fly in my boxes, which are the C&F brand. It is very important to use the right fly floatant for tiny midge patterns. I like to dress my fly initially with Hydrophobe. Fly Sauce will also work, but the former is better.

A healthy rainbow trout is finally brought to the net after a hard-fought battle.

Both seem to break down and absorb into the bodies of small midge patterns better than the other available floatants. It is also very important to use amadou or a good synthetic fly drier, like Ruby Cell. Since my dry midge patterns are dressed sparsely, it is important to keep them dry and floating in the surface film. If you don't have a good fly drier and use Frog's Fanny powder, you are not in the game. After taking a fish or two, I go to amadou or a Ruby Cell fly drier to dry tiny flies, and then brush on Frog's Fanny. Last season alone I went through a case of Frog's Fanny and always have two in my vest.

Trout love all stages of midges, from larvae to pupae to adults to mating clumps of adults. Several years ago, our good friend, the late Ross Merigold, introduced us to a fly called the Serendipity. We have made some modifications to the original, which year after year proves to be the most effective nymph pattern fished on the Madison, Gallatin, and several other area rivers. Our $3 Dipity, named for the $3.00 Bridge section of

the Madison River where the pattern was born, works the best. We like to fish the $3.00 Dip in brown, olive, and red.

Midges are subject to many emergence defects, and cripples and deformed adults are common during midge hatches. And since midges emerge at the surface and fish feed readily on such flies, we tie most of our midge adult and pupa patterns with trailing shucks. My favorite emerging midge flies are our Improved Zelon Midge and Griffith's Gnat Emerger. These two midges are the most effective dry-fly midge patterns I know of.

Adult midges assemble into mating clumps along the shoreline and behind rocks and logs. At times you might come upon clumps of midges with dozens of individuals making up the mating clump. These clumps might be a full size 14 and roll and tumble with the current downstream. A well-tied size 14 to 22 Griffith's Gnat is a great pattern to imitate these mating clumps.

Reading the River

Jerry Hubka

IF THERE ARE no signs of any actively feeding trout, that does not mean you should just go home. In my experience, trout feed below the surface 80 to 90 percent of the time. Fishing with dry flies is great fun and a real art form, but fishing blind or prospecting for trout under the surface and in the river's currents is also an art.

It's tough fighting a current all of the time, so in most streams and rivers, trout like to hold in slower water, spot their food and move into faster water to take it, and then return to the slower water. The trick is locating these spots. Here are some good places to try:

1. In front of large rocks. The current slows or hesitates and splits just before it goes around the rock. If you can get the fly to these trout, they are sometimes the largest and strongest in the river.

2. Behind the rock. Remember, the biggest fish is at the head of the food line. He is large and in charge of that feeding lane. Don't fish to him first; come up from behind and just

Author Jerry Hubka works a seam, which is a favorite feeding area where trout can feed easily out of the heavy current.

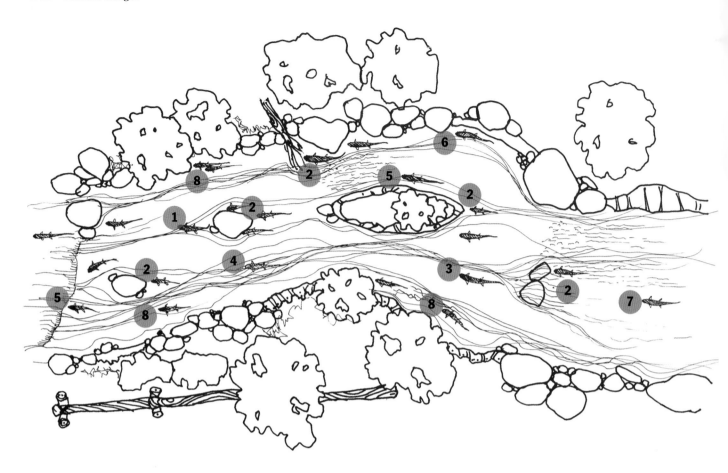

pick off the smaller ones behind him, one at a time. Logs, islands, and other structure provide the same scenarios.

3. Where two water currents come together, they collide, and that collision slows the flow of both currents so that a foam or bubble line usually forms on the surface. Trout seek out these lanes because any food in the water is forced into this narrow trough. Fish on top and under the surface in these current troughs.

4. Near, or on, the bottom of the stream. Sometimes trout just rest and wait for their favorite food to drift by and eat as much as they can. And it's all done in slow motion because currents on the bottom are much slower than they are on top.

5. Where a riffle drops into a pool or flat. Fast water dislodges food in the riffle and drops it into the slower water below. Trout just lay there and wait. They also wait just behind the edge of a ledge or dropoff.

6. On the inside of a bend in the river, or under the cut in the bank on the outside of the bend.

7. A "soft" or "gentle" section of a riffle. This is a smoother surface or flat part in or next to a riffle. These are sometimes the places anglers seek out to wade or stand in, because the water is slower here than in the fast part of the riffle, but they are often standing right in the middle of the fish.

continued on page 244

Obstructions in the stream's currents offer the trout respite from the constant flow and provide a safe haven from which to feed. Trout lie in front of, to the sides, and behind rocks and other structure, waiting for food to pass by.

The Natural Drift

Jerry L. Saiz

The trick to catching large, educated trout is in presenting a natural drift—where your flies are moving at the same speed as the current—but at the same time keeping the leader tight enough to detect when a trout takes the fly before it spits the fly. Fish on the San Juan River, for example, can spit your fly quickly, and with the longer leaders that are often necessary, you may never see the strike if there is too much slack between the fly and indicator.

I try to cast straight upstream to a specific target area and feeding lane. This cast must be made far enough upstream to allow the flies time to sink to the correct depth before reaching the target area. Make sure it's the flies that land in the feeding lane and not the strike indicator. Then, using a modified roll cast, I first try to roll my indicator downstream and over into the same lane as my flies. This is important to get your leader stretched out downstream from your flies, and your indicator in the feeding lane. Be careful not to allow the strike indicator to drag the flies downstream unnaturally.

After the flies, strike indicator, and leader are all in the fish's feeding lane, you must keep it all there, flowing at the same speed and direction as the current, with no movement near your target fishing area. I do this by immediately making an upstream modified roll cast and stacking my fly line directly upstream and in the same lane as my indicator, leader, and flies. You must make this roll cast without taking your indicator out of its lane, thus defeating all the work you have done in setting up the drift. Now you should have everything, including about 2 to 3 feet of fly line, all in the same feeding lane, and all floating at the same speed.

You can now make smaller right or left mends, as needed, taking care to feed this line into the same lane while also feeding sufficient slack to prevent disrupting the natural flow of your strike indicator. If you detect any movement or hesitation of the strike indicator, immediately set the hook.

Jerry Hubka concentrates on watching for the subtle hints of line movement indicating that a trout has taken one of his flies.

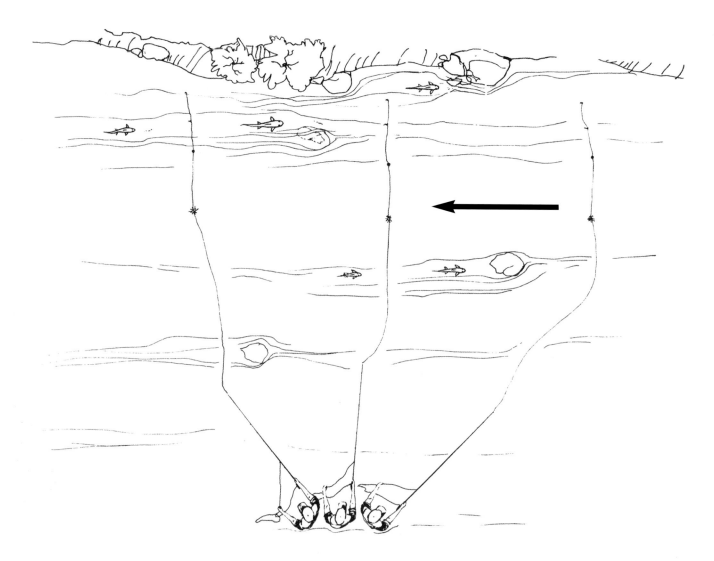

After an upstream cast, I mend immediately, so that my flies, strike indicator, leader, and fly line are in a straight line with each other as much as possible and floating together perpendicular to the current. If your strike indicator is dragging your weight and flies downstream at a rate faster than the current, the fish will ignore your flies. Continue to mend, if necessary, to keep everything in a straight line, but try to get the drift correct before the flies and weight get down to the fish. If you have a bad drift, pick it up well before it reaches the fish and re-cast, or leave it alone and let the drift run out and slowly lift the flies out of the water at the end of the drift. Sometimes the slow lifting of the flies at the end of the drift emulates the emergence of the midge. The fish see this and sometimes strike at them before they get to the surface.

8. Fish the seams. Seams are where fast water and slow water meet or run alongside each other. Trout rest in the slow water, and feed out of the faster water, and then return to the slower water. Trout biologist Dr. Robert Bachman has determined that all trout like to rest in water that is traveling one-quarter to one-half feet per second (fps), because they are not expending any energy and therefore not unnecessarily burning calories. Rainbow trout prefer to feed in water that is traveling about 6 fps. All other species of trout prefer to feed in water traveling much slower, at around 2 fps.

These are the obvious places where fish feed, but there are many more, like shallow riffles, deep runs, big pools, and gentle flats. Each of these types of water has special fishing techniques for angling success, but that's for another book. I'm always surprised when I catch a trout in an unlikely place on the river, so try all the likely and even the unlikely spots. But, if you want to maximize your chances, read the water and think about where the trout might like to rest, eat, and hang out.

Sight-Fishing Strategies

Carrot Midge Pupa

Rick Takahashi

MOST OF THE waters I fish allow me to see the fish as they feed. I'll watch to see if they are actively feeding and how they move as they take their food. My strategy is to determine at what depth they are feeding and to mimic a natural drift. Remember that the fish are not in exactly the same location as you see them, due to the parallax effect of the water. It may require some experimentation to determine their exact position, but I generally find that they are actually closer to me than they appear when viewed from above. Try to adjust for this and cast a little shorter to the fish than you think you should to put the fly directly in front of the fish or just to the side of the fish closest to you, which prevents dragging the tippet over the fish and putting it down or scaring it away from its feeding lane.

When casting to visible fish, I try to approach from the side, if possible, and walk and wade carefully so that I do not spook the fish. I keep a low profile and try to blend in with the background, moving slowly and making a minimum number of false casts. Using polarized sunglasses and a hat with a bill

This fat cutthroat fell for a midge larva drifted near the bottom of a weed-lined trough.

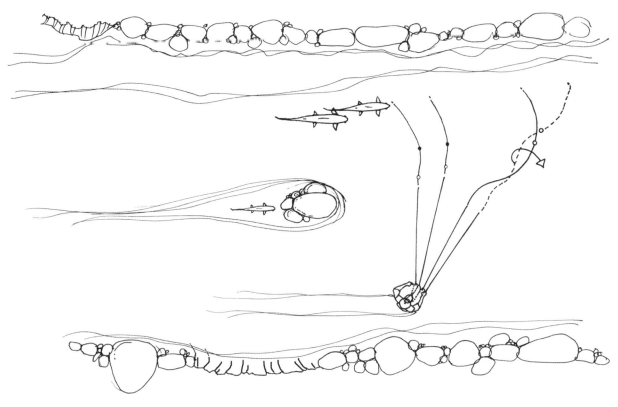

Cast your flies approximately 2 to 3 feet directly upstream of the fish. Mend the line upstream to allow your flies to sink to the fish's level. You may need to make several mends. Pull the flies into the feeding lane and follow the line with the rod tip. Watch for any signs that the fish has taken your fly such as the "wink" of a white mouth or movement.

Mending the line upstream or down is essential for a drag-free drift.

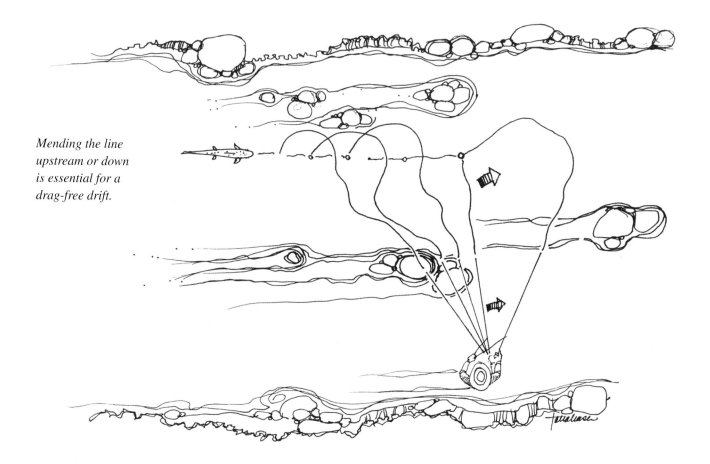

to shade my eyes helps me to see into the water. If I can't approach the fish from the side, I'll try to throw a curve or reach cast to either side of the fish. This may require making several casts to the fish. If I make a bad cast, I generally allow the flies to pass well beyond and behind the trout before I pick up the line for the next one. Even then, I pick up the line gently and false-cast in a different direction and away from the fish, if possible.

When sight-fishing, the strike indicator is more of a placement tool than something that actually indicates a strike. After casting, I make a large mend upstream (or downstream, in slow flows) and immediately turn my concentration to the feeding fish. I mend the line for two reasons: To allow the fly to get to the proper depth and to compensate for the effects of the current. I watch the fish for telltale signs that it has intercepted the fly—such as the wink of an open mouth, or an up-and-down or side-to-side motion—and gently lift the rod tip to see if the fish has taken the fly. Oftentimes the strike indicator

Keep Your Flies Clean

Some of the rivers and streams I fish have algae or other debris in them, which my flies pick up. Trying to clean the flies by picking off this "junk" by hand can be difficult and time consuming. I use a circular cast, best described as a circular whipping motion, slapping the flies on the water to dislodge any junk on the hook. I do this far away from the trout I've already targeted to avoid spooking the fish.

doesn't move. It's important to remember to constantly adjust your setup to adapt to the present fishing conditions. I change weight, adjust my strike indicator, or make any other changes necessary as conditions evolve. This also means that I have to make changes every time I move from my position.

Alternative Nymphing Strategies

Rick Takahashi

UVZ Midge

ACROSS THE COUNTRY, the most common way of fishing a nymph is by what is called "high-sticking." High-sticking is a technique that allows you to bounce your flies off the bottom. You hold your rod tip high to keep line off the water for a better drift. This close-range technique is deadly; however, I use two other less common techniques when fishing midges subsurface: straight-line nymphing and the induced take.

STRAIGHT-LINE NYMPHING

Straight-line nymphing is a technique I've used since I first started nymph fishing as a kid. Back in the day, I didn't know what a strike indicator was, so I had to rely on my sense of touch to feel when trout took my flies. I still like this technique for fishing all the way across a stream, if required, from shallow water to deep runs. Without an indicator you can fish at different depths easier.

In straight-line nymphing you cast upstream then lower the rod tip and pull the sunken flies toward you—opposite of indicator and dead-drift tactics.

The beauty of this river must be ignored when guiding a large trout through tricky pocketwater.

A large rainbow inhales several midge pupae at a time.

Let the Fish Settle Down

Once I've hooked the fish, I keep light pressure on it, and during the first few minutes of the fight, I allow it to do whatever it wants. I try not to put too much pressure on the fish, because in my experience this either causes the hook to pull out of the fish's mouth or I break the tippet. After the fish settles down a bit, I begin to play it and then, hopefully, land it.

I cast directly upstream, then immediately lower my rod tip to the surface while pulling in all the slack line. This allows me to put tension on the fly as it drifts toward me. This is in direct conflict with the notion of creating a dead-drift; in fact, I'm pulling the flies ever so slightly toward me. I sometimes get caught on the rocks because I'm fishing with more weight than I would usually use while nymph fishing. That's one reason I tie my own flies—I lose so many.

INDUCED TAKE

When fish flash in the current or rise to intercept ascending insects (but not break the surface), and my dead-drift tactics aren't working, I'll try this technique that I learned from a guide on the San Juan. Fishing a midge pupa or larva as a dropper and a pupa as the point fly, I add a heavier weight and move the strike indicator a little higher. I cast quartering well upstream of the fish's position, mend upstream to get the fly down, then immediately mend downstream. As my strike indicator passes where I think the fish is holding, I start jigging the rod tip while pulling in the fly line. This action causes the flies to rise erratically to the surface, which sometimes induces the fish to take the flies. It doesn't always work, but it works enough for me to keep it in my bag of tricks.

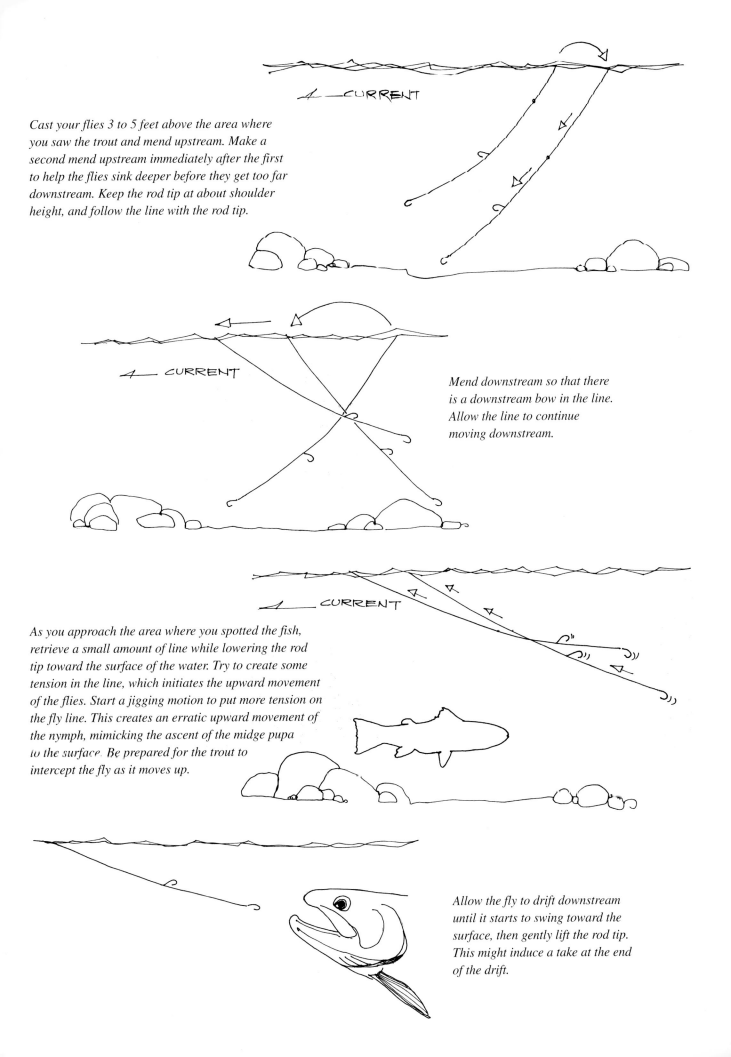

Cast your flies 3 to 5 feet above the area where
you saw the trout and mend upstream. Make a
second mend upstream immediately after the first
to help the flies sink deeper before they get too far
downstream. Keep the rod tip at about shoulder
height, and follow the line with the rod tip.

CURRENT

Mend downstream so that there
is a downstream bow in the line.
Allow the line to continue
moving downstream.

CURRENT

As you approach the area where you spotted the fish,
retrieve a small amount of line while lowering the rod
tip toward the surface of the water. Try to create some
tension in the line, which initiates the upward movement
of the flies. Start a jigging motion to put more tension on
the fly line. This creates an erratic upward movement of
the nymph, mimicking the ascent of the midge pupa
to the surface. Be prepared for the trout to
intercept the fly as it moves up.

CURRENT

Allow the fly to drift downstream
until it starts to swing toward the
surface, then gently lift the rod tip.
This might induce a take at the end
of the drift.

Strike Indicator Strategies

Rick Takahashi

Virus Midge

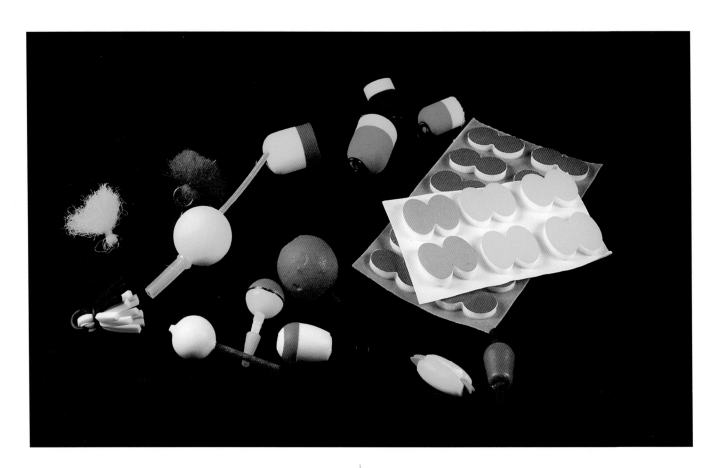

I USE A VARIETY of indicators to match the conditions in which I'm fishing. The color of the strike indicators sometimes bothers the fish, so I try to use darker or more natural colors such as black, white, brown, or tan.

PALSA PINCH-ON STRIKE INDICATORS
I like to use two Palsa indicators at the same time. I attach the first according to the depth and speed of the water, and then attach another 6 to 10 inches above the first. After casting, I mend the line to manipulate the indicators so they are in a direct line. As the drift begins, I watch the first indicator closely. If it moves out of line with the other, I set the hook.

SPIRIT RIVER HOT HEAD INDICATORS
These indicators come in several color combinations: yellow and black, yellow and green, yellow and red, and red and yellow (top color listed first). They float high, are easy to see, and can be adjusted easily (see illustration).

From left to right, homemade yarn indicators, Spirit River Hot Head indicators, Palsa Pinch-On indicators, Orvis Oval indicators, Slotted EZ indicators, Betts's pear shaped slip indicators, Betts's round slip indicators, foam ball indicators, Umpqua foam indicator, Spirit River Pop Top indicators.

BALLOON INDICATORS

Ron Yoshimura, who guides the Colorado and Platte rivers, inflates a black balloon with just enough air to make a small bubble, and then ties it off with an overhand knot. He ties another overhand knot in the leader, pulls the balloon's end over the knot, tightens the overhand knot, and trims the excess balloon. The black color contrasts well against the water and is sensitive to the slightest tug of the line. As long as it is kept small, the balloon does not interfere with your casting.

You can use another trick to make the balloon indicator adjustable up and down along the leader, by stretching the excess balloon material and making one wrap around the leader. Then make a second wrap on the opposite side of the first wrap, and make a knot by placing the end through the second wrap. Tighten the end, and trim the excess.

LOON OUTDOORS BIOSTRIKE INDICATOR MATERIAL

When I want to create a small indicator that is visible on the surface, I like Loon's Biostrike, which has a puttylike consistency and can be molded to the desired shape and applied to the leader. When you dip it in water, it hardens. When fishing patterns just under the surface in conditions where you can't see the fly, try adding a little Biostrike. I generally use this material when I'm fishing stillwaters.

YARN STRIKE INDICATORS

Though you can purchase yarn indicators, I prefer to make my own from poly yarn, which is the same material used in macramé. You can find it in most hobby or craft stores, or you can usually purchase smaller amounts from your favorite fly

Attaching Hot Head Indicators

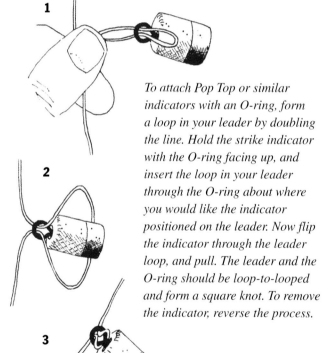

To attach Pop Top or similar indicators with an O-ring, form a loop in your leader by doubling the line. Hold the strike indicator with the O-ring facing up, and insert the loop in your leader through the O-ring about where you would like the indicator positioned on the leader. Now flip the indicator through the leader loop, and pull. The leader and the O-ring should be loop-to-looped and form a square knot. To remove the indicator, reverse the process.

Making a Balloon Indicator

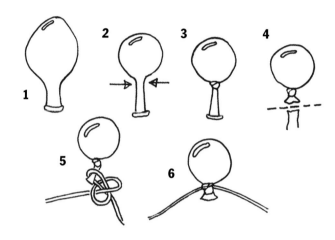

Take a small round party balloon and blow in a small amount of air to create the desired size. Squeeze the balloon stem with your fingers, tie it off with a simple overhand knot, and trim the excess. Form a simple slip knot in the leader at the desired indicator position and tighten the slip knot above the balloon stem knot. Please properly discard the balloon stem and balloon when removed.

Yarn Indicator and Slip Knot

Form a slip knot in the leader where you want the indicator to go. Tighten the slip knot slightly, but leave a large enough loop to easily accommodate the yarn. Slide a piece of yarn through the loop and pull the slip knot tight around the yarn. Trim the yarn if needed. Fluff out the yarn with a small brush or comb and add floatant.

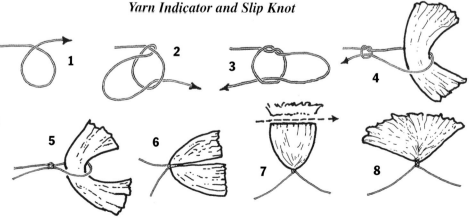

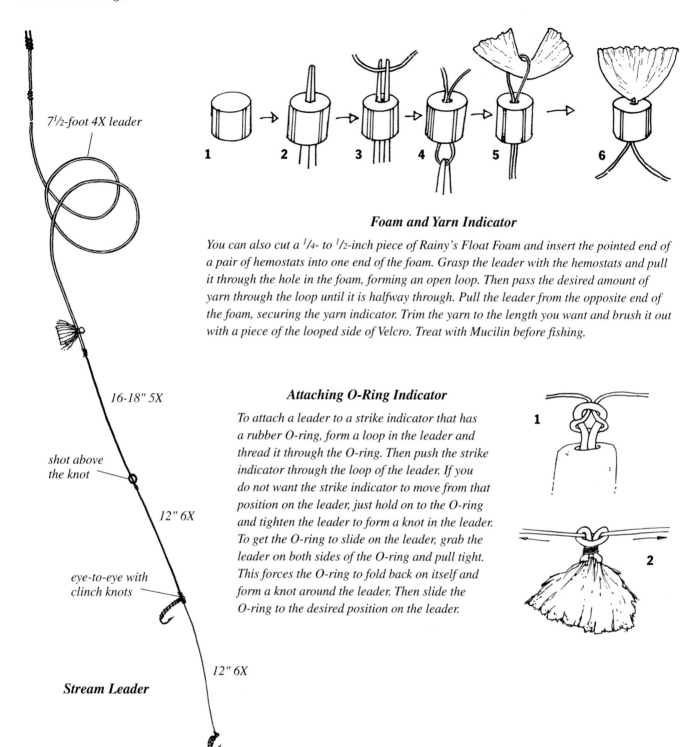

7½-foot 4X leader

16-18" 5X

shot above the knot

12" 6X

eye-to-eye with clinch knots

12" 6X

Stream Leader

Foam and Yarn Indicator

You can also cut a ¹/₄- to ¹/₂-inch piece of Rainy's Float Foam and insert the pointed end of a pair of hemostats into one end of the foam. Grasp the leader with the hemostats and pull it through the hole in the foam, forming an open loop. Then pass the desired amount of yarn through the loop until it is halfway through. Pull the leader from the opposite end of the foam, securing the yarn indicator. Trim the yarn to the length you want and brush it out with a piece of the looped side of Velcro. Treat with Mucilin before fishing.

Attaching O-Ring Indicator

To attach a leader to a strike indicator that has a rubber O-ring, form a loop in the leader and thread it through the O-ring. Then push the strike indicator through the loop of the leader. If you do not want the strike indicator to move from that position on the leader, just hold on to the O-ring and tighten the leader to form a knot in the leader. To get the O-ring to slide on the leader, grab the leader on both sides of the O-ring and pull tight. This forces the O-ring to fold back on itself and form a knot around the leader. Then slide the O-ring to the desired position on the leader.

shop. Yarn indicators are useful because you can make your own on the spot depending on lighting, water conditions, and the amount of weight on your rig. For low, clear water, a small pinch of yarn is one of the stealthiest indicators that you can use. I coat these indicators with Mucilin, but you can use any gel fly floatant.

A guide once shared with me his theory that the trout is more likely to see the two flies placed together in its window of vision than if the flies are placed further apart. This seems plausible to me, so I like to keep the flies 12 inches apart for

that reason. I've fished all my midges with this setup, and have not found any reason to change unless I'm fishing stillwaters.

Micro split-shot in various sizes is critical for fishing your pattern anywhere from just under the surface to right on the bottom. I attach my weight above the blood or surgeon's knot connecting the 5X to 6X, so that the knot prevents it from sliding down the leader. If using a strike indicator, I attach it at a point on the leader one to two times the water depth (determined from the weight to the indicator, not the indicator to the flies).

Micro-Indicators

Jason Borger

WHEN FISHING MIDGES, a strike indicator of even average proportions may be overkill. Micro-indicators can be the answer. Micro-indicators are tiny indicators that cause little or no interference with casting and do not make much disturbance when they hit the water.

When using any micro-indicator, remember that you are really fishing the indicator more than the fly. If you can't see your fly, you can't tell what it's doing. But if you can see your indicator, you know what your leader, and thus likely your fly, is doing. But don't depend on your indicator alone. There are times, especially when using long leaders and slack-line presentations, that a fish may take your fly and your indicator(s) may not relay the message fast enough. Watch where you think your fly is, and be ready to strike if you sense that a fish has taken it.

STRIKE PUTTY
Rubbing putty into the interstices of the knots of your leader (or directly onto the leader itself) creates a dot-to-dot connection to your fly. If the dots suddenly stop, or dart upstream, strike. In addition, the putty dots illuminate your drift. If the dots are dragging, what do you think your midge pupa is doing? This is a modern update to the practice of painting the knots in a leader, or tying bits of floss in, at various points. To get maximum visibility in varied light conditions, try using a different color of putty for each knot. This system also works well for small dry flies and emergers, especially in rougher water.

GREASED LEADER
A greased leader works best in slack water where you don't want anything extra attached to the leader. The idea is to coat the leader with a paste-type floatant down as close to the fly as is necessary. The track of the leader on the surface is visible and, in essence, creates a long monofilament "bobber" that can hold a small larva or pupa at a pre-determined depth. This old technique is a favorite of mine when fishing midge pupae in slow or still waters, since the slightest change in leader position, such as when a fish subtly samples the fly, is immediately visible. Drag issues also become obvious. The downside is that the high-floating leader may spook fish in some circumstances.

Indicators are often an enormous help for detecting strikes, but on pressured fisheries or in low, clear water you do not want to use large ones. For small flies that aren't that heavy, such as a #22 midge pupa that fooled this rainbow, micro-indicators can be the ticket to success.

HOLLOW LINE
A short piece of fly line with the core stripped out of it (available over the years under various brand names, or you can make your own) can not only help to suspend small pupae and such, but it can also reduce the overall indicator "footprint" on the surface. I grew up using core-stripped line, and still use it today when I need an indicator for flies like midges and small nymphs.

COLORED MONO
Another style of micro-indicator, and one that can be incorporated directly into the leader, is a piece of brightly hued monofilament. The idea is to tie a segment of the material in at one or more places in the leader, preferably in the butt or mid-sections. To get a bit more visibility, you can also use a furled or braided section of bright monofilament or thread.

Adjusting Your Rig

Jerry Hubka

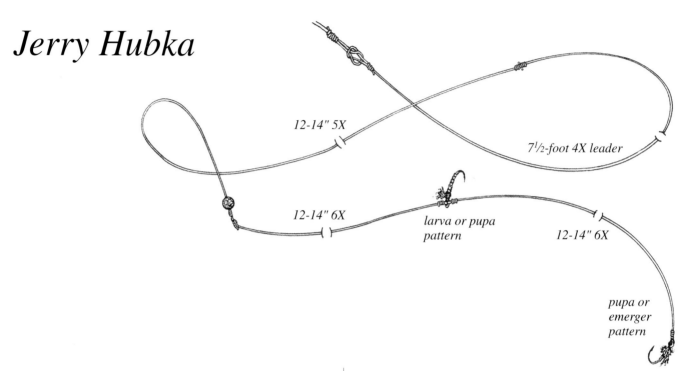

12-14" 5X

7½-foot 4X leader

12-14" 6X

larva or pupa pattern

12-14" 6X

pupa or emerger pattern

IT IS GENERALLY GOOD practice to adjust the strike indicator to one to one-and-a-half times the estimated depth of the water in relation to the weight on the leader. Fish as deep as possible, because fish mostly feed and rest on the bottom of the stream. When fish are porpoising (moving up from the bottom and taking midge pupae and emergers, then returning to the bottom) move the indicator closer to the actual depth of the water so that the dropper fly is drifting in the middle or top

Photographer and midge designer, Brian Yamauchi, shows off a bright rainbow from Eleven Mile Canyon on the South Platte.

area of the stream's current, and the point fly is drifting near the bottom. When the fish are feeding exclusively on emergers, remove the weight or put on a small weight.

I usually start with one size 4 or 6 split-shot, and change as conditions dictate. However, when the fish are feeding on midge emergers or midges that are floating near or just under the surface, I use smaller 8 or 9 split-shot. I sometimes slide the strike indicator all the way up to the top of the leader and remove the weight altogether, using the natural ability of the fluorocarbon leader and tippet to sink the midge just below the surface of the water.

The first fly drifts closer to the bottom because it is closest to the weight, and the dropper fly will drift higher up in the water column because it is farther away from the weight. This dictates the order of the flies on the rig and where they drift in relationship to the bottom, middle, and top of the stream's current. As midges drift in the current, they float at different depths depending on their life cycle stage. Larvae and pupae drift nearer the bottom; pupae and emergers in the middle and up near the surface.

When it looks like trout are feeding on adults, they are sometimes taking midges just below the surface that have not broken through the surface film. By taking the weight off of the fluorocarbon leader, you can put emergers and pupae right in the trout's feeding lane. If you remember this, you will hook more fish.

A Better Two-Fly Rig

Jeff Ehlert

This setup has two advantages over just tying the lower tippet to the upper fly: you can change your upper fly with only one snip and one knot, and the nonslip mono loop allows you to use larger-diameter tippet with small flies, because the loop allows more natural movement of the nymph. When you want to change your upper fly, grab the bottom tippet section and slide it up the upper tippet. Clip off your upper fly, tie on a new one with a nonslip mono loop, and slide the bottom tippet back down.

Attach your indicator (I prefer a small balloon or yarn) above the weight 1 to 1½ times the average depth of the water you plan to fish. The weight, which can be anything from split-shot to a weighted or beadhead midge, will be at this depth as long as it gets to the bottom early in your drift.

This is also a great rig for tandem streamers, or what I call "salt and pepper" (a light-colored streamer followed by a dark streamer). This setup works best with fluorocarbon since monofilament nylon tends to cut through itself after a while.

A lively trout puts on an aerial display as it tries to throw the hook. In Ehlert's two-fly rig, the length of the tippet from the first to the second fly should be longer than the length of fish you expect to catch, otherwise the second hook can pierce the fish during the battle.

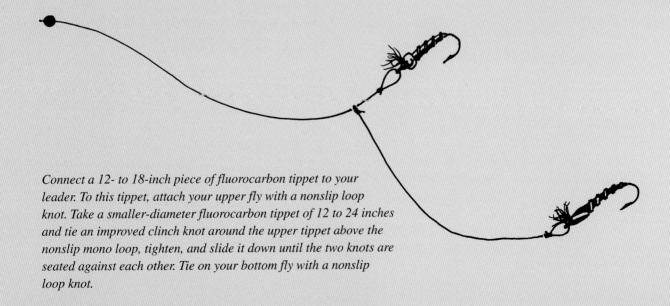

Connect a 12- to 18-inch piece of fluorocarbon tippet to your leader. To this tippet, attach your upper fly with a nonslip loop knot. Take a smaller-diameter fluorocarbon tippet of 12 to 24 inches and tie an improved clinch knot around the upper tippet above the nonslip mono loop, tighten, and slide it down until the two knots are seated against each other. Tie on your bottom fly with a nonslip loop knot.

Fluorocarbon Advantages

Jerry Hubka

IN THE LAST four years, I have replaced all my monofilament leaders and tippet material with fluorocarbon. I firmly believe that I hook more fish and have fewer tippet and knot mishaps with fluorocarbon than with nylon monofilament. I like the stiffness of fluorocarbon and the fact that it sinks quicker than monofilament since most of my midge fishing is below the surface of the water.

Fluorocarbon leaders have some important advantages over monofilament leaders. Specific gravity is the ratio of the density of a substance to the density of water. Water has a specific gravity value of 1.0, so materials that are denser (heavier) than water sink, and those with less density than water will not readily sink. Even materials with specific gravities above 1.0 will not sink unless they can overcome the water's surface tension. That's why lightweight tippet material made from monofilament with a specific gravity of only 1.1 refuses to sink much of the time. Fluorocarbon leaders, on the other hand, are almost twice as dense as water. With a specific gravity of 1.9, fluorocarbon easily overcomes the water's surface tension and sinks just below the water's surface.

Another advantage of fluorocarbon over monofilament is the refractory index. Water has a refractory index of 1.33, and if your leader had that same refractory index it would be totally invisible in water. Fluorocarbon leaders have a refractory index of 1.42, compared to an index value of 1.62 for nylon monofilament, thus making the fluorocarbon leaders as invisible in water as current technology allows.

Fluorocarbon has a harder coating than monofilament, which makes it more abrasion resistant. Also, it retains its strength longer, because nylon monofilament becomes weaker over time as it it exposed to sunlight, whereas fluorocarbon does not. Lastly, fluorocarbon material has higher knot strength than monofilament. Whenever I used to have a leader or tippet failure with monofilament, it was usually at the knot.

Fluorocarbon is more expensive, but why would you buy a $600 fly rod, a $350 reel, and a $65 fly line, and then go cheap all of a sudden with the most important connection between you and that large trout?

Jerry Hubka inspects his fly box and prepares to fish the pocketwater of the Cache LaPoudre River.

Stillwater Tactics

Brian Chan

CHIRONOMIDS, OR MIDGES, represent the most significant source of food for trout and other fish species inhabiting lakes and ponds. The estimated 2,000 species of Chironomidae identified within North America are ecologically and biologically diverse and can be found living in a wide variety of environments, from shallow marine waters to arctic ponds to sewage treatment lagoons. Chironomid species found in shallow, nutrient-rich lakes can be large, with larvae and pupae reaching over 20mm, or ¾ inch, in length. Chironomid pupae are found in a wide variety of colors, with the most common being black, maroon, green, and brown, and various shades of each color. There are various sizes and colors of pupae, and trout can be selective about both. The proper and selective use of a throat pump can provide you with samples of still-live

This rainbow trout from a high mountain reservoir grew fat feeding on midges. Most midges in lakes are large. Pupal patterns tied on size 16 to 10 shrimp/pupa hooks, such as the Mustad Signature C49S or Tiemco 2457, are the norm for these lakes. The largest pupal patterns are dressed on 3XL size 8 to 12 hooks.

Brian Chan releasing a big rainbow. In the early season, the midges hatch in shallow water; later in the season, they hatch in deeper water. As with many other flies, chironomid larva and pupa patterns fish better when tied on with a loop knot. This style of knot allows the fly to move much more naturally, whether being retrieved or suspended under a strike indicator.

pupae from the esophagus of the fish. This is invaluable information for determining and changing pupal pattern size, as feeding selectivity changes throughout the day.

Several significant factors produce the exceptional chironomid fishing found in lakes and ponds. First, there are many species of chironomids, which means they hatch from ice out well into late summer. Second, during a hatch, thousands upon thousands of pupae ascend to the surface, and trout literally breathe in pupae because of the sheer densities of them. Third, many of the chironomid species are relatively large, so they can make up a significant proportion of the trout's annual diet. As an added bonus, trout and other gamefish species eat so many of these insects that they will take imitations of them even when there is no actual emergence, or when only minor ones are occurring, such as in the late fall.

Larval and pupal stages typically attract the greatest attention from stillwater trout. The fish are often so stuffed with pupae that they are no longer in search of an evening meal of the egg-laying adults. It is also much safer for a fish to be feeding closer to the lake bottom than at or nearer the surface, so that predators such as osprey and loons can be avoided. This is especially true in lakes with clear water. With that said, on some stillwaters, newly emerged and egg-laying adults can also be important food sources.

Trout feed most heavily on the pupal stage, due in large part to the sheer numbers that can be present during an emergence. Historical diet studies done on numerous Kamloops-

area lakes have shown that a 3-pound trout could easily have well over 1,500 pupae in its stomach, all of which would have been ingested during a single morning or afternoon feeding period. Pupal emergences occur over a wide range of depths, but most larvae live in water from 8 to 25 feet deep, which coincides with the extent of the littoral, or shoal, zone of a typical lake. Generally, the earliest emergences of the season begin in shallow water and gradually move out deeper as water and air temperatures increase. Therefore by mid to late summer, some of the best hatches will be in the deepest parts, which on many lakes can be between 25 and 50 feet in depth. Chironomids start emerging within days of the ice coming off a lake, but the most intense emergences begin once the surface water temperature reaches between 50 and 55 degrees F. This tells us that water temperatures at the bottom of the lake have been warm enough to complete the transition from larval to pupal life stage. In the Kamloops area, the most intense chironomid emergences occur from early May through the end of July. Intense means heavy, multiple-species emergences that leave windrows of shucks on the water. On many bodies of water, smaller and shorter duration emergences continue through at least the end of September.

Larvae are also an important trout food source, especially those of larger species that can easily reach almost an inch in length. In most feeding situations, trout cruise along the lake bottom and suck out the larvae from their tubecases. It is common to pump a trout's throat and retrieve live larvae and remnants of their muddy cases. Larval densities can be high, and they make easy meals. There are also situations when larvae float on the surface of the lake or suspend in the water, often after spring or fall turnover. Turnover is the complete mixing of the water column, a process that creates currents that sweep across the lake bottom and can pull the larvae out of their tubes, making them even easier meals. Also, larvae that overwinter in the lake often move from shallow water to deeper water and re-establish their tubecases in the late fall. This migration ensures that the larvae develop under ideal conditions during the winter. Migrating larvae can get swept up into the water by wind moving across the littoral or shoal areas. Trout are often moving back onto the shoal or shallow-water areas at the same time, as they are looking for as much food as possible before a long winter.

TACTICS

The most effective way to fish lakes is from some type of watercraft. Just as important, though, is having an anchor (or two) to ensure that your fishing platform does not move, particularly when the wind is constantly changing direction. Anchoring your boat at both bow and stern is the best way to minimize movement. The goal is to have as much control as possible over your retrieve, so that even the most subtle takes by the trout can be detected. It is also important to know the depth you are fishing, so that flies representing specific life stages can be presented at the right depth. Estimating depth can be as simple as marking anchor ropes at 3-foot intervals, or, better yet, using a depth sounder or fish finder.

A variety of fly lines can be used to effectively fish larva, pupa, and adult patterns, but the floating line is the most versatile and often the most effective. This is because most pupae hatch in water less than about 25 feet. A floating line and long leader, with or without a strike indicator, effectively covers these depths.

Rainbows, brook trout, and kokanee all prefer to feed on the larvae and pupae closer to the bottom than near the surface of the lake. To present larvae and pupae imitations as close to the bottom as possible, use a floating line and tapered leader that is at least 25 percent longer than the depth zone being fished. Cast your weighted or unweighted pattern out, let it sink to within about a foot of the bottom, and then begin a painfully slow hand-twist or strip retrieve to move the larval or pupal pattern horizontally through the water while the fly stays in the desired depth zone. This technique is extremely effective, but it requires considerable patience to wait for the fly to sink and then to maintain the slow retrieve. Though the real pupae are moving slowly up through the water, your goal is to keep the fly at the depth where the trout are actually feeding. Strikes are often soft, as the trout are just inhaling pupa after pupa while lazily swimming along or near the lake bottom. This is why it is so important to be as stationary as possible. This same setup can be used to wind-drift your fly from the anchored position. With a gentle breeze at your back, cast out to either side and allow the floating line and fly to be pushed downwind. The undulating motion caused by the wave action imparts a natural up-and-down action to the fly.

Floating lines and strike indicators, which suspend your fly at a precise depth, are also a deadly combination and the easiest way to learn how to catch fish with chironomid pupae. Hard foam indicators are durable, easy to cast, and visible. Set the depth of the fly at between 12 and 18 inches off the lake bottom, and gradually move it higher in 6- to 12-inch intervals until you get a strike. Sometimes the trout only want the pupa if it is sitting almost perfectly still, and other times a slight bobbing action of the fly is enough to trigger a strike. A slight riffle or chop on the water often provides the perfect amount of action to a pattern suspended under an indicator. You can enhance movement by wind-drifting with the indicator setup. Indicators are ideal to use when fishing depths of between 5 and 15 feet. They can be used effectively in deeper water, such as 20 to 25 feet deep, but in these cases a quick-release indicator makes it a lot easier to land a fish (see page 265). Some days the trout will pull the indicator quickly under; other days all you'll see is a slight quiver. Watch your indicator closely at all times.

You can also imitate the pupae's ascent with slow-sinking or intermediate lines, particularly the clear intermediate lines, in water that is 15 to 25 feet deep. Allow the pupa pattern to

This rainbow took a pupa pattern suspended under an indicator. Standard indicators work well in depths of between 5 and 15 feet. For deeper water, use a quick-release indicator system.

sink to the bottom before beginning a continuous slow hand-twist or strip retrieve that brings the fly to the surface. This technique presents the pupa pattern through the entire depth zone that the fish may be feeding in. Often the strikes occur just as the fly is still within a few feet of the bottom, or when the fly is within a few feet of the surface. Those strikes that occur within about 10 feet of the lake surface are from fish that have followed the fly up from the lake bottom.

Hatches in deep water, from 25 to 50 feet, generally take place in mid to late summer. Fast-sinking fly lines are effective in imitating the pupae's ascent from these depths. Take a Type III or IV full-sinking or density-compensated sinking line, and cast out an amount of line equal to the depth you are anchored in. Allow the fly line and pupa pattern to sink until the line is straight up and down. Begin a slow but continuous hand-twist retrieve, bringing the fly to the surface. Strikes generally occur within a few feet of the bottom or within about 10 feet of the surface of the lake. The takes are often hard, which makes this an exciting way to fish.

FLY PATTERN SELECTION

As with any fishery, a host of local and generic patterns will fool the fish. Numerous commercially tied chironomid larva and pupa patterns work on these waters. Refinements to pattern selection should take place on the water, where larvae and pupae can be observed and color and size can be matched on the spot, making a small aquarium net and throat pump essential tools. However, some basic color combinations cover the major chironomid pupae found in these lakes. Pupa bodies with ribbings of red copper, silver, and gold wire are always reliable. These can be tied with white metal bead heads to imitate the gills, or tied with a traditional shellback and white Antron or ostrich herl gills. Remember the common pupae body colors of black, maroon, brown, and shades of green. Excellent body materials include Stretch Flex, Stretch Floss,

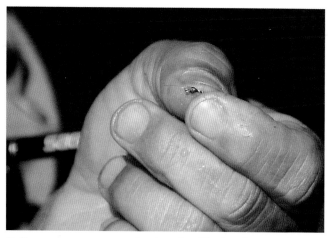

Refinements to pattern selection should take place on the water, where larvae and pupae can be observed and color and size can be matched on the spot.

Flashabou, Krystal Flash, and traditional flosses. One of the most consistent chironomid pupae color combinations is a fly with a black body and red wire rib tied on a Mustad Signature C49S or a Tiemco 2457, in sizes 10 to 16.

Some of my most productive and fun fishing while imitating chironomids is using an indicator dry fly with a pupa. This is also my favorite method for rivers. Normally, most fish can be taken below the surface, however I use a dry-fly rig whenever possible. It is easier to cast all day long than a heavier nymph rig, and it disturbs the water much less. This is especially important in clear, slow-moving water. Light presentations are a must when fishing in shallow water. Also, a strike indicator flying above the water will send fish scurrying away from their shallow feeding lanes into the perceived safety of deep water.

Basic Lake Techniques

Rick Takahashi

Tav's Larva

DURING RUNOFF IN the Rockies, many of the streams and rivers are running high with swift water, and fishing is marginal at best. Because of the high water and hard wading, many of us wait until runoff is over to get back to fishing the rivers and streams. But at this time, the lakes and reservoirs are just starting to turn on. If you are willing to put in the time it takes to learn to fish lakes, this will add a whole new dimension to your fishing.

What follows are some techniques that I use with floating and sinking lines. But, if only one line is in your budget, then I would suggest making it a floating line. Floating fly lines allows you to fish almost any situation you might encounter. When fishing subsurface flies, adjusting the length of the leader allows you to reach down deep, while the use of a strike indicator allows you to fish vertically.

SINK AND DRAW AND SINK AND TEASE
Let the fly sink to the bottom of the lake, if possible, and then strip in line with 1-inch retrieves. Count the seconds, changing

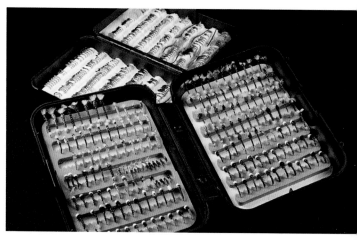

Trout feed on more pupae than any other stage, so I concentrate my tying efforts in developing a variety of patterns that represent the pupa. Chironomid pupae I've collected indicate they have a silvery surface and prominent breathing structure (commonly referred to as gills). I tend to tie mine in black, gray, tan, and olive.

Author Rick Takahashi leads a large Delaney Butte cutthroat, caught on a black Bow Tie Buzzer, to the net.

the amount of time you let the fly sink before retrieving the fly. Once you locate the fish, use the same count each time before retrieving the fly. Vary the amount and length of retrieves. Stopping the retrieve might also induce strikes. Draw the fly to the surface, and recast. When using this technique, I am usually fishing on an inclined plane.

For the sink and tease, allow the fly to sink to the bottom and then hand-twitch the line, giving life to the fly without retrieving any of the line. Move in your belly boat, slowly teasing your fly until you get a strike.

DEAD-DRIFT

I usually use this technique with dry flies. Cast to where you think a trout will be rising, allow the fly to rest, and then twitch it. Sometimes I just let it sit for a short period before retrieving the fly. I often cast directly to the spot where a fish has taken a natural. I do this within seconds of the rise-form. Sometimes, the fish will turn around and take the new offering.

BOW-TIE BOOGIE

I use this technique when I want to move the fly straight up and down. To a long leader and tippet (length to be determined by the water depth or depth at which the fish are suspended) attach a slip-type indicator large enough to suspend the flies. Attach a considerable amount of weight to quickly get the flies to the fish's level about 18 inches above the point fly. After you cast the rig out, allow the flies to sink and settle. After the flies have settled, take two to three sharp and short strips of the fly line and let the flies settle down for a few seconds, then slowly hand-twist retrieve. Be prepared for the take.

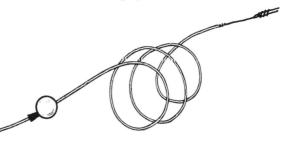

In stillwaters, I tend to use a longer leader tapering to heavier, 1X to 3X tippets to better handle the larger trout, though I go down to 4X if the fish seem leader-shy. When fishing on the surface, I'll go down to 5X. I use as long a leader as I need to reach any depth of water with a subsurface fly, unless I switch to a sinking line.

Essential Lake Equipment

Float tubes or pontoon boats allow you to reach water that you can't reach when wading the shoreline. Some equip their pontoons with fish finders and electric motors. If you decide to use an electric motor, your state may require you to register your pontoon boat.

Chest waders. Whether boot- or stocking-foot models, chest waders are essential. I wear breathable waders year-round, layering under them in the early spring or fall. Be sure to wear a wading belt to keep the water out, if you should happen to fall in.

Fins help propel you in the water. They come in a variety of styles, from fins that attach to your wading boot, to fins that scuba divers use and that might fit over a boot-foot or stocking-foot wader. Safety straps reduce lost fins. Safety note: The most dangerous time when belly boating occurs while getting in and out of the water. Always walk backward into the water, and try to enter where you have a fairly solid lake bottom. If the lake bottom is soft, you can sink in with your fins and lose control, which may result in an accident or, worse yet, drowning.

Rain gear is critical to have onboard. Storms can arrive quickly and you don't want to be caught out in the middle of a lake without a jacket. Also, wind seems to be a constant factor when fishing lakes, and it's nice to keep the water off your upper body.

A **hat** and **polarized glasses** reduce glare and help you spot fish.

Personal floatation devices (PFDs) are essential, and some states require them by law. I keep several on hand, including one that looks like a fly-fishing vest and another that goes around my neck and looks like a pair of suspenders. When I pull a cord, it inflates.

Nets make landing fish from a belly or pontoon boat a lot easier, and I always carry one.

Large-arbor reels allow you to retrieve line quickly and are light in weight. The best reels for midge fishing have smooth, dependable drags. Standard or medium-arbor reels may be a better choice for stillwater fishing, because you will need the extra backing capacity.

A large stillwater rainbow is guided to the net. Use heavier rods and tippets to land the fish quickly, so you do not play them to exhaustion.

Brian Yamauchi releases a beautiful rainbow that took his Latex Chironomid Pupa.

DEEP STRIP

Use a full-sinking fly line to get the pattern deep, or to the level of where the fish are feeding. Cast out, and allow the fly to sink to the desired depth, using the countdown method. Try several retrieve rates, starting with stripping in line as fast as you can, and then slowing down the retrieval rate.

SLIP-STRIKE INDICATOR

If you are fishing depths greater than the length of your fly rod, the slip-strike indicator allows you to land the fish without the strike indicator inhibiting your ability to reel the fish in closer to the net. The slip indicator will come loose from the post that holds it in place, and slide down the leader until it hits something that stops it, such as a split-shot or point fly.

The leader slides through a hollow peg and is held in place by looping up the leader and inserting one end into the peg, which is then inserted into the opening of the strike indicator. When you set the hook, the weight of the fish and the strike pulls the loop out of the indicator and it slides down the leader.

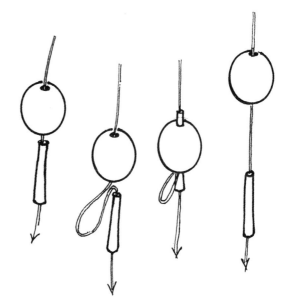

Buzzer Fishing

Alex Ferguson

Tak's Buzzer

A cloud of midges during a midmorning hatch provides a clue to the buzzer's onomatopoetic name.

WALK THROUGH a cloud of midges or get one stuck in your ear, and you'll soon understand why, in the United Kingdom, "buzzer" is the onomatopoetic name for adult chironomids. There are around four hundred different species in the UK, which differ widely in size from about $1/8$ inch to just under an inch in length. They are predominantly black, brown, or olive, but can come in other more exotic colors, including silver-gray, bright green, red, and a beautiful orangey ginger. With so many varieties, a wide distribution, and a tolerance for variations in water quality, the buzzer is as important to stillwater trout as mayflies or stoneflies are to river trout.

When most UK anglers talk about fishing buzzers, they are usually referring to fishing pupae rather than adult imitations. Listed below is a basic introduction to methods that we commonly use that are equally useful from bank or boat.

STANDARD NYMPHING

"Standard" nymphing, if there is such a thing, is fishing a single or team of nymphs unaided by any means of floatation other than the floating line itself. Buzzer nymphs can be found anywhere in the water column, so if you don't have a clue where the fish are feeding, you can search with a floating line, a 15- to 18-foot leader, and a team of quill or epoxy nymphs, with the heaviest on the point. These would be fished with a slow figure-eight retrieve or slow 4- to 6-inch pulls, counting down until you made contact with fish or the lake bed. If you know the sink rate of your line or flies, you can judge what depth the fish are at and keep your flies there longer. Trout tend to look upward for food, so it's sometimes useful to lower the count. It's also worth lowering the count after some time has passed, because the rising nymphs and feeding fish will probably be moving higher in the water. As with all wet fly/nymph fishing, depth is a major consideration, and being above the fish with your fly is preferable to being below them. The importance of keeping your flies at the right depth has spawned a couple of methods, known as the bung and the washing line.

THE BUNG

While not being the number-one method for the purist, the bung can be a effective method of putting fish in the net. The chironomid nymph's ultimate goal is to reach the surface, but in trying to attain this it doesn't shoot straight up like a Polaris missile. It wriggles its way up, has a bit of a rest, then wriggles some more. At times, it hangs almost lifeless, possibly undergoing some form of change in the pupal stage. The bung method is perfect for imitating this sort of movement.

Starting at the top of the setup, we have an indicator of some sort. I use a bit of foam tied to a size 8 or 10 standard wet hook. The color of foam depends on the lighting conditions. Sometimes I use bright red or yellow, sometimes white or black—whatever I can see best. Some glue different colors of foam together. Below that, I have either two or three chironomid nymphs, which are usually a heavier black on the point and a mixture of brown and olive further up, depending on conditions.

Fishing this method is best with a crosswind as you can drift the team around, a bit like wet-fly fishing. Takes can come on the drop, so it's a good idea to give the line a quick pull after the cast to tighten everything up. Once the flies have settled and are drifting nicely, begin a slow figure-eight retrieve with the occasional medium 6- to 12-inch draw to imitate the rising and falling action of the pupae. After a draw, let things settle down for a few seconds so that the nymphs drop back down, and keep an eye on the indicator. If the indicator is too far away to see or is obscured by ripples, watch the fly line between the rod tip and the water's surface for movement.

If no action is forthcoming, try swapping the fly colors, but keep a heavier fly on the point. Once you locate feeding fish, you can vary the distance between flies by retying to the tippet rings so that the flies are closer together and in the fishes' feeding zone, or you can swap all the flies to the color that's working, varying sizes or types.

THE WASHING LINE

The washing line suspends flies between the floating line and a floating fly—rather like clothes on a washing line—and works well when fish are feeding on pupae in the top few inches of water or breaking through the surface film. The floating fly may be something big like a Booby with large foam eyes at the head, but I prefer the Parachute Hopper Midge with a foam post or a Sugar Cube Buzzer with foam at the head.

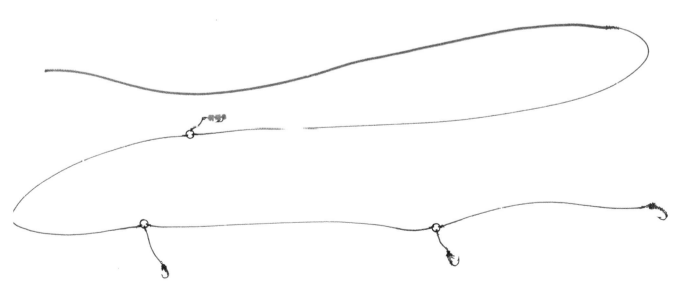

To fish the bung, use three 1.5mm tippet rings to connect your dropper flies. Connect the rings to your tippet with clinch knots, leaving 2 to 4 feet between each ring. The distance between the top ring and the point fly should not be greater than the length of your rod. Attach the indicator fly on a short dropper, and the chironomid nymphs on 3- to 5-inch droppers.

Brian Chan prepares to land a trophy fish at his favorite British Columbia lake. Fishing flies just under the surface can be deadly at the right times.

The standard method is to attach the Booby on the point and two or three pupae on droppers farther up the leader. Cast this rig out, give it a quick pull to tighten everything up, and then begin a slow figure-eight retrieve to keep the flies within inches of the surface. Halting the retrieve intermittently to allow the flies to sink a little and then tightening up with a slow draw, causing the flies to rise slowly toward the surface, can also induce takes. You can use heavier or lighter flies in different positions on the leader, so that one fly fishes deeper than the others and rises farther with the draw. It's really something to be experimented with on the day.

Another method, and my personal favorite, is to suspend one or two pupae between either two Sugar Cube Buzzers of different colors or a Sugar Cube Buzzer and a Parachute Hopper. Admittedly, this only leaves one or two flies under the surface, but the weight of the flies usually pulls the Sugar Cube Buzzer on the top dropper just below the surface where it can be deadly at times. If you halt the retrieve and let the flies sink, the Sugar Cube Buzzer on the top dropper pops up into the surface film, which again can trigger takes.

Dry-Fly Tips

Bubba Smith

Griffith's Gnat

FOR A LOT OF fly fishers, trying to catch trout rising to midges can be intimidating. It shouldn't be. Here are a few tips that might help.

1. Try to work in close to the fish—this will help your presentation and your ability to see the fly. Dress in drab colors, since you need to get pretty close to the fish to successfully present your fly.

2. When stalking fish, stay low to reduce your profile. Knee pads are a good idea in shallow water, allowing you to maintain a low profile.

3. Use the best polarized sunglasses, period.

4. Learn to understand the riseform. If you see a trout's nose and then its dorsal fin breaking the surface, the fish are on the midge dun. If all you see is a dorsal fin, then they are eating emergers just below the surface.

5. When fish are feeding on the surface, their field of vision is reduced to 6 inches or so around them. Be prepared to cast a dozen times or more to get your fly into their feeding window.

6. A lot of fly fishers like to use a bigger fly in front of the small midge dry. I don't. This larger fly can cause microdrag, and the fish will refuse it. Watch where your fly line and tippet land on the water. If anything rises in this area on the drift, gently lift.

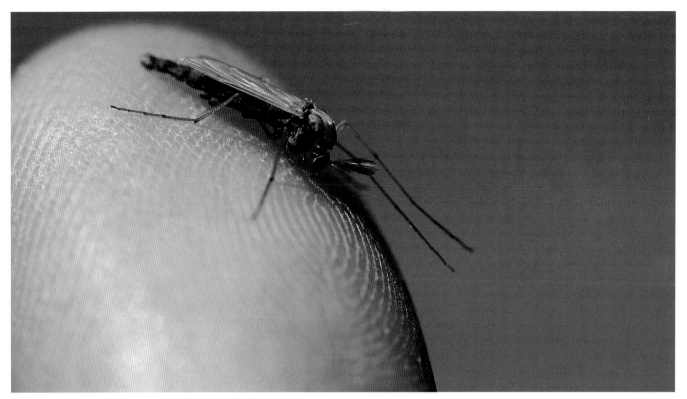

Fishing to trout rising to midge adults can be the ultimate challenge in dry-fly fishing.

7. Rising fish have a rhythm to their feeding. Try to present the fly when they are starting to come back up.

8. Don't cast too far upstream of the fish. Lead the fish 12 inches or so.

9. I like a downstream presentation, as the fish will see the fly first and not the line. You can also drag the fly into the proper position if your cast is a little off. You need to set the hook to the side parallel with the water. If you lift straight up, you will likely pull the hook out.

10. If you are getting refusals, go down a size or two in tippet before you try a smaller fly.

11. I like to use about 6 inches of fluorocarbon to the dry. It will sink slightly, helping you set the hook.

12. On small hooks (size 28 to 32), bend an offset in the hook to get the point away from the shank.

13. Use a soft rod. Fiberglass or bamboo is my choice, but a slow graphite rod will also do. A fast rod breaks light tippet, such as 6X or 7X, too easily.

14. When there are a lot of fish rising, pick one and cast to it. Shotgun casting into a pod will put all the fish down.

Keeping High and Dry

Rick Takahashi

Following are some items that I consider essential for fishing midge dry flies.

Amadou
Amadou is from a fungus that grows on trees and is noted for its absorbent properties. When fishing dry flies such as midge adults and clusters or any CDC patterns, I'll often rinse them clean in the water, then dry them with amadou before treating them with a powdered desiccant. It's a little expensive, but well worth the additional cost.

Dessicants and Floatants
I treat most of my dry flies with Shimizaki Dry-Shake. It puts a light coat of desiccant on the fly, helping to refloat it. I also put it on my midge pupa patterns in order to form tiny air bubbles on the flies when they are submerged. I also use Frog's Fanny to refloat a fly, and the handy little applicator brush helps to get into the nooks and crannies.

For flies that don't have CDC in them, I like to use BT's Float EZY, Umpqua's Bug Float, Loon Aquel, or Gink floatants.

Drift-Boat Tactics

Ron Yoshimura

WD-80

WHEN FISHING MIDGES from a drift boat, you can get long, drag-free drifts and cover lots of water, some not accessible to wading anglers. The key to fishing midges and other subsurface flies from a drift boat is using long drifts with the flies in the feeding zone. To accomplish this, it is important that the anglers and the boat handlers both do their parts.

Anglers should fish to the side of the boat, perpendicular to the boat's line of travel. Both anglers should fish the same distance from the boat, so that in theory both sets of flies drift at

the same speed and small channels or currents don't entangle the flies, which can be a real mess.

Anglers need to position their strike indicators to take advantage of the trout's feeding lane, and mend slightly upstream or downstream of the indicator, depending on the river currents, to prevent drag on the flies. When floating and fishing a run, remove excess slack from the fly line then lift the rod straight up. If the sinkers and flies are behind or upstream of the strike indicator, try removing some weight. If the flies are

Anglers take a rest in the late afternoon light on the Bighorn River. Fishing from a boat allows you to reach unpressured water and get long, drag-free drifts.

270

downstream of the strike indicator, try adding some weight. I want my flies and sinkers to float directly beneath the strike indicator. Point the rod tip toward the water, and try to remove as much slack between the rod tip and strike indicator as possible. Do not pull too tightly or this will create drag on the flies. This will also help with the hookup.

The boat handler should keep the boat parallel to the run. I want my boat to run right next to the hole for as long as possible. I also want the boat to drift at the same speed as the flies. This may take small sideways adjustments, as well as possibly rowing forward or backward. Of course, this is much harder when there is a strong wind. Position the boat a reasonable casting distance from the hole. I don't want the boat to run directly over the hole.

An effective method for fishing a productive hole is to make multiple passes through the same hole. We call this the "merry-go-round." We float and fish through the hole, and at the bottom of the hole, the fishers pick up their flies, and I row back upriver to the head of the hole, where we start all over again.

RIGGING

I typically use a 9-foot leader tapered down to the same size tippet I'm going to use. I prefer to use regular monofilament leaders because they are less expensive and then I don't feel as bad when a client develops a horrendous wind knot. I attach about 24 inches of fluorocarbon tippet using a blood knot. Though it is stiffer than monofilament nylon, fluorocarbon is virtually invisible in the water, has great knot strength, and is abrasion resistant. By the time I have tied knots at both ends, this tippet section should be around 18 to 20 inches.

I attach my first fly, the point fly, using a loop knot. I like the Rapala knot, which is easier for me to tie, especially in the wind and when the fish are biting, but I know others who use the nonslip mono knot. I tie on my second piece of tippet material above the loop knot. Again, the goal is to have about 18 to 20 inches between flies, after the knots are tied. I use the improved clinch knot for both the knots to the first tippet section and to attach the second fly.

Next, I attach split-shot to the leader just above the blood knot. The blood knot will stop the sinkers from sliding down. I use as much weight as a client can comfortably cast. The heavier weights get the flies down quickly, and the balloons will float anything short of a small boulder and still be sensitive to takes.

I prefer to use the water balloons found at party stores, and blow them up to about the size of a quarter. Any bigger, and they can be hard to cast. Black ones are much easier to see in the bright glare off the water. Attach the balloon to the leader

Gordon Waldmier and Brad Bischoff drift in the snow, braving a brief winter storm on the Big Horn River. Midges were the main fare for the trout that day.

Rick Takahashi and Ron Yoshimura take a 20-inch 'bow on Colorado's Blue River.

using a slipknot. To tie the slipknot, simply take a section of leader, twist it in your hand forming a loop, and pull the line closest to the fly line through the loop. You want the fly end of the knot to pull tight. Place the balloon on the leader so that the flies are $1\frac{1}{2}$ times the depth of the water you are fishing.

Splatting the Midge

Kevan Evans

TO CATCH TROUT feeding on midges, you must be able to get a fly that you cannot see right over their noses. So I offer you a simple yet effective way to overcome this problem. Let's say your target is just 20 feet away. The fish are keyed in to size 22. First, pull out 30 feet of fly line. The extra 10 feet will help to keep your fly floating down to the target. Next, make your cast do the work for you in one of two ways, the choice of which will depend on whether the water is glassy or contains multiple currents.

We'll start with glassy, smooth waters. The splat cast is a speedy, steep-angled cast more commonly used for fishing grasshopper and cricket imitations, but when using it with a small fly, the fly hits first and creates a ring on the water. Until the ring dissipates, it will show you where the fly is floating for the first 5 to 7 feet of the drift. Now that extra 10 feet of line comes into play. The moment the fly hits the water, mend your line upstream so that it is in line with the fly by flipping your fly line up into the air at a 45-degree upstream angle. When the timing is right, let the extra line go. You can get as much of a natural drift as necessary.

The dimple on the water will move downstream faster than your fly. Though you can't count on your fly being in the ring, the ring on the water shows the speed of the surface currents, which enables you to judge the timing of your fly to the fish's mouth. I hold back for a couple of seconds (depending on water speed) to figure out where my fly is. This is not going to be a 100-percent certain calculation (more like 60 to 80 percent)—I have often set the hook on nothing.

When fishing multiple currents you can use these same techniques, albeit in a different way. In this situation, I shoot all my line, overcasting by 10 feet and casting 10 feet upstream of my target. Then all I need to do is pull my fly into the feeding lane. Use the same big-belly upstream mend, and use the rest of the slack line to create a multiple-current mend. As you pull the fly in, the wakes will show you where the fly is located on the water. I have caught a good number of fish that I didn't even know were there while pulling my fly across the surface of the water.

A large fish comes to the net green.

Midges for Migratory Trout

Landon Mayer

Rojo Midge

IN THE SPRING, large rainbows, cutthroat, and cuttbows migrate from many of Colorado's reservoirs into streams to spawn. When fishing for these large trout you can gain an advantage by matching foods that the fish are most familiar with rather than what they encounter in the rivers.

Many anglers use midges ranging in sizes 20 or smaller, but these large fish will not shy away from larger chironomid imitations in sizes 14 to 18. The larger fly hooks and holds larger fish a lot better than the smaller patterns, giving you a better shot at landing them.

My three favorite chironomid patterns to use in these situations are red and black Frostbite Chironomids, Frostbite Chronomids with the brass tungsten bead in red, black, and cream; and Garcia's Rojo Midge in red, black, and orange. This range of patterns gives you the option of fishing different depths without using split-shot, which I think causes the flies to drift unnaturally. I use fluorocarbon to rig these flies (from the hook bend), spacing each fly approximately eighteen inches apart so that I know where my flies are as they are drifting downstream. Strike indicators are useful in deep water for detecting takes, and in shallow water, a strike indicator placed four feet or higher above the main fly helps suspend the flies at the fish's level as they drift downstream.

In deep water, I use the tungsten bead pattern below a midge, egg, or other pattern to get the fly deep to staging trout. If the trout are holding directly on the bottom I use two tungsten patterns. For shallow water, Garcia's Rojo Midge is ideal trailing below a nonweighted Frostbite Chironomid because the plastic bead allows the flies to sink enough without snagging the river bottom and spooking the fish.

Fish grow fat feeding on chironomids in lakes. They don't forget this important food source when they travel upstream to spawn.

Midge Musings

Ed Engle

Red Blood Worm

WHAT I LIKE most about fishing midges has to do with refinement and persistence. There was a time when I would have said simplicity. But if you've ever fished midges, you know that it is anything but simple. I believed in minimalism back then, because I thought that when the trout were feeding on midges I needed to strip everything I knew about fly fishing down to the bare essentials. I wanted a fly rod that *became* my casting arm—because this was one less thing to think about when I had fifteen trout sipping pupae right in front of me, and

everything depended on fly presentation. At times like that, a fly rod shouldn't be an impediment to fishing success no matter how fond you are of it.

My idea was to have as few distractions between me and the trout as possible. Fishing midges makes you condense everything you know. You do this by refining your fly-fishing knowledge in the same way that a raw material is refined, in the hope that what remains is pure and reliable. It sounds like hocus-pocus, but it isn't.

Brian Yamauchi makes his way in the early morning mist to his favorite stretch of the Dream Stream.

Find a leader design you like and stick with it. Learn a few modifications to that basic design that can help you overcome the commonly encountered changes of conditions, such as wind or water flow changes, but fight the urge to believe that a finer tippet will solve all your problems. The goal, most of the time, is for the fly to look as if it dropped onto the water unattached to your leader. If the size of the leader interferes with that illusion of naturalness, you may have to reduce it, but remember that a well-designed, slack-line leader built from the most soft and supple nylon you can find will make it unnecessary for you to go below 7X in all but the most unusual situations. So what's the secret slack-line leader formula? You are the only one who can determine that. Start with a basic George Harvey type of design, and go to work. Mold it to your casting style. Make it the most comfortable leader you've ever cast.

For fishing the river, you should strive to know all the basic slack-line and drag-reducing casts—parachute casts, check casts, downstream-and-across reach casts, S-curves, and any other useful combinations, such as a reach cast with S-curves.

Always get into your casting position, and then just observe the fish for a while. Give yourself time to internalize their behavior, get dreamy, or just have a little quiet time. It will pay off, because your unconscious angler's mind will be spinning at warp speed, figuring out the right cast to use and the right distance to cast.

Always get as close to the fish as you can. Make every cast count. Be persistent; then be more persistent. With midges, it's almost never about the magical silver bullet. Keep the good presentations coming. A trout taking midges may not take any of a hundred perfect presentations. So make one hundred and one perfect presentations. Don't waste time, keep casting. The fly has to be on the water. If the trout are midging below the surface and a dead-drift fails, try adding movement to the fly. Lift it, slow swing it, wiggle it, strip it. It's not heresy. It works.

Good flies represent the insect, but don't necessarily match it. Pay attention to color. Pay attention to size. Pay attention to shape. But remember the best flies are triggers. They make trout strike. Try the color blue in winter. Use prominent seg-

Hooking, and landing, a fish on a midge is a true accomplishment, the rewards heightened by the skill and patience required.

mentation on larva and pupa imitations. Experiment with trailing shucks. Add flash. Try everything and pay special attention to accidents, mistakes, and the butt-ugly stuff you just want to throw out. The discovery of a trigger is almost always unexpected, and never complicated. Remember that good proportions make for a good-looking fly, but that overemphasized features often make that fly a trigger. Case in point: extra-large wingcases on pupa imitations. For tiny flies, use hooks with the heaviest wire and the largest gap you can find.

For everything, I believe in repetition. Tie lots of flies. Make lots of casts. Get into the trout's space. Come out of it when you hook up.

Déjà Vu Rainbow

Gary A. Borger

Biot Chironomid

MIDGES HAVE ALWAYS been magic for me. I've used them successfully in trout streams across the angling world. There was a particularly fine 26-inch brown on a hidden New Zealand spring creek, a series of browns from Blagdon Reservoir in England, big rainbows in Tasmania, a really fine brown that my wife, Nancy, took in the early morning on the Bighorn, and numerous other memories as bright as new coins, but it is the déjà vu rainbow that burns brightest of all.

The trout was feeding steadily, positioned next to a large rock in a narrow current. The fish rhythmically tipped up its snout and sipped tiny insects from the surface film. A low, stone dam just upstream of the fish's lie afforded an avenue upon which to make a stealthy approach. The sharp-edged rocks cut at my hands and knees as I cautiously inched toward the big rainbow. Thirty feet from the feeding fish, I stopped and rose to a casting position.

A glittering rainbow takes a realistic midge pupa pattern.

To minimize the visual impact of the line, I added a fifteen-foot, clear nylon leader; its last section, to which I knotted a little Griffith's Gnat, was a mere .004 inch in diameter—a delicate 1½ pound breaking strength. I cast with a sidearm motion so the line wouldn't throw a shadow across the fish.

The fly dropped softly upstream of the trout, but unseen currents quickly dragged the imitation out of the fish's feeding lane. If the pattern moved unnaturally, the fish wouldn't take it; in fact, a dragging fly might have frightened the trout. I threw a curved line to compensate for the currents, but even though the pattern floated drag-free over the rainbow, it ignored my offering. Several more attempts were likewise ignored.

Perhaps the fly was wrong, or perhaps my timing was bad and the tiny imitation had not reached the fish during one of its evenly spaced rises. I trimmed the pattern with my scissors to give it a slightly different silhouette and cast again. The fly and the timing were right.

Unaware of the duplicity, the trout rose and took the imitation. Bewildered by the pressure it felt from the rod, the rainbow cartwheeled into the air then rushed headlong about the pool. But the tiny hook was firmly embedded in the fish's lower jaw, and the long, delicate rod cushioned the head-shaking rushes of the trout and prevented it from snapping the leader. At last, the fish submitted to the pull of the line. A hemostat removed the hook cleanly. As I held the fish in the water, I noted that one of its maxillary flaps was missing, long ago lost to incident or accident. Fully recuperated, the three-pound male dashed back into the sanctuary of the pool.

In the excitement of stalking, playing, and releasing the fish, I had been aware of nothing else. Although my knees now complained of the reckless treatment I had given them, this interlude had been like a poultice on the soul; all cares had drained away leaving me fresh and deeply satisfied. Watercress grew at the stream's edge, and I twisted off a sprig, then headed upriver, munching the peppery herb and watching for another trout.

Nearly five hours passed before I returned downstream. My then-eight-year-old son, Jason, was with me. He'd gone upstream earlier in the day to fish with my wife, Nancy, and we had now rendezvoused for lunch. I pointed out the rock where the big trout had been. And there, as we looked, was a ring on the water. Inching closer, we saw a large rainbow feeding in the same place as the fish I had taken earlier. The midges were still emerging; perhaps it was the same fish, lured back to feeding by this extremely abundant fare. "Come on Jason," I whispered, "you try him."

We crawled out on the stone dam and knelt where I had knelt earlier. "Use my rod, Jas," I offered, "the fly and leader are the same ones I used right here earlier today. Remember, if it's the same fish, he'll be more wary than when I fished for him. Make a few practice casts way upstream until you get it

A midge pupa takes another beautiful rainbow. Many of the best patterns are not only representative of the natural but they also dramatize key features that trigger strikes.

right." His first casts betrayed the nervous excitement that he felt—not only was the fish a substantial one and the hook small, but Dad was watching.

Soon, however, he had accurately calculated the distance and had figured out the correct throw to get a drag-free float over the fish. Several times the trout rose close to the artificial. Then, there it was, backing downstream under the fly and examining it closely. We could only watch, holding our breaths, as if exhaling would somehow spook the trout. Again the fly and the timing were right, and the rainbow took the tiny imitation.

As a little boy, my greatest longing had been to catch a big trout, but it didn't happen until I was in my teens. Now, as my son drew the rod back and pulled the hook home, those feelings came rushing from the past in a torrent of vicarious excitement. I found myself standing and shouting instructions, my mouth dry and my stomach drawn into a tight little ball that forced my pounding heart into my ears. He had to land that fish—for himself, yes, but also for me.

In a repeat performance, the big rainbow tumbled into the air and dashed about the pool. But Jason had been fishing since he was less than three years old, and was already a seasoned angler. He played the fish skillfully, and the long rushes and wild leaps were replaced with a dogged swimming, then surrender. It was the same male that I had caught earlier; the missing maxillary flap was our confirmation.

Jason's pride of accomplishment shone in his youthful face as he received my praise. And if he had only known to look beyond the love in his father's face, he would have seen another little boy whose dream had at last been fulfilled by this deja vu rainbow.

INDEX

Note: Originator listed in parentheses; if originator is unknown, the person or company that provided the pattern is listed. See entries for originator and tier.